AS/A-LEVEL

Psychology

Cara Flanagan

ESSENTIAL WORD

DICTIONARY

To Janny, Lesley and Sue. How could I do it all without you?

Philip Allan Updates, an imprint of Hodder Education, part of Hachette Livre UK, Market Place, Deddington, Oxfordshire OX15 0SE

Orders
Bookpoint Ltd, 130 Milton Park, Abingdon, Oxfordshire, OX14 4SB
tel: 01235 827720
fax: 01235 400454
e-mail: uk.orders@bookpoint.co.uk
Lines are open 9.00 a.m.–5.00 p.m., Monday to Saturday, with a 24-hour message answering service. You can also order through the Philip Allan Updates website:

ISBN 978-0-86003-371-4

Printed in Malta

Hachette Livre UK's policy is to use papers that are natural, renewable and recyclable products and made from wood grown in sustainable forests. The logging and manufacturing processes are expected to conform to the environmental regulations of the country of origin.

P01266

Introduction

This is a concise dictionary of essential terms used in AS and A-level psychology. Each word has been carefully chosen and is explained in detail to enhance your knowledge and understanding of this subject.

Many other dictionaries will contain words which are not relevant to students of AS and A-level psychology. This dictionary, however, only lists the most important terms and does not include words on the periphery of the subject. This will help you learn the key terms more efficiently.

In the dictionary, each word is defined in up to four parts: (1) a brief definition; (2) further explanations of the word; (3) an example (where relevant); (4) an examiner's tip, such as where a word is commonly misunderstood, confused with another word, used in error, or found in conjunction with other words in the dictionary. In many cases, all four parts are not needed and the entry has been amended accordingly. Finally, for each term it may be necessary to make a cross-reference to the words in italics in order to understand fully the entry you are reading.

In some cases the names and publication dates have been given when referring to studies in the extended explanations. The full references for such studies should easily be found in textbooks should the reader wish to research the topic further.

Acknowledgements

Writing this dictionary has been a most interesting and enjoyable task. I was reminded of a scene once described to me of Samuel Johnson, who compiled the earliest dictionary in the English language. He would walk around a long table set out at the top of his house in London, where clerks sat scribbling. Each clerk in turn would say a word to Johnson and then he would declare a definition. Unlike Johnson, I have had no scribes but it felt much the same — I typed a word on the screen and then set about trying to provide a useful and appropriate definition from my own store of (imperfect) knowledge and a large pile of books.

Every effort has been made, through careful re-reading, to eliminate errors and omissions in the text. I am especially grateful to Anthony Curtis for his assistance in this inglorious task. I am also indebted to my daughter Pip for her help in generating useful terms, as well as Mike Cardwell for sharing insights. Finally, my thanks to my partner and children who continue to tolerate the endless stream of work.

ablation: removal of a part of the body as a means of investigating *cortical* functioning.

- This operation may be performed to treat a condition, such as a tumour, or to study the role of a part of the body or brain.
- ***e.g.*** HM required bilateral ablation of his hippocampus because of severe epilepsy.
- ***TIP*** 'Functional' ablation can be achieved through the use of *lesions*, i.e. it appears as if a section of the brain was ablated whereas only a connection is cut.

abnormal behaviour: a behaviour that differs from the *norm*.

- A norm is a standard that can be used as a means of comparison. The difficulty lies in defining this standard.
- ***e.g.*** The 'norm' can be defined in terms of statistical *deviation*, deviation from social norms, a failure to function adequately and/or deviation from ideal mental health.
- ***TIP*** *Cultural relativism* is an important issue as all definitions are not absolutes; each is inevitably related to cultural norms and practices.

abnormal psychology: the branch of psychology that is concerned with abnormal or atypical behaviour.

accommodation: in *Piaget's theory of cognitive development*, the process of changing existing *schemas* because new information cannot be *assimilated*.

- Accommodate means 'to adjust or change'. The driving force behind this cognitive change or 'adaptation' is the principle of equilibrium. The intellect strives to maintain equilibrium or a sense of balance. If an experience cannot be assimilated into existing schemas then there is a state of imbalance. Cognitive development is the result of adaptation between the individual's existing schema and environmental 'demands' for change, such as the 'demand' made by new experiences which do not fit existing schemas.
- ***e.g.*** A child may have the schema 'four legs, fur and wet nose (dog)'. Every new instance of a creature with the same characteristics is assimilated into this schema. However, one day someone uses the word 'cat' and this challenges the current schema. This new information cannot be assimilated into the

existing schema; instead the child's schemas must alter to accommodate the new information — a new schema is formed.

acetylcholine (ACh): a *neurotransmitter* released in the brain and throughout the body. It generally has an excitatory effect.

■ In the brain it is related to *REM sleep*. Drugs that block ACh prevent the continuation of REM sleep. Drugs that stimulate ACh synapses start REM sleep. In the body, ACh is released at the synapse between motor neurones and muscles.

action potential: the wave of potassium–sodium ion changes that passes down an *axon* when a *neurone* fires.

■ This is the basis of transmission in the nervous system.

action slip: the performance of an unintended action as a result of inattention.

■ Action slips can be explained in terms of open- versus closed-loop modes of action. A person who is operating in open-loop mode (*automatic processing*) may fail to return to closed-loop mode (direct attention) when necessary, resulting in an action slip because the wrong motor programme is activated or runs on.

activation–synthesis model: Hobson and McCarley's (1977) theory of dreaming (*REM sleep*) whereby dreams are the result of the random firings of *neurones*.

■ There are two parts to the theory: (1) the neural 'noise' (activation) plus (2) the synthesis or putting together of these random images. In other words, we impose meaning on fleeting images and this gives us the subjective experience of dreams.

activity theory: the view presented by Havighurst et al. (1968) that psychological well-being in old age is promoted by continuing to be an active member of society and even finding new interests.

■ This is in contrast to *social disengagement theory*. The extent to which an individual is active or disengaged may depend on personal preference, economic position and physical health.

actor–observer effect: a kind of *attributional bias*. Individuals tend to explain their own behaviour (the actor) in *situational* terms whereas, when observing the same action in another, they would use *dispositional* terms.

■ This acts as a self-serving bias, i.e. it increases one's own sense of control and enhances *self-esteem*.

■ ***e.g.*** If you are asked to explain why you chose a particular A-level, you might explain your own choice in terms of what the course had to offer (situational) but would explain someone else's choice in terms of their personality (dispositional).

acute: describing a disease/disorder of rapid onset, severe symptoms and brief duration.

adaptive: a way to describe behaviours that promote an individual's survival and reproduction, and thus the potential survival of their *genetic* line.

■ This concept is derived from the principle of *natural selection*.

■ ***e.g.*** *Stress* is adaptive because it ensures that the animal is ready to respond to any demand.

■ ***TIP*** It is wrong to talk about any animal choosing to behave in a particular way because the behaviour is adaptive. No individual chooses adaptive behaviour, it evolves because it is advantageous for the individual and their genetic line.

adolescence: a transitional period between childhood and adulthood.

■ Biologically, this period begins when the individual enters puberty and ends on reaching sexual maturity. Psychologically, there are a number of levels on which the individual makes the transition to adulthood (e.g. social, emotional and cognitive) which do not have clear beginnings and endings. There is some debate over the extent to which the transition is necessarily 'stormy' or not. See *focal theory*.

adrenal gland: an *endocrine* gland located adjacent to and covering the upper part of each kidney.

■ The adrenal medulla (inner region) produces *adrenaline* and *noradrenaline*. The adrenal cortex (outer region) manufactures glucocortoids (such as *cortisol*) and various sex hormones, such as *androgens*.

adrenaline: a hormone produced by the *adrenal glands* which increases physiological arousal.

■ To be precise, adrenaline is produced in the adrenal medulla, the inner area of the adrenal gland. The effects of adrenaline parallel the activity of the *sympathetic nervous system* generally (e.g. increases heart rate). It also reduces activity in the *parasympathetic nervous system* (e.g. decreases digestive activity). See also *noradrenaline*.

■ ***TIP*** Americans use the term epinephrine (norepinephrine) instead of adrenaline.

adrenitogenital syndrome: a condition where a normal female (*genetically* XX) receives excess male hormones during *prenatal* development. This causes external male genitalia to develop and may also affect brain development.

adrenocorticotropic hormone (ACTH): a hormone released by the *pituitary gland* which stimulates the *adrenal glands*.

aetiology: the study of what causes a mental or physical disorder.

affect/affective disorder: related to mood and emotion.

affectionless psychopathy: a psychological condition where individuals appear to experience little guilt or emotion, lack normal affection, and are unable to form permanent relationships.

■ Bowlby linked the condition to early and frequent separations between a child under the age of 2½ years and his or her primary caregiver. According to Bowlby, the resulting *bond disruption* means that the child fails to form an *internal working model* and emotional development suffers as a result.

afferent nerve: conveys impulses from sense organs to the spinal cord or brain, as distinct from an *efferent nerve*.

affiliation: the *drive* to associate with others.

■ Some individuals have a greater need for affiliation than others. It is a basic human need which is useful for reproduction, social comparison and coping with uncertainty.

agentic state: feeling under the control of an *authority* figure and therefore lacking a sense of personal responsibility.

- This has been used to explain *obedience* to unjust authority. The individual becomes an 'agent' of the individual in authority. The key is to identify those *situational* and *dispositional* conditions that determine when an individual behaves in an agentic state and when he/she behaves in an *autonomous state*.

aggression: an act of hostility with the deliberate intention of harming another against their will.

- Aggression is a form of *antisocial behaviour*. It is a highly emotional behaviour relying mainly on *nonverbal* cues. It may be expressed in a ritualised form to prevent actual harm (e.g. raising your arm as a threat), or as anger, or self-assertiveness. It is helpful to distinguish between aggressive motives and an aggressive act. Motives can be distinguished in terms of different kinds of aggression: instrumental aggression which is a means to an end, hostile aggression which is senseless, and legitimate aggression which is performed for *prosocial* reasons such as defending a child. They all result in aggressive acts, but the motives are different and therefore the psychological explanations for the behaviour should be different. Explanations for aggressive behaviour in humans are either social/psychological (e.g. *social learning theory, frustration–aggression hypothesis*), or genetic/physiological (e.g. the *ethological* and *psychoanalytic* approaches, and the effect *hormones*).
- ***TIP*** An important way to evaluate any explanation of aggression is in terms of the reduction of aggression.

agonist: a drug that has the same effect as a naturally produced *neurotransmitter*.

- See also *antagonist*.
- ***e.g.*** Diazepam (Valium) enhances *GABA* activity and therefore decreases anxiety. Large amounts of alcohol also act as a GABA agonist.

agoraphobia: a *phobia* about being in open places or being alone in public places.

alpha bias: see *gender bias*.

alpha rhythm: a *brainwave* that is characteristic of the relaxed, awake state.

alternative (alternate) hypothesis: the alternative to the *null hypothesis*.

- It is another term for the *experimental hypothesis*. If we can reject the null hypothesis as a consequence of obtaining a significant result from an *inferential* test then we can accept the alternative hypothesis.
- ***TIP*** The abbreviation for the alternative hypothesis is H_1.

altricial species: animals whose young are relatively helpless at birth and require considerable care, as contrasted with *precocial species*.

altruism: putting the interests of others first, potentially with some risk or cost to the altruist.

- Reward should not be the primary motive. If reward is involved this is called 'egotistic altruism'. See also *reciprocal altruism*.
- ***e.g.*** Giving blood, saving a drowning person.

■ **TIP** It is important to distinguish between *biological altruism* and *psychological altruism*.

altruism, biological: altruism that develops as a means of promoting survival and reproduction (i.e. it is *adaptive*).

■ **e.g.** One form of biological altruism is explained in terms of *kin selection*: an individual will behave selflessly in order to protect their kin and thus promote the survival of their *genes* (the 'selfish gene') as is the case with the lapwing, which walks away from its nest feigning a broken wing so that a predator is drawn away from the young.

altruism, psychological: human altruistic behaviour is influenced by personal choice, *empathy*, *morals* and social *norms*.

amenorrhoea: the absence or cessation of menstruation.

■ This condition is associated with *anorexia nervosa* and may be either caused by a *hormonal* imbalance or due to the reduced intake of calories.

amnesia: a partial or total loss of *long-term memory*, as a result of brain damage or a psychological trauma.

■ Two kinds are distinguished: (1) Anterograde amnesia affects long-term memory. Permanent memories remain intact but sufferers cannot remember any new information for more than the normal *short-term memory* span. This is probably because transfer from short- to long-term memory is lost. (2) Retrograde amnesia affects short-term memory. Events immediately prior to the trauma are permanently forgotten, presumably because information is lost from short-term memory at the time of trauma. This may occur as the result of, for example, an accident or electroconvulsive shock therapy (*ECT*).

amygdala: a region located in the *temporal lobe* of the *cerebral cortex*. It is part of the *limbic system*.

■ The amygdala is associated with memory, emotion, sleep, *arousal* and the *fight or flight* response.

anaclitic depression: a severe form of depression in infants who experience prolonged separations from their mothers/primary caregivers.

■ The term 'anaclitic' means 'arising from emotional dependency on another'.

anal stage: in *psychoanalytic theory*, the second stage of *psychosexual development* when the organ-focus of the *id* is on the anus.

■ This developmental phase occurs around the age of 18–36 months. *Fixations* may be caused by strict toilet training, or by intense pleasure associated with, for example, smearing faeces on the wall. The anal-retentive character wants to make a terrible mess and therefore builds up defences against this, such as being very orderly, rigid and hating waste. The anal-expulsive character is very generous and may also be creative and productive.

analysis: to examine in detail the components or elements of an argument or theory.

■ **TIP** Analysis is an important skill in writing essay answers (*Skill AO2*).

analysis-by-synthesis model: Neisser's (1976) model of *perception* that combines *bottom–up* and *top–down processing.*

■ We start by sampling available information (bottom–up). Then cognitive *schema* direct our attention towards likely features (top–down). If our *hypothesis* is not confirmed we look for further data (bottom–up).

■ ***e.g.*** Your initial perception is of four legs and a wet nose; this generates the hypothesis 'it is a dog'. However, the roar alerts you to the fact that this hypothesis is not correct and you search for further cues.

analysis of variance (ANOVA): a method of *inferential statistics* which analyses the interactions between more than two variables.

■ This is a more sophisticated technique than those used at A-level. It is also a more realistic measure than the simple relationship investigated in tests of difference or correlation.

androcentric theory: a theory that is based on male behaviour but applied to females as well and therefore is biased.

■ ***e.g.*** Kohlberg's research on moral development used male participants only, yet was offered as an explanation of all moral development.

androgen: a male *hormone.*

androgyny: a mixture of feminine and masculine behaviour in the same individual.

■ Bem proposed that androgyny was a more healthy psychological state than the traditionally held view that males and females should engage in distinct *gender roles*. Narrow gender concepts inevitably limit a person's repertoire of behaviours. A man who feels strongly that he must behave in a masculine fashion is more limited in terms of his behaviour than a man who is less rigid about doing things that might be seen as feminine.

animal behaviour: the study of non-human animals in their own right.

■ See *comparative psychology.*

animal language: a specialised form of communication between members of the same species.

■ The debate is over whether such communication can be called '*language*' or whether even sophisticated animal communication systems are just that, communication not language.

■ ***e.g.*** The honey bee waggle dance, birdsong, warning cries of vervet monkeys.

■ ***TIP*** There have been many attempts to teach human language to non-human animals (e.g. Washoe, Nim Chimsky, Kanzi). There is no doubt that they can communicate using words but the question is whether they can acquire the *grammar* of human language, which would be evidence that Chomsky's *LAD* is not a biologically-determined system.

animism: a willingness to give lifelike qualities to inanimate things.

■ *Piaget* claimed that this kind of thinking was typical of a child in the preoperational stage of development because their thinking lacks formal logic.

■ ***e.g.*** Saying 'The moon wants to hide behind the clouds'.

anorexia nervosa: literally a 'nervous lack of appetite'.

■ An eating disorder in which the individual has an intense fear of becoming fat despite being seriously underweight due to gross undereating. The *DSM-IV* lists four criteria for the diagnosis of anorexia: less than 85% of normal weight, intense anxiety about weight gain, distortion of body-image, and *amenorrhoea*. It is a condition that is most common in adolescent girls. Explanations include *genetic, learning theory, psychodynamic* and social causes.

■ **TIP** It may be possible to distinguish between anorexia nervosa and *bulimia nervosa* in terms of desire for perfection: anorexics are more concerned with perfection, whereas bulimics suffer from a constant craving for food/attention. However, recently it has been suggested that the two conditions are not in fact easily distinguishable and it may be more appropriate to consider the eating disorder as a condition 'bulimarexia', a continuum of the disorder ranging from restricting anorexics at one end of the spectrum, through to obese bulimia at the other.

ANS: see *autonomic nervous system.*

antagonist: a drug that prevents the effects of a naturally produced *neurotransmitter.*

■ See also *agonist.*

■ ***e.g.*** Chlorpromazine blocks both *dopamine* and *noradrenaline* receptors, acting as an antagonist. Lithium just blocks noradrenaline receptors.

anterograde amnesia: see *amnesia.*

antibody: a protein in the blood that is part of the *immune system.*

■ Antibodies are produced in response to *antigens*. They then attach themselves to these invaders, marking them out for subsequent destruction.

■ **TIP** This system of natural defence is the basis of childhood vaccination programmes. It is possible to inject small doses of a virus (which is usually in a de-activated state). Your body copes with a small invasion and produces antibodies which then remain in your system. If, at some later time, you are exposed again to the virus your body can fight it off — you are immune to it.

anti-conformity: behaviour which is in opposition to group *norms.*

■ However, the individual is still responding to such norms and therefore this is not truly *independent behaviour.*

antidepressant drug: a stimulant drug which has an *agonist* effect by increasing the production of *serotonin* and *noradrenaline.*

■ ***e.g.*** *Selective serotonin reuptake inhibitors.*

antigen: a foreign body, such as a virus.

anti-psychiatry: the view that traditional conceptions of mental illness are dangerous and mistaken, and that alternative therapies should be pursued.

■ Szasz (1960) challenged the *medical model* of mental illness by suggesting that the medical approach was scientifically crippling and that the concept of mental illness was a myth. Socially expressed symptoms, he felt, are better represented as problems in living.

antipsychotic drug: a drug used to reduce psychotic symptoms.

■ **e.g.** Chlorpromazine (for *schizophrenia*), lithium (for *manic depression*).

antisocial behaviour: behaviour which is harmful to others.

■ Social behaviour is any behaviour involving one or more members of the same species, therefore antisocial behaviour disrupts this in some way.

■ **e.g.** *Aggression*, *discrimination* and *anticonformity* may all be antisocial — but they can also sometimes be *prosocial*.

antisocial personality disorder: an individual who lacks a conscience and lacks *empathy* for others, making it likely that they will commit crimes and have difficulty forming relationships.

anxiety disorder: a mental disorder characterised by levels of fear and apprehension which are disproportionate to any threat posed.

■ **e.g.** *Obsessive–compulsive disorder*, *post-traumatic stress disorder*, *phobias*.

■ ***TIP*** Anxiety, like *stress*, is an adaptive response to certain situations.

anxiolytic drug: a drug that reduces anxiety.

■ They are also called sedative hypnotic drugs.

■ **e.g.** Alcohol, *barbiturates*, *benzodiazepines*, *busipirone*.

AO1 and **AO2:** see *Skill AO1* and *Skill AO2*.

APA: the American Psychological Association.

aphagia: when an animal stops eating, thought to be caused by a *lesion* in the *lateral hypothalamus*.

aphasia: a partial or complete loss of language functions due to brain damage.

■ **e.g.** Broca's aphasia is a disruption of speech production caused by damage to *Broca's area*. There are many other aphasias, each related to a different aspect of language.

applied psychology: areas of psychology where psychological research is applied to real-world settings.

■ **e.g.** *Educational psychology*, *clinical psychology*, *criminal* (*investigative*, *forensic*) *psychology*, *environmental psychology*, *health psychology*, *organisational psychology*, *sport psychology*.

arousal: being stirred to activity, a state of readiness. The de-aroused state is *sleep*. A moderate level of arousal is required for the awake state and this is increased if the situation demands it. For example, stress or any emotional state results in an activation of the *sympathetic branch* of the *autonomic nervous system* so that the animal is ready for *'fight or flight'*. This is an *adaptive* response.

arousal–aggression hypothesis: a more generalised version of the *frustration–aggression hypothesis*. Instead of suggesting that frustration causes aggression, it is simply arousal that predisposes an individual to release pent-up psychic energy.

■ **e.g.** Arousal may be created by pain, extreme temperatures, overcrowding, physical exercise, loud music, intense physical activity.

arousal — cost–reward model: Piliavin's explanation for *psychological altruism* and *prosocial behaviour* which suggests that the primary motive for helping is to reduce the arousal created by seeing someone in distress.

- Piliavin's original model of prosocial behaviour just focused on the decision about whether to help or not which, he suggested, was determined by a *cost–benefit* analysis. The 'costs' might include time spent helping, effort, damage to personal belongings, risk of harm and also of not helping (e.g. others may think less well of you). The benefits might include social approval, increased self-esteem and feeling good because you helped someone. The 'arousal' component was introduced as a further element in the decision of whether to help or not. High arousal increases the likelihood of helping. The model can account for both emergency and non-emergency helping behaviour. However, it is a rather *mechanistic* approach to behaviour and people may not have the time for such apparently logical decisions.

articulatory (phonological) loop: the part of *working memory* that holds information for a short period of time in a phonological (sound) or speech-based form.

- The loop is divided into: (1) a phonological store, which is directly concerned with speech perception; and (2) an articulatory process, which is linked to speech production.

assimilation: in *Piaget's theory of cognitive development*, the process of fitting new information and experiences into existing schemas, as distinct from *accommodation*.

- Assimilate means 'to take in'.

association cortex: an area of the cortex involved with sensory processing.

- It is located in the *temporal* and *parietal lobes*. The term 'association' comes from the original belief that this part of the brain was involved with forming associations between motor and sensory areas, because the region is located between the sensory and motor regions. However, it is now thought that this was a mistaken assumption and that the association cortex is an additional sensory area that deals with higher-order processing of sensory information.

association hypothesis: an explanation offered for *parental investment* by Williams (1975), that the adult who is left in closest proximity to the embryo is the one that tends to take care of the young.

- Where external fertilisation takes place this is generally the male; with internal fertilisation this is the female.

attachment: a strong emotional and reciprocal tie that develops over time between an infant and its primary caregiver(s) and results in a desire to maintain proximity.

- Both *learning theory* and *psychodynamic theory* suggest that attachment occurs as a consequence of feeding; however, empirical research has found that children are not necessarily most attached to the person who feeds them or who spends most time with them. Bowlby's theory of attachment suggested that attachment serves an *adaptive* function: in the short term it ensures safety and closeness, and in the long term it is the basis of emotional development (the *internal working model* acts as a template for future relationships). Infants are born with innate *social releasers* which ensure that attachments are formed, because these releasers (e.g. smiling) elicit caregiving. Infants become attached to the person who is most responsive to the social releasers (the *caregiver sensitivity hypothesis*). Bowlby also proposed the concept of *monotropy*, that children have one especially strong attachment which is important for emotional development, but they have a hierarchy of other caregivers.

■ ***TIP*** It is important to distinguish between Bowlby's theory of attachment and his earlier *maternal deprivation hypothesis* which focused on the effects of deprivation rather than the consequences of attachment.

attention: the concentration of mental effort, equivalent to consciousness.

■ Focused (selective) attention describes the ability to pick out (or focus on) a particular set of stimuli in a mass of information. Theories of focused auditory attention include the *filter* and *attenuator* (early selection) and *pertinence* (late selection) *models*. The *zoom-lens model* explains focused visual attention. Divided attention refers to our ability to allocate attention to two or more tasks at the same time. This is affected by task similarity, task difficulty and practice (where tasks are more similar, more difficult and less practised it is harder to divide attention). Divided attention is enhanced by *automatic processing*. Various theories have been proposed such as *central capacity theory* and the idea of *modules*.

attention-deficit disorder (ADD) or attention-deficit hyperactivity disorder (ADHD): a form of atypical behaviour characterised by inappropriate inattention and impulsiveness and by motor hyperactivity which is inappropriate for a child's age.

■ The causes of this disorder are not clear but suggestions include overarousal (and therefore continual switching of attention), underarousal (inability to maintain attention), or diet (high in additives or other food substances such as chocolate). The stimulant drug Ritalin is widely used to treat the disorder, although *behavioural therapies* are also effective.

attenuator model: Triesman's (1964) explanation for focused auditory *attention* in terms of a *serial processing*.

■ This model suggests that the incoming signals are weakened (attenuated) rather than being filtered on the basis of physical characteristics (the *filter model*). The weak signal can still trigger an individual's 'dictionary' of important words so that attention can be diverted to important things. This model is more flexible than the *filter model* but it is still a single-channel model, ignoring *parallel processing* (see the *pertinence model*).

attitude: a liking or disliking of something which leads to certain behaviours.

■ The structural approach stresses three factors: the affective component (liking or disliking) plus a behavioural component (a readiness to behave in a certain way) plus cognitions (beliefs about things). The functional approach considers the functions served by attitudes, such as being *adaptive*, providing knowledge, being self-expressive and also acting as an *ego defence*.

attitude scale: a psychological test for measuring people's *attitudes*.

■ **e.g.** *Likert scale, semantic differential technique, projective tests.*

attributional bias: a systematic way of behaving when making attributions, which leads to mistakes in explaining one's own behaviour and the behaviour of others.

■ **e.g.** *Actor–observer effect, defensive attribution, fundamental attribution error*, self-serving bias.

attribution theory: how we explain the causes of behaviour to ourselves.

■ When observing behaviour (our own or someone else's) we provide explanations for the behaviour. These explanations will be *dispositional* or *situational*.

■ **e.g.** *Causal schemata, correspondent inference theory, covariation theory, self-perception theory.*

atypical psychology: the study of behaviour that is not representative or characteristic of a group of people.

■ This is an alternative way of describing *abnormal behaviour* but without the more negative connotations of abnormality. For example, it is more helpful to think of a child with *Down's syndrome* as atypical rather than abnormal because it changes our perceptions and hopefully prevents negative expectations affecting the child's development. It is also more appropriate to use the term 'atypical' because there are some 'abnormal' behaviours which are not necessarily problem behaviours (such as children who are gifted).

audience effect: see *social facilitation*.

augmentating principle: a concept in Kelley's *causal schemata* model of attribution, that people tend to place greater importance on a causal explanation if the behaviour occurs in the presence of inhibiting or restricting factors.

■ This principle is used in cases where there is only a single instance of behaviour on which to make an attribution, so that an analysis of *covariation* is not possible.

■ **e.g.** If you hear that a friend's daughter received a first-class honours degree in philosophy you are especially impressed by her abilities. The fact that it is in philosophy augments the attribution and makes it more likely that you would give a *dispositional* rather than a *situational* attribution.

authoritarian personality: a person who tends to hold rigid beliefs, be hostile towards *outgroups*, and be submissive to authority.

■ It is possible that such characteristics are associated with a parenting style characterised by *conditional love*, strict discipline and expecting unquestioning loyalty. Such experiences would create an insecure adult who respects authority and power, conforms more readily to group norms, and who may increase their self-esteem through *ingroup favouritism*. In addition, people who find ambiguity hard to cope with search for simplistic interpretations of reality and deny negative feelings in order to maintain consistency. Authoritarian individuals are likely to be *prejudiced, conformist* and *obedient*. Adorno used the *F scale* to investigate the authoritarian personality.

authoritarian style of leadership: see *leadership styles.*

authority: the power or right to direct others.

autism: a mental disorder characterised by 'self-orientation'.

- The disorder becomes apparent in early childhood and typically involves avoidance of social contact, abnormal language and so-called 'stereotypic' or bizarre behaviours. An example of stereotypic behaviours would be incessant rocking or an obsessive routine. There are two broad groups of autistics: the Kanner-type (first identified by Kanner in the 1940s) and the Asperger-type (first identified by Asperger about the same time). The Kanner-type tend to be mentally retarded and to have associated neurological problems such as epilepsy and insensitivity to pain. The Asperger-type have normal or even superior intelligence and few neurological problems.

autokinetic effect: a visual illusion where a small spot of light is viewed in a darkened room and appears to be moving, though it is in fact stationary.

automatic processing: *processing* that occurs without attention or consciousness.

- The advantage is that prolonged practice means we no longer have to think about what we are doing because the information can be supplied directly from memory, and memory retrieval does not require attentional control. The disadvantage is that *action slips* may result, sometimes with disastrous consequences.
- ***e.g.*** All the activities involved in driving are fairly automatic which means that you can talk and do other things while changing gear, signalling, looking in your rear-view mirror and so on. However, a sudden unexpected event, such as a branch blowing in front of you, requires a return to *controlled processing.*

autonomic nervous system (ANS): this controls the body's involuntary activities and is thus largely automatic and self-regulating (or autonomous). If this was not the case we might forget to carry out vital activities such as breathing and digesting.

- The ANS controls involuntary muscles, such as those of the stomach and the heart, and also controls the *endocrine system,* which produces and distributes hormones. There are two branches of the ANS that work in a correlated but antagonistic fashion to maintain internal equilibrium (*homeostasis*): the *sympathetic branch* (activity) and *parasympathetic branch* (the relaxed state).
- ***e.g.*** The ANS controls heart rate: the rate is accelerated by sympathetic activity and slowed down by parasympathetic activity.

autonomous morality: a stage of moral development described by Piaget as relying on internal judgements, where the person's intentions are used as a basis for judgement.

- Younger children operate a heteronomous morality where they base their judgement on the severity of outcome.

autonomous state: being aware of the consequences of one's own actions and therefore taking voluntary control of one's own behaviour.

■ ***TIP*** This can be used to explain why some individuals act independently rather than obediently, as in an *agentic state*.

availability heuristic: a mental shortcut (*heuristic*) that tells us to make decisions based on the information that is most readily available.

■ One's judgements are related to the ease with which we can bring instances of some group or category to mind (i.e. their availability).

■ ***e.g.*** In one experiment participants were given a list of 19 men's names and 20 women's names. The women's names were better known (e.g. Mrs Thatcher as opposed to Denis Healey). When asked later to estimate the number of male and female names in the list, participants greatly overestimated the number of women, presumably because the names were more available.

average: see *central tendency*.

aversion therapy: a form of *therapy* based on *classical conditioning* in which undesirable behaviour is eliminated by associating the behaviour with something unpleasant.

■ ***e.g.*** Giving alcoholics a drug which makes them vomit every time they have a drink. The learned association between pleasure and drinking is extinguished and replaced by a new association between drinking and feeling sick.

aversive stimulus: anything that is unpleasant to an *organism*.

avoidant attachment (called 'type A')**:** a type of *insecure attachment* of an infant to its caregiver.

■ In the *Strange Situation* the infant shows apparent indifference when the caregiver leaves, and does not display *stranger anxiety*. At reunion the infant actively avoids contact with the caregiver. The caregiver tends to be insensitive and may ignore the infant during play. Research has found that adults who were ambivalently attached as children tend to describe their adult love experiences as involving obsession, a desire for reciprocation, emotional highs and lows, and extreme sexual attraction and jealousy. They worried that their partners did not really love them or might abandon them.

awareness: a state of being conscious of one's own existence and one's behaviours.

axon: a single nerve fibre that projects from the cell body of a *neurone* and transmits the *action potential* to another neurone or target organ.

balance theory: an explanation of *attitudes* and attitude change in terms of consistency, proposed by Heider (1946).

- Individuals prefer to be in a state of balance where their attitudes are consistent. For example if P likes something (termed 'X') and so does O, then P and O are in balance (they have a positive relationship). If P likes something but O does not, then balance can be maintained if P does not like O. Alternatively balance can be restored if P differentiates between different occurrences of X.
- ***e.g.*** Mary likes dancing and so does Susan, so they are in a state of balance. Betty does not like dancing which creates a negative relationship between Mary and Betty except when Mary discovers that they both like disco dancing but not Highland dancing.

barbiturate: an *anxiolytic drug* used to treat anxiety disorders.

- Barbiturates are effective in depressing activity in the *central nervous system* because they are *GABA* agonists (enhancing GABA activity), which increase *serotonin* levels and thus decrease anxiety. However, they have undesirable side-effects such as poor concentration, lack of coordination and slurred speech. They also tend to be addictive. More recently the use of barbiturates has been replaced by *benzodiazepines,* such as Valium.
- ***e.g.*** Phenobarbitol.

bar chart: a kind of *graph* used to represent the frequency of data.

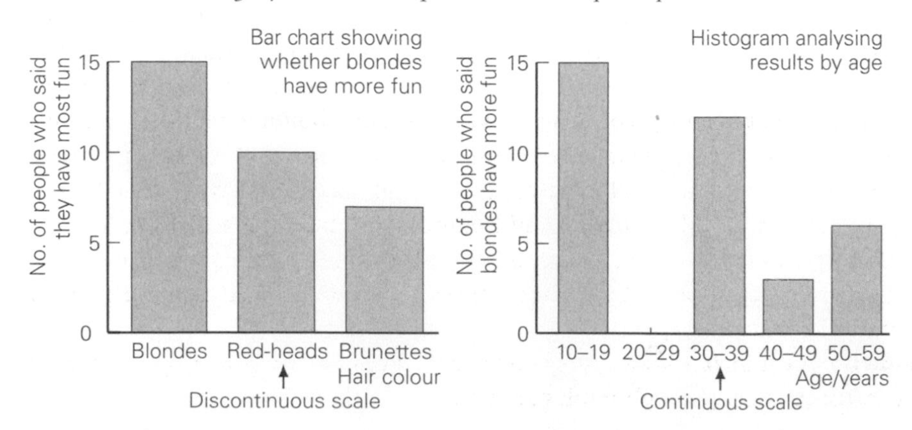

- It is suitable for use with any *level of measurement* because, unlike a *histogram*, the data on the *x*-axis are *discrete* rather than continuous, such as with *nominal* level data. These data cannot logically be ordered in any way. The *y*-axis represents frequency and these data are continuous.
- ***TIP*** The 'highest' bar is the mode.

basal ganglia: a group of *subcortical* structures located on either side of the thalamus, involved in aspects of memory and emotional expression as well as planning sequences of behaviour.

Batesian mimicry: see *mimicry*.

behaviour: any activity of a living organism.

- ***e.g.*** Attention, thought, emotion as well as the more obvious aggression, discrimination and imitation.

behavioural therapy: any form of *therapy* derived from the *behaviourist* model.

- One criticism of these therapies is that they are based on non-human animal research which may not generalise to human behaviour. On the other hand, such therapies have been successful for certain psychological problems, such as *phobias*.
- ***e.g.*** *Behaviour therapy* (*classical conditioning*) and *behaviour modification* (*operant conditioning*), as well as *cognitive–behavioural therapy*.

behaviour genetics: the study of the *genetic* causes of *behaviour*.

- This is a *deterministic* approach to explaining behaviour.

behaviourism/behaviourist: the view that all behaviour can be explained in terms of *learning theory*, referring only to the behaviours themselves rather than any internal mechanisms in order to explain behaviour.

- Behaviourists claim that environmental influences (*nurture*) can explain everything, largely rejecting *nature* explanations. *Radical behaviourists* completely reject the use of inaccessible, internal mental processes in psychological explanations (for them 'the mind' is a *black box*). They believe that it is both sufficient and more *empirical* to focus on observable, external events. In contrast *neo-behaviourists* use both learning theory and internal mental processes in their explanations. Behaviourism is criticised for being *determinist* (environmental determinism), *reductionist* and *mechanistic*. Research is largely conducted with non-human animals and therefore the findings may not generalise to humans (though a behaviourist would argue that one can generalise to humans because all animal behaviour is constructed with the same building blocks as demonstrated by the *theory of evolution*). Despite such criticisms it is true that many aspects of behaviour can be at least partly explained through learning theory (this view is called *methodological behaviourism*) and the approach has the advantage of lending itself to testing (a highly scientific and *empirical* approach). It also has given rise to many useful applications such as *programmed learning* and *behavioural therapies*.

behaviour modification: a form of *therapy* based on the principles of *operant conditioning*, i.e. through reinforcement.

■ ***e.g.*** *Modelling, token economy, social skills training.*

behaviour therapy: a form of *therapy* based on the principles of *classical conditioning*, i.e. through association.

■ ***e.g.*** *Aversion therapy, systematic desensitisation, implosion therapy, flooding, time out.*

Bem Sex Role Inventory (BSRI): a *psychometric test* for measuring *androgyny*.

benzodiazepine: a class of *anxiolytic* drugs used to treat anxiety.

■ They are *GABA* agonists, i.e. they act like a naturally produced *neurotransmitter*, and enhance GABA activity, thus reducing anxiety. Benzodiazepines (like *barbiturates*) have side-effects, such as drowsiness and memory impairment, and can be addictive. More recently they have been replaced by *buspirone*.

■ ***e.g.*** Diazepam, Valium, Librium.

bereavement: the emotional state arising from the death of someone close to you.

■ We also use the term to refer to coping with the loss of anything which is important to you, including coming to terms with one's own death. Kübler-Ross (1969) identified five processes which were characteristic of the bereavement process: denial (coping with the initial shock), anger ('Why me?'), bargaining (making promises to try to change things), depression (e.g. crying), acceptance (accompanied by a lack of emotion and becoming detached).

beta bias: see *gender bias*.

beta rhythm: a *brainwave* that is characteristic of the active awake state, such as when working on an activity.

bias: a systematic distortion.

■ (1) It is a problem in *research* studies (e.g. *experimenter bias, interviewer bias, sampling bias, social desirability bias*, volunteer bias, *observer bias*). (2) It is a problem in the design of psychological tests (e.g. *culture bias*). (3) It is also a term used to indicate the differential treatment of individuals in relation to some characteristic (e.g. ageism, *racism*, gender bias). Such biases can be positive or negative. (4) It is used to denote the human tendency to behave in certain predictable ways (e.g. *confirmatory bias*, and various *attributional biases* such as the self-serving bias).

bilateral: a description for behavioural functions that are equally represented in both cerebral *hemispheres*.

■ ***e.g.*** Vision is processed in the visual cortex of both hemispheres. The right hemisphere receives input from the right visual field of both eyes. As well as being *bilateral* this is also *contralateral* (input to opposite side) and *ipsilateral* (connection to same side of body).

bimodal: a distribution with two *modes*.

binocular: simultaneous functioning of both eyes.

biofeedback: a technique to learn how to control involuntary (autonomic) muscles through the use of feedback about current physiological functioning.

■ Patients are taught how to relax, which changes muscle tone and *autonomic* activity. The patients are given feedback by connecting them to biological monitoring devices. A light or tone signals when a correct alteration occurs.

- **e.g.** The technique has been claimed to be successful with, for example, migraine headaches, Reynaud's disease (constricted blood flow to the fingers or toes), asthma and high blood pressure (*hypertension*).

biological altruism: see *altruism, biological.*

biological clock: a biologically driven means of timing certain behaviours, such as the sleep–wake cycle. See the *suprachiasmatic nucleus.*

biological preparedness: see *preparedness.*

biological psychology (biopsychology): the study of how biological factors influence animal behaviour.

- This includes the influence of both *physiological* and *genetic* factors.
- **TIP** Contrast biological explanations with those using social and cognitive factors.

biological (bodily) rhythm: an *innate*, biologically driven behaviour that is periodically repeated.

- Biological rhythms may be *endogenous*, controlled by *hormones* and/or the *suprachiasmatic nucleus*. Or they may be *exogenous*, i.e. guided by external cues called *zeitgebers*.
- **e.g.** *Circannual, circadian, infradian* and *ultradian rhythms.*
- **TIP** A biological rhythm is not the same thing as a 'biorhythm', which is a pseudoscientific technique using biological rhythms to predict a person's behaviour on a given day.

biopsychosocial: an approach to studying the whole person by combining biological, psychological and social aspects of their life.

biosocial theory: any theory that combines *biological* (*genetic* and/or *physiological*) factors with social ones. See also *biopsychosocial.*

bipolar cell: the middle layer of cells in the *retina* between the layer of *photosensitive cells* and the *retinal ganglion cell* layer.

- Every photosensitive cell (*rod* or *cone*) is connected to more than one bipolar cell, and each bipolar cell is connected to several photosensitive cells.

bipolar depression: see *depression (bipolar).*

birth order effect: the suggestion that first-born children have certain characteristics as compared with subsequent children.

- **e.g.** First-born children have been found to be more intelligent and conformist and higher achieving.
- **TIP** The reasons for such an effect may be because such children have more parental attention during infancy.

black box: the term used by *behaviourists* to refer to the mind.

- Behaviourists regard the concept of the mind as an epiphenomenon, i.e. a secondary process which arises from the biological existence of the brain but does not explain behaviour. Therefore the concept of mind is an irrelevancy in understanding behaviour. Behaviourists are only concerned with what goes into the black box (a stimulus) and what comes out (a response).

blind spot: the region of the *retina* where there are no photoreceptors because the optic fibres collect to pass back to the optic nerve.

- It generally does not disrupt vision because the brain fills in gaps in data.
- ***TIP*** You can be aware of your blind spot if you draw two small black circles, about 15 cm apart, on a piece of white paper. Cover your left eye and focus on the left circle. Move the paper until it is about 25 cm from your face while staring at one circle. The other circle should 'disappear' because the image is falling on your blind spot.

bogus pipeline: a technique to trick respondents into giving truthful answers.

- In an experiment a participant is told that the experimenter can detect whether they are telling the truth or lying by using some direct physiological measure (such as the *galvanic skin response*). This tends to result in the participant providing more truthful answers.

bond disruption: when an infant or child is separated from a caregiver and no links are maintained.

- Separation may result in emotional damage if the bonds between caregiver and child are not maintained. If links are maintained damage may be avoided, for example through occasional visits, or even having a photograph of the caregiver.

bonding: the process of forming close ties with another.

- ***TIP*** There is some confusion between the idea of forming an '*attachment*' and 'bonding'. To some extent the terms are synonymous (as in the use of the phrase 'attachment bonds'). However, 'attachment' appears to involve more *cognitive* activity than 'bonding', and therefore applies exclusively to higher animals such as humans and monkeys. 'Bonding' is a less cognitive activity and is used to describe behaviour associated with *imprinting* in, for example, ducks and sheep, as well as the very early stages of the attachment process in higher animals (see the *skin-to-skin hypothesis*).

boredom effect: performance is depressed as a result of doing a repetitive task previously.

- This reduced achievement can be explained in terms of tiredness, lack of challenge, becoming less aroused, or being simply bored. Boredom effects can be overcome by using *counterbalancing* or leaving a time gap between conditions. It is also possible to make the conditions different but comparable so that participants do not lose interest (e.g. *test–retest*).

bottom–up processing: *processing* that is based on the physical stimulus or data itself, as distinct from *top–down processing* which is influenced by expectations.

- ***e.g.*** The *direct perception theory* is a bottom–up theory, as is the *template matching theory* of pattern recognition.

box-plot: a kind of *graph* used to represent dispersion.

- Three items of data are shown: (1) a line joining the top and bottom score; (2) a box shaded in to show the mid-50% of the scores; and (3) a further indication of where the median lies. The advantage is that this gives a visual picture of the *semi-interquartile range*, the middle section of the data, as well as a view of the extremes.

Set of scores 1

3, 4, 6, [7, 9, 10, 11, 14, 16,] 17, 18, 19

Mid-50% of scores

+

3
Bottom score

10.5
(Median)

19
Top score

In the case of skewed data, this would be apparent in the box plot.

Set of scores 2

3, 8, 9, [9, 10, 11, 14, 15, 16,] 17, 19, 19

Mid-50% of scores

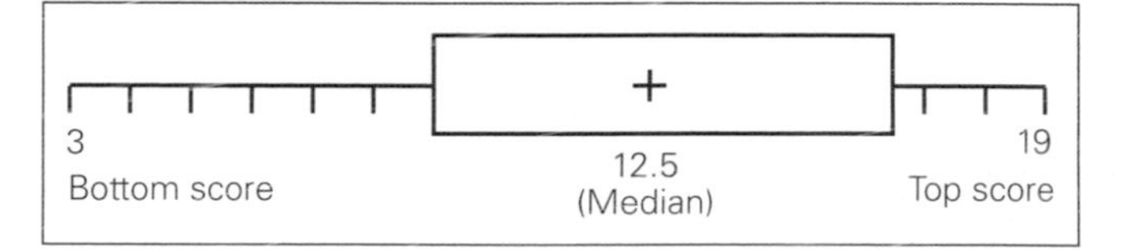

BPS: the British Psychological Society.

brain: the nervous system that is contained within the skull.

- Altogether the human brain contains about 12 billion nerve cells (*neurones*), and about ten times as many glia cells, which provide nutrition and waste removal. The brain is divided into three main areas: (1) The forebrain is the largest part of the human brain. It is also called the *cerebrum*. There are two halves or cerebral *hemispheres* joined by fibres including the *corpus callosum*. Each half of the cerebrum has four lobes: *frontal* (e.g. fine motor movement, thinking), *parietal* (bodily senses, e.g. pain), *occipital* (vision) and *temporal* (hearing, memory, emotion, language).

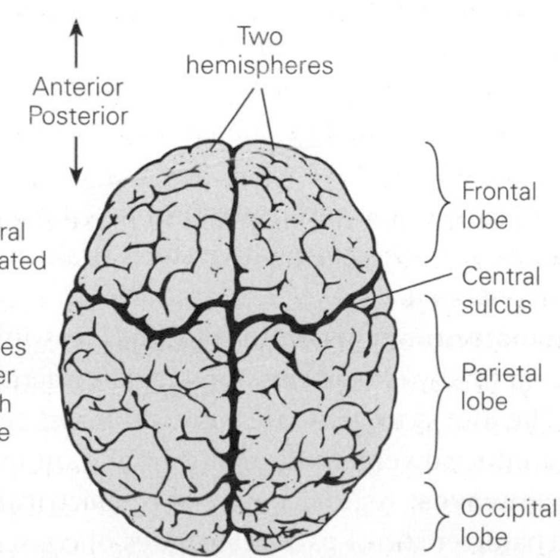

The outer 6 mm of the cerebrum is called the *cerebral cortex* and is grey in colour (your 'grey matter'). Also within the cerebrum are various *subcortical* structures including the *thalamus, hypothalamus, pituitary gland, hippocampus* and *limbic system,* and the *basal ganglia.* (2) The midbrain contains part of the *reticular formation,* and part of the *brainstem.* (3) The hindbrain contains the *cerebellum, pons,* and *medulla oblongata.*

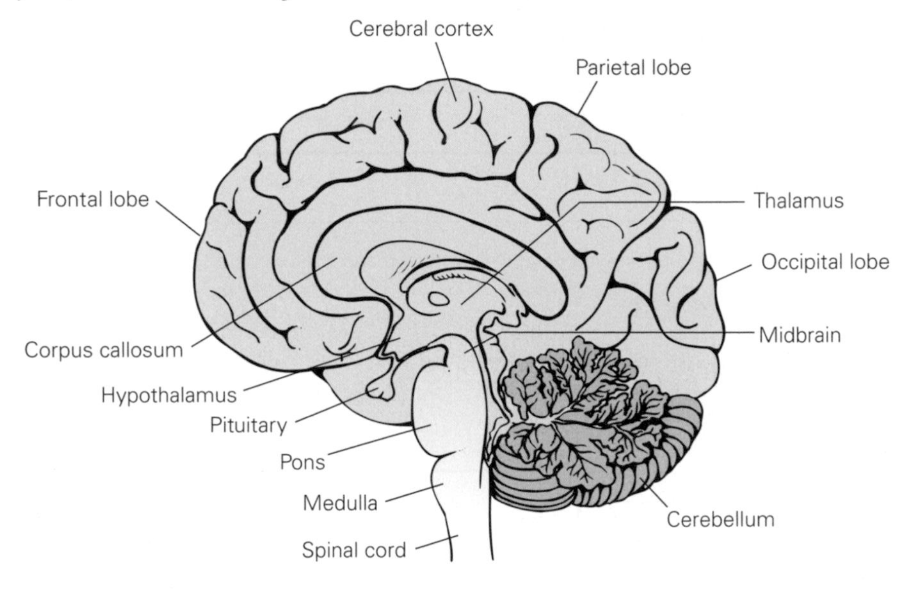

brain scan: a technique used to investigate *cortical* functioning by taking images of the living brain.

■ This technique makes it possible to match regions of the brain to behaviour by asking participants to engage in particular activities while the scan is done. Brain scans are also used to detect brain abnormalities, such as tumours. It is, however, an expensive technique and can be unpleasant (e.g. claustrophobia).

■ ***e.g.*** *CAT scan, PET scan, MRI scan.*

brainstem: the part of the brain that is left when you remove the *cerebellum* and the *cerebrum,* i.e. the *medulla,* the *pons,* the midbrain and some structures of the forebrain.

■ The brainstem monitors the vital life functions and is active even when someone is in a vegetative state. Brainstem death is a sign that life cannot be maintained.

brainstorming: generating lots of ideas uncritically, then evaluating the ideas and finally elaborating them again uncritically.

■ The aim is to generate new, *divergent* approaches to a problem. In order to produce divergent ideas it is important to be uncritical.

brainwaves: regular patterns of electrical activity from the brain which are characteristic of particular states of consciousness.

■ ***e.g.*** *Alpha rhythm* (relaxed wakeful state), *beta rhythm* (active wakeful state), delta, *slow-wave sleep* (deepest sleep).

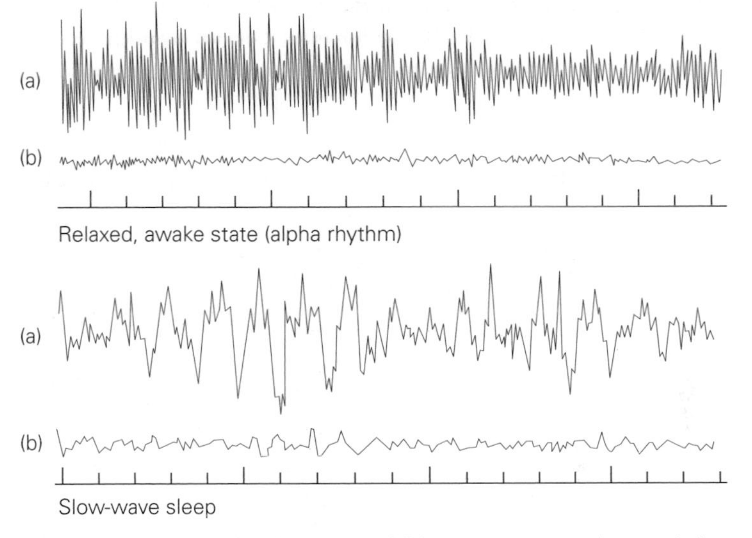

EEG traces showing (a) brainwaves and (b) eye movements characteristic of different states of awareness.

Broca's area: an area in the *frontal lobe* of the forebrain, usually in the left *hemisphere*, related to speech production. See also *Wernicke's area* and *aphasia*.

bulimarexia: a way jointly to describe the eating disorders *anorexia nervosa* and *bulimia nervosa* as one disorder located on a continuum.

■ It may not be possible to distinguish clearly between the two eating disorders as evidenced by the fact that there are anorexics who are classified as 'bulimic anorexics' and many anorexics become bulimic. A continuum would range from restricting anorexics at one end of the spectrum through to obese bulimics at the other.

bulimia nervosa: an eating disorder in which an individual regularly engages in excessive (binge) eating followed by compensatory behaviour such as self-induced vomiting or misuse of laxatives.

■ The *DSM-IV* lists five key characteristics of bulimia: bingeing, purging, both at a frequency of more than two times a week for a period of more than 3 months, distorted body-image and no diagnosis of *anorexia nervosa* (though it may not be so easy to distinguish the two eating disorders, see *bulimarexia*). Bulimia is a more common problem than anorexia and probably more related to dieting. Like anorexia it is more common in women and in the Western world, though this is changing. Explanations include learning theory, social factors and the *disinhibition hypothesis*.

burnout: the physical and/or emotional exhaustion caused by high levels of work stress.

■ It leads to ill health, and a sense of *deindividuation* and perceived inadequacy.

buspirone: a more recent anti-anxiety (*anxiolytic*) drug.

- It acts by increasing the production of serotonin and thus reducing anxiety. It has fewer side-effects than *benzodiazepines*.

bystander behaviour (also called 'bystander effect' or 'bystander apathy')**:** the observation that the presence of others (bystanders) reduces the likelihood that help will be offered in an emergency situation.

- Psychological research has shown that there is an inverse relationship between the number of people present and the willingness of those people to offer help. Many reasons have been suggested for this, including *diffusion of responsibility, evaluation apprehension* and *pluralistic ignorance*.

Cannon–Bard theory: a theory of *emotion* proposed by Cannon (1927) and modified by Bard, suggesting that when an emotionally arousing cue is perceived it leads to both *physiological* and *cognitive* changes which occur simultaneously and independently.

- This view was in opposition to the *James–Lange theory* of emotion.

caregiver sensitivity hypothesis: the explanation that an infant forms a primary *attachment* with one person because that person is most sensitive and responsive to the infant's *social releasers*.

- Caregiver sensitivity hypothesis emphasises the importance of the quality of care given to an infant. The opposite view would focus on the quantity of care, e.g. amount of time spent with the infant.

carpentered environment: the suggestion that people in some cultures are susceptible to certain *visual illusions* (such as the *Müller–Lyer illusion*) because they are exposed to straight lines in their buildings, whereas other cultures may lack such 'carpentering'.

case study: a detailed account of a single individual, institution or event.

- In a study of an individual, the data are likely to concern an individual's past experience and present abilities including, for example, the results of psychological tests. The information would come from interviews with the individual concerned as well as relatives and acquaintances. The advantages of this approach are that it enables us to gain unusual insights, especially into statistically rare behaviours. It is high in *ecological validity* because it is based on real-life experiences. However, the approach is inevitably subjective, unreliable and unreplicable, which challenges the *validity* of the findings. It is likely to be subjective because the investigator influences the kind of data collected and the interpretations put on the data. It is likely to be unreliable because data are often collected retrospectively and cannot be confirmed independently. It is likely to be unreplicable because it concerns rare behaviours. In terms of ethical considerations it is important that *confidentiality* and *privacy* must be protected. Individuals should not be named.
- ***e.g.*** Little Hans, Genie, HM, Kitty Genovese are all classic case studies of individuals. *Organisational psychology* uses case studies of companies and

institutions. *Health psychologists* might study the case of one hospital.

■ ***TIP*** A *single participant* study is not the same as a case study because the former does not involve a detailed record of individual's behaviour. The study of Little Albert is a single participant design experiment rather than a case study because an *independent variable (IV)* was manipulated and only one aspect of his behaviour was studied.

catecholamine: a group of neurotransmitters that are chemically similar.

■ They are also called *monoamines.*

■ ***e.g.*** *Serotonin, dopamine* and *noradrenaline.*

catharsis: the process of releasing pent-up psychic energy.

■ Such things as frustration or *repressed* wishes create pent-up psychic energy which must be released. One way is through *aggression* (see *frustration–aggression hypothesis*). Freud suggested that this energy can be channelled into more positive things such as sport. The problem with this is that sport sometimes makes people more, rather than less, aggressive because it creates rather than dissipates arousal (see *arousal–aggression hypothesis*). Catharsis is also an important component of *psychoanalysis.* During treatment the therapist seeks to make unconscious thoughts conscious, for example, helping the patient to recognise his/her repressed thoughts. This is cathartic because the fact that the repressed thoughts were unconscious prevented the associated emotions being released. By making them conscious, the psychic energy can be released.

CAT scan (computerised axial tomography scan)**:** a method of detecting activity in the living *brain* to determine the function of different regions.

■ Participants are asked to engage in an activity, such as reading. The CAT scan passes X-rays through the head. See *brain scan.*

causal relationship: when one thing is contingent upon another. This is a deterministic relationship.

causal schemata: Kelley's theory of *attribution* that suggests that we determine the causes of behaviour on the basis of a set of general ideas (schemata) about how causes interact to produce certain behaviours.

■ This theory grew out of Kelley's earlier *covariation theory* as a means of explaining how people make attributions when they only have a small amount of information. There are two main kinds of causal schemata. (1) Multiple necessary causes: the idea that a group of behaviours are jointly necessary for a particular cause to be attributed. For example, you only attribute the character of lateness to a person if they are always late. (2) Multiple sufficient causes: the idea that any one of several behaviours is sufficient to arouse an attribution. This is necessary when one only has a single instance of behaviour; people rely on either the *discounting principle* or the *augmenting principle* to make attributions.

CBS: see *culture-bound syndrome.*

ceiling effect: this occurs when a *psychometric test* or other measure of behaviour is too easy and therefore nearly everyone gets a high score.

- The end result is a failure to discriminate between individuals, which also occurs with the *floor effect*.

central capacity theory: a model for divided *attention*, proposed by Kahneman (1973), suggesting that divided attention can be understood in terms of having one central processor that allocates a central pool of attention.

- The amount of capacity varies with circumstances, for example if you are wide awake you have more attentional capacity, different tasks take up different capacity, and motivation increases capacity.
- ***TIP*** This theory has the advantage of being able to explain both focused and divided attention, and incorporating *parallel processing* into the model. However, it cannot explain the effect of task similarity, which can be accounted for by the notion of *modules*.

central executive: the key component of *working memory* which directs activity.

- The executive has limited capacity and is a modality-free system (i.e. it is not visual or auditory). It is roughly equivalent to 'paying attention' to something.

central nervous system (CNS): this comprises the *brain* and the spinal cord.

- The nervous system consists of the central nervous system and the peripheral nervous system, which is further subdivided into the somatic nervous system (all the nerves that control voluntary activity) and the *autonomic nervous system* (which controls involuntary activity).

central sulcus: one of the deepest grooves in the *cerebral cortex*, lies at the top of the *brain*.

- The frontal cortex lies in front of the central sulcus, and the parietal cortex lies behind it.

central tendency: a type of *descriptive statistic* which indicates the mid-point of a set of data.

- It is a way of expressing the typical or 'average' value of a set of data.
- ***e.g.*** *Mean*, *median* and *mode*. Each of these is appropriate in certain circumstances.
- ***TIP*** The word 'average' is a rather vague term for any of these measures and should not be used. It is not mathematically precise.

centration: thinking that is centred in one aspect of a problem (e.g. height) and ignores other important features (e.g. width).

- *Piaget* claimed that this kind of thinking was typical of a child in the concrete operational stage of *cognitive development*. Both *egocentric thought* and the lack of ability to *conserve* are examples of centration.

cerebellum: a large structure at the back of the *hindbrain*, which has many deep folds.

- It is involved with motor control. Recently it has been recognised that the cerebellum is probably more involved with organising the sensory information that guides movement, rather than just controlling the movement itself.

cerebral commisures: fibres that connect the left and right *hemispheres* of the forebrain.

■ The largest bundle of nerves which connects the two hemispheres is called the *corpus callosum*. There are other, smaller, hemispheric connections collectively called commisures.

cerebral cortex: the surface layer of the forebrain or *cerebrum*.

■ It is grey in colour and it is highly folded to make it possible to fit the massive amount of material inside the skull. The folds are called sulci. Mammals have a large amount of cerebral cortex, whereas there is very little in reptiles and fish. Some mammals, such as dolphins, have large skulls and thus the cortex is less folded. See *brain*.

cerebral hemisphere: see *hemisphere*.

cerebrum: the forebrain, the largest part of the human *brain*.

■ It consists of two *hemispheres* joined by the *cerebral commisures*. The outer layer (*cerebral cortex*) is grey. The inner core is white and consists of *myelinated* fibres and the grey *basal ganglia*.

■ ***TIP*** The forebrain is not the same as the frontal lobe (see the *brain*).

chemotherapy: treating illness using *drugs*.

■ ***e.g.*** *Antidepressant* and *antipsychotic drugs*.

chi-squared test of association: an *inferential* test of the association between two or more discrete variables.

■ The test uses nominal data given in frequencies.

■ ***e.g.*** Data in the following form can be analysed using the chi-squared test, to see if obedience to traffic signals is associated with gender:

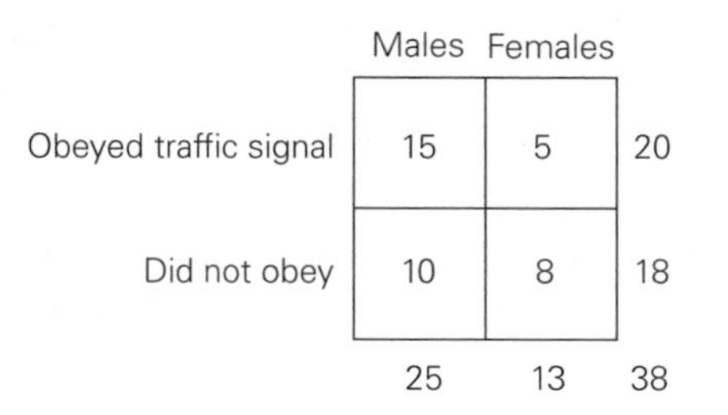

	Males	Females	
Obeyed traffic signal	15	5	20
Did not obey	10	8	18
	25	13	38

chromosomes: the X-shaped bodies that carry all the *genetic* information (*DNA*) for an organism.

■ In humans there are 46 chromosomes arranged in pairs. Each cell of your body contains these chromosomes and they instruct the cell what to do. One member of each pair comes from one's mother and one from one's father, which explains why you have 50% of your mother's genes and 50% of your father's. The gene for any trait, such as eye colour, is represented on both members of a pair. Whichever gene is dominant is the one that is expressed. For example, if you have a gene for blue eyes (recessive gene) from your mother and a gene for brown eyes (dominant gene) from your father, then, because brown is dominant, you will have brown eyes. One pair of chromosomes are called the 'sex chromosomes' because they determine your sex, and other things as well. The sex chromosomes are described as XX for normal females and XY for normal males. The symbol 'Y' is used because this chromosome in males carries very little genetic information.

chunk: an integrated unit of information that forms one unit of memory.

- The amount of material that can be stored in *short-term memory* can be increased through chunking. For example, we can remember more or less the same number of five-letter words as ten-letter ones. Chunking also assists *long-term memory* because it gives meaning to the data.
- ***e.g.*** The list S O S I B M A Q A B P S can be remembered much more easily if we chunk the data: SOS IBM AQA BPS (and it helps even more if you are familiar with the abbreviations, which involves accessing long-term memory).

circadian rhythm: a *biological rhythm* that occurs approximately every 24 hours ('circa' and 'dies' = around the day).

- ***e.g.*** The sleep–wake cycle, body temperature. See also *circannual, infradian* and *ultradian rhythms.*

circannual rhythm: a *biological rhythm* that occurs in a cycle of around a year.

- ***e.g.*** Migration, hibernation. See also *circadian, infradian* and *ultradian rhythms.*

circular reaction: a concept in *Piaget's theory of cognitive development* to describe the repetition of sensorimotor actions which enable the infant to learn new *schema.*

- Primary, secondary and tertiary circular reactions are a feature of the first (sensorimotor) stage of Piaget's theory of cognitive development.

classical conditioning: learning through association.

- Organisms produce *innate* responses to certain stimuli, such as blinking when air is blown in your eye or salivating at the smell of food. These are reflex responses. Neither the stimulus nor the response has been conditioned and thus they are called an unconditioned stimulus (UCS) and an unconditioned response (UCR). An example could be the response of salivation (UCR) to the presence of food (UCS). If a neutral stimulus (NS) becomes associated with a known stimulus–reflex response, then a new link may be formed, i.e. learning or conditioning takes place. Classical conditioning has useful applications, such as *behaviour therapies.*
- ***e.g.*** A bell is rung (NS) just before food (UCS) appears, so that the NS (bell) is associated with the UCS (food). The NS comes to elicit the salivation (UCS) so that a new link is formed (bell and salivation are linked). The NS is now a conditioned stimulus (CS) and the response is now a conditioned response (CR).
- ***TIP*** The other form of conditioning is called *operant conditioning.* In practice the apparently clear theoretical distinction between the two forms of conditioning is not always apparent. Consider the following question: in a classical conditioning experiment, is the food a UCS or a reward?

classificatory system: a system for classifying mental disorders on the basis of diagnostic criteria. See *DSM-IV* and *ICD-10.*

client-centred therapy: a form of *humanistic* therapy that focuses on the problem as the client sees it.

■ The aim of client-centred therapy, or counselling, is to increase the client's *self-esteem* through *unconditional positive regard* from the therapist. This is based on the concept that maladjusted behaviour or unhappiness occurs as a result of receiving conditional love in childhood and, as a result, continuing to strive for acceptance. Such striving blocks the ability to self-actualise. Client-centred therapy allows the individual to accept themselves, increase their sense of self-esteem and thus reduce incongruence between self and *ideal self*. Ultimately this results in self-acceptance and *self-actualisation*.

clinical interview: a form of unstructured interview (see *survey*).

■ The interviewer starts with a predetermined set of questions, but as the interview proceeds these questions are adapted in line with some of the responses given. This allows for the possibility that the interviewee will give unexpected answers and that questions generated from the interviewee's responses will lead to new discoveries about behaviour, thus maximising the amount of information that is gained. The more informal atmosphere is good for some participants but the method is highly susceptible to *interviewer bias*.

■ ***e.g.*** It is the method used by *clinicians* when interviewing their patients. Piaget used the same method in his research with children.

clinical psychology: the branch of *applied psychology* concerned with the diagnosis and treatment of *abnormal behaviour*.

clinician (also called 'clinical psychologist')**:** a person whose profession is concerned with the diagnosis and treatment of *abnormal behaviour*.

closed question: on a *questionnaire survey*, a kind of question that has a limited range of answers.

■ The advantage is that such questions are easy to score, and they reduce respondents' tendency to give socially desirable answers. On the other hand, closed questions reduce the richness of data collected and they may force respondents to misrepresent what they feel/think. The opposite is *open-ended questions*.

■ ***e.g.*** 'What are your dreams like? Nonsensical/meaningful/cannot remember them.'

cluster sample: a *sampling technique* where participants are selected from specific geographical regions, groups or classes.

■ This saves time (and money) when trying to locate participants because you are targeting specific clusters who can be found together. However, the sample tends not to be representative.

CNS: see *central nervous system*.

co-action: see *social facilitation*.

cocktail party effect: in relation to focused *attention*, Cherry's (1953) observation that people at a cocktail party are aware of the physical features of non-attended conversations.

■ ***e.g.*** If participants in an experiment are questioned about the non-attended message, they can report the sex of the speaker (male or female) but not whether the non-attended message was in a foreign language.

- ***TIP*** Sometimes this effect is described as the ability to detect your name being spoken in the general hubbub of a cocktail party. However, this was not what Cherry described.

cognition: knowing, perceiving or believing.

cognitive appraisal theory: an extension of the *cognitive labelling theory* of *emotion* that emphasises the role of cognitive appraisal.

- The experience of an emotional state depends on an assessment of its quality. Cognitive appraisal theory offers a set of rules for working out what emotion you will feel given a certain set of circumstances.
- ***e.g.*** Smith and Ellsworth (1987) suggested that an experience is appraised in terms of the desirability of the situation, the effort one anticipates spending, the certainty of the situation and control one feels. For example, an unpleasant situation may lead variously to anger (if caused by another), to guilt (if brought about by self), or to sadness (when controlled by circumstances).

cognitive–behavioural therapy: a form of *psychotherapy* which combines the cognitive and behavioural approaches. It has come to be equivalent to *cognitive therapy*.

cognitive development: the cognitive (mental) changes that take place as a person grows older.

- This generally refers to childhood changes in abstract thought processes but can apply to many areas of behaviour, such as moral and gender developments which also involve mental changes. The two main approaches are *Piaget's* and *Vygotsky's theories of cognitive development*, both of which contrast with the more traditional approach of *learning theory* (where cognitive development is seen as being due to *reinforcement* and *association*).

cognitive–developmental theory: any theory of development that focuses on how a child's thinking changes with age.

- Such theories are typically stage theories, suggesting that development proceeds through a sequence of innately determined stages which follow an invariant sequence. Each stage is defined by the kind of thought (*cognition*) used at that age.
- ***e.g.*** *Piaget's theory of cognitive development*, Martin and Halverson's *gender schema theory*.

cognitive dissonance: an explanation for attitude change based on the concept that dissonance is an unpleasant state which occurs whenever an individual holds two cognitions (ideas, beliefs, attitudes) which are psychologically inconsistent.

- The drive to restore balance results in attitude change.

cognitive interview: an interview technique based on our knowledge about the way human memory works.

- ***e.g.*** Using knowledge about retrieval cues.

cognitive labelling theory: a theory of *emotion* proposed by Schachter and Singer (1962) suggesting that all emotional experiences are preceded by a generalised state of physiological arousal; this arousal is then 'labelled' on the basis of *situational* cues and past experience.

cognitive map: a mental representation of spatial relationships.

■ This concept is a challenge to *learning theory* which cannot explain how an animal can become familiar with the plan of a maze in the absence of any rewards. Under such conditions no learning should take place but research has shown that it does. See *latent learning*.

cognitive miser: a term used to describe the fact that people generally prefer to reduce mental (*cognitive*) effort.

■ When processing large amounts of data, we try to reduce the associated mental activity by finding shortcuts such as *heuristics* or *stereotypes*.

cognitive psychology: this uses internal mental processes to explain behaviour.

■ The word 'cognitive' is derived from a Latin word 'cognitio' meaning 'to apprehend' or 'understand'. See also *information processing approach*.

■ ***e.g.*** Cognitive psychology is concerned with topics such as *memory*, *perception*, thought, *language* and *attention*. There are various associated areas of psychology such as *social cognition* and *cognitive–behavioural therapy*. There are also many applications of cognitive psychology such as in air traffic control (improved attention, avoidance of error) and methods of improving memory.

cognitive restructuring therapy: a *cognitive therapy* developed by Beck which aims to reformulate faulty thinking.

■ The therapist identifies the patient's self-defeating assumptions and substitutes more adaptive ones. This therapy has proved useful for treating anxiety and depression (see *cognitive triad*).

■ ***e.g.*** You may feel very anxious about exams and this anxiety causes you to fail exams. If you take on new beliefs about your exam performance, this will reduce your anxiety and improve your examination performance.

cognitive style: an individual's characteristic way of thinking.

■ ***e.g.*** A tendency towards *convergent* or *divergent thinking*, use of imagery, *field dependence*, or independence.

■ ***TIP*** It has been suggested that people who study science subjects tend to have a cognitive style that involves more convergent thinking, ability to reason logically, preference for 'closed' tasks and are more conformist, as contrasted with individuals who choose arts subjects.

cognitive therapy (also called 'cognitive–behavioural therapy')**:** a form of *psychotherapy* which attempts to change a client's thoughts and beliefs as a way of treating *maladaptive* behaviour.

■ This is based on the assumption that maladaptive behaviour is due to faulty cognitions (thoughts and beliefs), i.e. the way the individual thinks about the problem, rather than the problem itself. Cognitive therapy aims to change the individual's cognitions and thus 'cure' the problem. The advantage of such therapies is that they are quick and lend themselves to assessment because there are measurable outcomes. They are also client-centred. The limitations are that they require effort on the part of the client and they do not always address underlying problems.

■ ***e.g.*** *Rational–emotive therapy* (Ellis), *cognitive restructuring therapy* (Beck), *stress inoculation therapy* (Meichenbaum), *personal construct therapy* (Kelley).

cognitive triad: negative thoughts about the self, the world and the future, found in depressed patients.

■ This is a core concept in Beck's *cognitive restructuring therapy*. The depressed client must learn to replace negative thoughts with positive ones in all three areas.

cohort: a group of individuals who share common characteristics such as being the same age.

cohort effect: in a *cross-sectional* research study, where participants of different ages are compared, observed differences may be due to social changes from one generation to another rather than age per se.

■ ***e.g.*** If you studied attitudes towards music and compared young people of 15, 25 and 35, their attitudes would probably reflect what music was popular when they were young rather than age-related differences.

collective unconscious: see *Jungian*.

collectivist: a culture where individuals share tasks, belongings and income.

■ The people may live in large family groups and value interdependence, unlike *individualist* societies. The emphasis is on 'we-ness' rather than 'I'.

■ ***e.g.*** Israeli *kibbutzim*, many African cultures, communes.

commisurotomy: a surgical procedure where the *cerebral commisures* are severed.

■ See *split-brain procedure*.

companionate love: *love* which is on a continuum with liking, as distinct from *passionate love*.

■ Companionate love suggests a more entwined relationship than 'liking'. It is the kind of love you feel for your friends and family. Companionate love is quite different from passionate love. It develops through mutual rewards, familiarity, steady and positive emotions, and tends to deepen over time; whereas passionate love is based on intense emotions which often become diluted over time, novelty and a mixture of emotions (joy and anxiety, excitement and deep despair).

comparative psychology: the study of non-human animals in order to gain insights into human behaviour by making comparisons.

■ In practice a lot of comparative psychology also involves making comparisons between different species of non-human animals, as well as studying non-human animals in their own right (the study of *animal behaviour* and *ethology*).

■ ***e.g.*** Studies of *reproductive* strategies in non-human animals have led to *socio-biological* explanations for the formation of *interpersonal relationships* in humans.

compliance: conforming with the majority in spite of not really agreeing with them.

■ Kelman identified this as one of three types of *conformity* (the other two are *identification* and *internalisation*). In the case of compliance, conformity to majority or minority influence is only superficial; it stops when there are no group pressures to conform.

concordance: the extent to which a twin pair share similar traits or diseases.

■ ***e.g.*** The degree to which twins both have the same condition such as schizophrenia (if 20 twin pairs are studied and in 16 of them, both twins exhibit schizophrenia, this would produce a concordance of 16/20 or 0.80, which is very high concordance).

concrete operation: a stage in *Piaget's theory of cognitive development.*

concurrent validity: a means of assessing the validity or trueness of a psychological test.

■ It aims to demonstrate the extent to which performance on the test correlates positively with other tests of the same trait. If the test is a good one we would expect a high *positive correlation.*

■ ***TIP*** See other forms of establishing validity: *content, construct, criterion, face,* and *predictive validity.*

conditional love: see *unconditional positive regard.*

conditioned reinforcer: see *secondary reinforcer.*

conditioning: when one response is made dependent on another.

■ ***TIP*** It is important to remember that conditioning takes place with no conscious or mental activity.

cone: a cone-shaped *photosensitive cell* in the *retina* that responds to certain wavelengths of light and thus reports colour. Most cones are found in the central region of the eye (*fovea*).

■ There are three types of cone: those which are most sensitive to red, blue or green hues. Colour vision is explained by both the *trichromatic* and *opponent-process theories.*

confabulation: when memory fails, you manufacture something appropriate.

■ This is likely to be a problem in *eyewitness testimony.*

confederate: a colleague of the experimenter who pretends to be a participant during an experiment but is in fact simply following instructions.

■ ***e.g.*** In Milgram's study both the 'experimenter' and the 'learner' were confederates following pre-written scripts.

confidentiality: the requirement that information provided by participants in research or during therapy is not made available to other people, without *informed consent.*

■ With some information this is a requirement of the Data Protection Act.

confirmatory bias: we prefer information which confirms rather than challenges our beliefs and *stereotypes.*

■ The consequence of this is that stereotypes are *self-fulfilling* — because you ignore information which is inconsistent, it appears that your beliefs were correct.

conformity: a form of *social influence,* where group pressure (real or imagined) results in a change in behaviour, but not necessarily attitudes.

- One may conform publicly to group pressure but not change one's attitudes (*compliance* and *identification*). Sometimes conformity may involve a private change of opinion (*internalisation*). The pressure may be due to majority or *minority influence.* Majority influence works through pressure of number whereas minority influence relies on conversion. Conformity occurs through either *informational* or *normative social influence.*
- ***TIP*** Conformity and *obedience* both involve changing behaviour in response to social influence. Conformity is a response to group pressure (majority or minority). Obedience is to a single individual or law. Sometimes both are involved as in Zimbardo's prison study. In this study the prisoners were obeying the guards and were conforming to social roles (identification).

confounding variable: a *variable* that is not the intended *independent variable* but which has an effect on the *dependent variable.*

- This may happen because the variable in question is mistakenly manipulated or allowed to vary along with the independent variable. If a confounding variable is controlled then it is called an *extraneous variable.* There are two kinds of confounding variable: *constant errors* (which need to be controlled) and *random errors* (which can be assumed to affect all conditions equally and therefore do not need to be controlled).
- ***e.g.*** Testing two groups of participants on recall of organised and disorganised word lists but testing one group in the morning and the other in the afternoon. Any difference in performance may be due to the time of day (confounding variable) rather than the extent of organisation of the word list (independent variable). Both variables may affect recall (the dependent variable). *Order effects* are an example of a confounding variable.
- ***TIP*** A confounding variable continues to confound the experimental finding. An extraneous variable is extra to the independent variable.

congenital: behaviours that are present at birth but are not *innate.*

- ***e.g.*** Cerebral palsy is a congenital condition. Some children are born with cerebral palsy, but it is not inherited; it occurs because of brain damage resulting from a lack of oxygen.

conscience: a moral sense of right and wrong.

- In *psychoanalytic* theory it is suggested that the conscience develops through identification with a same-sex parent during the phallic stage of psychosexual development. At this time the *superego* is formed.

consciousness: being aware.

- In *cognitive psychology* consciousness is a form of *attention.* In *psychoanalytic theory,* it is one of three levels of mind (the others being the *preconscious* and the *unconscious*). The concept of consciousness is also one of the criteria for distinguishing humans from other animals. It is suggested that only higher animals have a sense of consciousness or self-awareness. One way to test this is to put a red mark on an animal's nose and show them a mirror. A child aged under 1½ years typically touches the mirror, whereas an older child demonstrates self-awareness by touching their own nose. Chimpanzees and orangutans also touch their own nose, but monkeys and elephants do not appear to recognise themselves in a mirror.

conservation: the logical rule that quantity does not change even when a display is transformed, i.e. the quantity is conserved.

- *Piaget* claimed that this kind of thinking was typical of a child in the concrete operational stage (over the age of 7). The pre-operational child's thinking is guided more by external appearances than internal consistency or logic, which is why they are unable to conserve (they are 'fooled' by external appearances). This is not to say that children of this age are not using rules but that their rules lack internal logic. Piaget demonstrated the conservation of numbers by showing a child two rows of counters. He asked the child if there were the same number of counters in each row. He then spread out the counters in one row so it looked as if there were more, and asked them the question again. Children under the age of 7 said the one row did have more counters, demonstrating an inability to understand the principle that quantity cannot be changed in this way. Piaget also tested the conservation of mass (balls of clay) and volume (beakers of water).
- ***TIP*** Subsequent research has found that younger children may be able to cope with the conservation task if, for example, they are only asked one question. However, there are still age differences.

conspecific: an animal that is a member of the same species as another animal.

constant error: any *confounding variable* that has a systematically different effect on the dependent variable in different conditions.

- Constant errors do need to be controlled whereas *random errors*, which are also confounding variables, do not need to be *controlled* because they do not have systematic effects.
- ***e.g.*** When testing two groups of participants, a group of girls is tested in a sunny, clean room whereas a group of boys is given the same test in a dingy corridor. Pleasantness of surroundings is a constant error. Better performance might be due to the conditions rather than gender.

constructivist theory: Gregory's (1966) theory that suggests that *perception* is the result of constructing *hypotheses*, on the basis of past experience and testing these against the sensory data.

- This is a *top–down processing* theory, as distinct from the *direct perception theory*. The theory can explain how we cope with often incomplete and ambiguous sensory data and can explain *perceptual set* and *perceptual constancy*. It cannot explain why vision is so fast and accurate, even in novel situations.

construct validity: a means of assessing the validity or trueness of a psychological test. It aims to demonstrate the extent to which performance on the test measures an identified underlying construct.

- **e.g.** We would expect a test of intelligence to measure our theoretical view of intelligence, i.e. the 'construct'.
- **TIP** See other forms of establishing validity: *content, concurrent, criterion, face,* and *predictive validity.*

content analysis: a kind of *observational study* where behaviour is observed indirectly in written or verbal material.

- A detailed analysis is made of, for example, books, diaries or TV programmes. It is possible to count the frequency of particular behaviours using categories. Counting is a *quantitative* activity but categorising is *qualitative.* Such categories are determined either by: (1) the researcher, using past theoretical research and/or collaboration with other researchers; (2) using 'indigenous categories', i.e. naturally occurring categories found in the text or by the participants.
- **e.g.** Studies which assess the contents of television advertisements may be used to show that men and women still play sex-stereotyped roles. The study would draw up lists of different behaviours, such as a list of feminine and masculine-type activities, and record whether males or females are seen doing the activities.

content validity: a means of assessing the validity or trueness of a psychological test. It aims to demonstrate that the content of the test represents the area of interest.

- **e.g.** On a test of intelligence we would expect the content of the test to cover all aspects of what we think of as intelligence.
- **TIP** See other forms of establishing validity: *construct, concurrent, criterion, face,* and *predictive validity.*

context-dependent recall: related to *cue-dependent forgetting,* where recall of some material is improved if recall takes place in the same context as where the material was first learned.

- **e.g.** You may be better able to recall your school work if you are tested in the classroom where you had the lesson. It is possible that features in the room provide cues for accessing memories.
- **TIP** This phenomenon can be applied to improving the recall of potential eyewitnesses. The police often stage reconstructions to jog people's memories, such as getting someone to dress like the victim and retrace his/her footsteps so the people watching might recall new details.

contingency theory: Fielder's (1965) theory of leadership based on the notion that certain leaders are effective in certain situations.

- In other words, effective leadership is contingent on certain other factors, chiefly the favourability of the situation for the leader. Fielder used the concept of the 'least-preferred co-worker (LPC)' to assess how potential leaders deal with subordinates. (1) Socio-emotional leaders had good relationships with subordinates (high LPC rating). They are good in situations of clearly defined tasks and moderate favourableness. Such leaders encourage confidence and loyalty, and ease interpersonal conflicts. (2) Task-oriented leaders have low LPC ratings, and are best when the conditions either are highly favourable or highly unfavourable. In such situations either there are fewer interpersonal conflicts or they can be overlooked because the task demands are high.

continuous reinforcement: when *reinforcement* is received every time the right response is made.

■ This is a less effective *reinforcement schedule* than *partial reinforcement* because the individual expects it on every trial and therefore 'notices' as soon as it stops, leading to *extinction*.

contralateral: a description for behavioural functions that are controlled by the opposite side of the cerebral *hemisphere*, as distinct from *ipsilateral*.

■ ***e.g.*** All sensory and motor processes are contralateral — the right hemisphere controls the left side of the body.

■ ***TIP*** Most people have a dominant cerebral hemisphere; the left side is dominant for right-handed people.

control: this refers to the extent to which any *variable* is held constant or regulated by the *researcher*.

■ In an experiment the experimenter manipulates (controls) the *independent variable*, measures the *dependent variable*, and also tries to control any *confounding variables* so that they do not interfere with the findings. The *laboratory experiment* provides the best situation for controlling any *variables*.

control condition: in an experiment with a *repeated measures design*, the condition which does not include the *independent variable* and acts as a comparison to the *experimental condition*.

■ This makes it possible to study any effects of the independent variable and also control for *participant variables*. See also *control group*.

■ ***e.g.*** In an experiment that seeks to compare the effects of noise or no noise on doing homework, the experimental condition will be conducted with noise (independent variable) and in the control condition the same participants will be tested in no-noise conditions to provide a comparison.

■ ***TIP*** The drawback of using this approach is the problem of *order effects*.

control group: in an experiment with an *independent measures design*, the group of participants who do not receive the *independent variable* and act as a comparison to the *experimental group*.

■ This makes it possible to study any effects of the independent variable. In some studies participants in the control group may receive a *placebo* or substitute treatment without any effect so that they think they are receiving the independent variable. If this is not done, participants may behave differently in the *experimental condition* as a consequence of a *confounding variable* such as attention.

■ ***e.g.*** If an experiment seeks to find the effects of organisation (independent variable) on short-term memory recall, participants in the experimental group would be given an organised word list to remember, whereas participants in the control group would have the same words, but not in an organised manner. (The same words would be used to control for the possibly *confounding* effects of word familiarity.)

controlled observation: an *observational study* that is conducted in a controlled, *laboratory* environment.

- This method gains in terms of *internal validity* (greater control) but loses *external (ecological) validity* because it becomes more artificial.
- ***e.g.*** The *strange situation* involved observations of children with their caregivers where the procedures were standardised and highly controlled.

controlled processing: *processing* that requires conscious *attention*, as distinct from *automatic processing*.

- This kind of processing is required during skill acquisition and for unpractised or difficult tasks. It reduces the capacity available for other simultaneous tasks.
- ***e.g.*** When one is learning to drive it seems hard to imagine ever being able to do it all and talk at the same time.

controlled variable: any *variable* other than the *independent variable* that is held constant or controlled by the experimenter.

convergence: turning the eyes inward to focus on an object *binocularly*.

convergent thinking: thought that focuses on one correct solution.

- The aim is to bring information together as a means of solving a problem, as in *deductive reasoning*. It is contrasted with *divergent thinking*.
- ***e.g.*** Calculating the area of a triangle using a formula.
- ***TIP*** Neither convergent nor divergent thinking is 'better' — each is appropriate for a different problem.

core sleep: a term to indicate those aspects of sleep that are critical.

- ***e.g.*** *Slow wave sleep* and possibly some parts of *REM sleep*.

corpus callosum: a bundle of nerve fibres in the *brain* that connects the right and left *hemispheres* of the *cerebral cortex*.

correlation: a measure of the extent to which two variables (*co-variables*) are related and jointly change together. See *correlation coefficient*.

- The covariables may increase together (*positive correlation*), or as one increases the other decreases (*negative correlation*). In both cases the covariables are changing in a consistent relationship. A complete lack of relationship is called *zero correlation*. These relationships can be illustrated on a *scattergram*. Positive and negative correlations are linear (in a line) but it is also possible to have a *curvilinear correlation* (i.e. not linear).
- ***e.g.*** It is likely that age and height are positively correlated (as you get older you get taller) and that age and number of brain cells are negatively correlated.

correlational analysis: this is conducted using either descriptive statistics (a *scattergram*) and/or *inferential statistics* (a test of correlation).

correlational study: an investigation that uses *correlational analysis*.

- NB. Strictly speaking a correlation is a statistical procedure and not a type of design. Therefore we should say an 'investigation using correlational analysis' rather than a 'correlational study'. Nevertheless the latter phrase is sometimes used. The terms *independent* and *dependent variables* are not used because there is no direct manipulation of variables as in an *experiment*. The variables in a correlational study are called *covariables*. The main drawback of using correlational analysis is that cause and effect relationships cannot be identified. Correlational studies are used when experimental manipulation would be unethical or impractical. It means that we can discover possible causal relationships between covariables and the findings might suggest future research ideas for investigating causal relationships.

■ ***TIP*** There is a temptation in correlational research to impute a *causal relationship* between the covariables whereas it may be that a third factor (or more) acted as a causal factor. However, if there is a lack of relationship between the covariables, this means that one cannot have caused the other. So, a correlation can demonstrate **no** causal relationship.

correlation coefficient: a numerical value that represents the degree to which two sets of data are correlated.

■ It is calculated using a test of correlation, such as *Spearman's rho* or *Pearson's product–moment test of correlation*. The number produced by such a test will lie between +1 and –1. A perfect *positive correlation* is +1.00 and perfect *negative correlation* is –1.00.

correspondent inference theory: a theory of *attribution* which suggests that we explain behaviour by making observations of others and inferring a corresponding attitude or disposition.

■ This is based on the assumption that behaviours are caused by underlying attitudes or personality characteristics (a *dispositional explanation*).

■ ***e.g.*** If someone shouts at a cyclist, we might assume that they are a hostile person who feels aggravated by cyclists. Correspondent inference theory predicts that we make dispositional, rather than situational, explanations when (1) the actor (person doing the behaving) appears to act intentionally and (2) the behaviour is uncommon, low in social desirability, has hedonic relevance (had specific effects for the perceiver) and/or has personalism (is seen as being aimed at the perceiver personally). In real life the attribution process may be more complex. In addition the theory is restricted to actions that are intended and voluntary.

cortex: the outer part of an organ.

■ ***e.g.*** The *cerebral cortex*, the *adrenal* cortex.

cortical: related to the *cortex*.

corticotropin-release factor (CRF): a hormone produced by the *hypothalamus* in response to stress. CRF stimulates the anterior *pituitary gland* to secrete its hormones.

cortisol: a *hormone* produced by the *adrenal gland* that is associated with stress.

■ Cortisol elevates blood sugar levels and enhances metabolism, acting in a similar fashion to activity of the *sympathetic nervous system*. Raised levels of cortisol in the urine are used as an indicator of stress.

cost–benefit analysis: a comparison between the costs of something and the related benefits, in order to decide on a course of action.

- If the costs are too great or the benefits too small, then no action will be taken.
- ***e.g.*** This form of analysis has been applied to *helping behaviour* (the 'cost–reward' model) and to making *ethical* decisions.
- ***TIP*** The limitation with using a cost–benefit analysis for ethical decisions is that it is difficult to predict both costs and benefits prior to conducting a study. And even then it is hard to quantify them, or to decide on whose perspective to use: the participant, the researcher or society in general. A cost–benefit analysis may lead to precisely the same ethical dilemmas that it is trying to avoid. See *arousal — cost–reward model* of prosocial behaviour, and *social exchange theory* of relationships.

cost–reward model: see *arousal — cost–reward model.*

counselling: see *client-centred therapy*.

counterbalancing: an experimental procedure used to overcome *order effects*.

- The method ensures that each condition in an experiment is equally likely to be used first and second by participants, so that *order effects* are balanced.
- ***e.g.*** If there are two conditions in an experiment, A and B, then some participants do A–B and others do B–A. Ideally participants should be *randomly allocated* to either pattern. A further possibility is to use the ABBA design, where everyone does both conditions twice but the order effects are counterbalanced by A being first and last.

counter-conformity: see *anti-conformity*.

counter-stereotype: a *stereotype* which is deliberately constructed to be opposite to traditional stereotypes.

- ***e.g.*** Portraying a judge as a Black woman, or portraying a thief as a young woman with a baby.
- ***TIP*** This is done in the media to alter *prejudices*.

covariables: the *variables* in a *correlational study* that may vary together (covary).

- ***e.g.*** If a researcher studies the relationship between IQ and age, the covariables are IQ and age.

covariation theory: Kelley's theory of *attribution*, which suggests that the explanations for behaviour are based on the tendency for two things to vary jointly (i.e. to covary).

- Covariance is determined by consistency, distinctiveness and consensus. When all three are high, external (*situational*) attributions will be made. When distinctiveness and consensus are low but consistency is high, internal (*dispositional*) attributions are made. However, the three types of information are not always available to the attributer and it is difficult to assess covariation. Kelley developed the idea of *causal schemata* to explain how we make attributions in the absence of detailed information, such as when observing a single event.

creativity: *problem solving* which results in a novel solution to a problem.

■ There are *psychological tests* of creativity or *divergent thinking*. Such tests include tasks such as: to think of novel uses for everyday objects, to think of consequences such as 'What would happen if national laws were abolished', or to write as many meanings for a word as you can. Such tests would be useful, for example, in selecting individuals to do creative jobs. The drawback with the tests is that the evaluation is mainly subjective, for example are the testee's novel uses for a paperclip good ideas?

CRF: see *corticotropin-release factor*.

criminal psychology: the branch of *applied psychology* that seeks to explain antisocial and criminal behaviour.

■ Concerns of criminal psychology include offender profiling, *eyewitness testimony*, behaviour of juries, the study of social influences on criminal behaviour, effects of media on violence, ways of controlling aggression, crime prevention, crime–victim interactions, and issues related to policing.

criterion validity: a means of assessing the validity or trueness of a psychological test. It aims to demonstrate the extent to which people who do well on the test, do well on other things that you would expect to be associated with the test.

■ ***e.g.*** Does someone who does well on an intelligence test also do well at school? The 'criterion' is doing well at school as a means of establishing the validity of the test.

■ ***TIP*** See other forms of establishing validity: *content, construct, concurrent, face*, and *predictive validity*.

critical period: a biologically determined period of time during which an animal is exclusively receptive to certain changes.

■ The term is derived from embryology. An embryo is the earliest stage of prenatal development. At this time of development, certain events must take place during a particular window of time or they will not happen at all. For example, in human development the arms begin to develop between day 24 and 26. Any interference with development at this critical stage will permanently affect the limb's development — it will not happen. *Ethologists* adopted the concept as a way to describe certain aspects of psychological development such as *imprinting*. Critics, however, have suggested that the term 'critical' is too strong because psychological developments do take place outside the specified 'window' of time, though less easily. Therefore the term *sensitive period* is preferred.

■ ***e.g.*** Critical periods have been proposed for *attachment* and *language acquisition*.

critical value: numerical values found in statistical tables that are used to determine the *significance* of an *inferential* test.

■ The *observed value*, obtained from the data collected in a research study, is compared with the critical value in the statistical table in order to determine statistical significance.

■ ***TIP*** In most cases the observed value must exceed the critical value in order to reject the *null hypothesis*.

cross-cultural study: a research study that compares different *cultures* with regard to certain practices (e.g. child-rearing practices) or behaviours (e.g. aggression).

■ Different cultures use different methods of *socialisation*. If these different methods nevertheless result in the same behaviours (e.g. men are equally aggressive in many different cultures), then this is evidence of universal and *innate* behaviours. The study of different practices also gives us insight into our own cultural practices. There are numerous limitations to cross-cultural studies. For example, practices may not be directly comparable, we cannot know how representative any *sample* of behaviour is of the whole culture, observers may misunderstand language or behaviours, and the methods used may be an *imposed etic* and thus inappropriate.

■ ***e.g.*** Margaret Mead's studies of Samoan girls growing up and of New Guinea tribes such as the Arapesh have been a rich source of data for psychology and anthropology.

cross-generational effect: in a *longitudinal* research study the sample used may be unrepresentative of people in general because of events specific to that generation.

■ ***e.g.*** Studies of infant deprivation conducted during the Second World War may involve other factors than deprivation alone.

cross-sectional study: a research method that enables comparisons over time.

■ Groups of individuals of different ages are compared at the same moment in time. Age is the *independent variable* and since age is not actually manipulated by the experimenter, this form of research is a *quasi-experiment*. Cross-sectional studies have the advantage of being quick (in comparison with *longitudinal studies*) and therefore less expensive. They also avoid the *cross-generational effect*. On the other hand, the method cannot control for *participant variables* and may suffer from the *cohort effect*.

■ ***e.g.*** This method is often used in developmental research, such as in studies that have investigated Piaget's concept of *conservation*.

crowd: a large but temporary gathering of people with a common focus.

■ The adjective 'crowded' refers to being in a crowd and closely pressed together, which is different from *crowding*.

crowd behaviour: the result of being a member of a crowd.

■ ***e.g.*** Being in a crowd may lead to *deindividuation*, *conformity*, *aggression* or other *antisocial behaviour*.

crowding: the psychological response to some situations of population density.

■ Population density leads to increased sensory stimulation, because of all the people and therefore physiological arousal. Explanations for the effects of crowding include *arousal–aggression hypothesis*, *density–intensity hypothesis* and social pathology hypothesis. Crowding can be controlled by the use of *territories* and *defensible spaces*.

cue-arousal theory: an explanation for aggression that is an extension of the *frustration–aggression hypothesis*.

■ Individuals who are frustrated do not express aggression unless they are 'triggered' by some environmental cue.

■ ***e.g.*** Guns may act as a cue, as may the sight of anything associated with aggression.

cue-dependent forgetting: forgetting as a result of the absence of suitable retrieval cues.

■ ***e.g.*** People are able to remember more (forget less) if they are given the category names (cues) of words they have to memorise. See also: *context-dependent* and *mood-dependent recall.*

cued-recall: a form of memory test.

■ Participants are given material to be learned, and then when recall is tested, they are given cues (such as category names) to enhance recall. This permits one to discover all the words that are available, not just those that are currently accessible.

cultural determinism: the belief that behaviour is determined by one's culture more than by innate, biological factors.

cultural relativism: the view that one cannot judge a behaviour properly unless it is viewed in the context of the culture in which it originates.

■ ***e.g.*** When trying to define a standard for distinguishing abnormality from normality the behaviours are inevitably relative to cultural context, such as the question of statistical frequency — anxiety may be more common in one culture than another.

culture: the human-made part of the environment.

■ The set of rules, morals and methods of interaction that bind a group of people. These rules, morals and so on are the products of *socialisation,* that is we learn them through our social interactions with other members of our culture. Cultural identity is an important part of personal identity (see *social identity theory*). See also *sub-culture.*

■ ***TIP*** The concept of different cultures does not just apply to cultures of people living in different countries but also to different historical cultures.

culture bias: the tendency to judge all people in terms of your own *cultural* assumptions.

■ This distorts or *biases* your judgement and is a problem in *observational studies* and the design of *psychometric tests.* See also *ethnocentric.*

culture-bound syndrome (CBS): a mental illness that is specific to a particular culture.

■ ***e.g.*** 'Koro' is a disorder diagnosed in China (the feeling that one's penis is retracting into one's abdomen and the belief that this will result in death).

■ ***TIP*** Such culturally bound syndromes raise questions about the universality of mental illnesses and the usefulness of classification schemes such as the *DSM.*

culture-free test: a goal for a *psychometric test,* to ensure that the test is not biased towards one culture.

- The danger is that if, for example, IQ tests are not culture-free, then inevitably some individuals will perform less well. This means that they might appear to be less intelligent, whereas in fact their poorer performance was due to the fact that test items did not make sense to them, i.e. the items were not culture-free. See *imposed etic*.
- **e.g.** One of the earliest IQ tests, the Army Alpha tests, had the following item: 'Crisco is a: patent medicine/disinfectant/toothpaste/food product?' [It is a food product.] This item is not culture-free both in terms of ethnic and historical differences.

cupboard-love theory: an explanation offered for *attachment* in terms of feeding.

- Both the *behaviourist* and the *psychoanalytic* explanations for attachment centre on the role of feeding in establishing the primary attachment object, in contrast with Bowlby's view that it is sensitivity to *social releasers* which underlies attachment. Behaviourists suggest that being fed is rewarding and this reward comes to be associated with the person doing the feeding, who thus becomes a *secondary reinforcer* and a source of reward in themselves. However, Harlow's research with monkeys suggested that food is not the primary basis for attachment.

curvilinear correlation: a consistent relationship between two variables which is not linear (in a line).

- If a set of data has a curvilinear correlation the *correlation coefficient* will be low because the data fits a good curve rather than a line. This means that it appears that there is no relationship between the covariables although there is one.
- **e.g.** The relationship between age and brain cell death is curvilinear because brain cells are always dying, but this cell death increases after the age of 30, producing a curve rather than a linear correlation.

CVC (consonant-vowel-consonant): see *nonsense syllables*.

Darwinism: see *theory of evolution*.

debriefing: information provided for a participant at the end of the study by the researcher.

- During debriefing, the participant should be informed of the true aims of the study, if they had been deceived. The participant should be given an opportunity to express any concerns about the experiment and advised of his/her right to withhold data. The researcher should try to reduce any distress caused by the study. Researchers may use this opportunity to obtain feedback from participants. This might result in excluding data.
- ***TIP*** It is generally not possible to debrief participants in a *field experiment* or some *observational studies* because that would alert other potential participants to the existence of the study.

decentration: the ability to focus on more than one aspect of a problem, overcoming the problem of *centration*.

- *Piaget* claimed that this kind of thinking was typical of a child in the pre-operational stage of *cognitive development*. The ability to *conserve* is an example of the ability to decentre.

deception: in some circumstances it is necessary to deceive a participant about the true aims of a research study because this knowledge would affect their performance and render the research procedure useless.

- The central issue is one of *ethics*. Deception can be excused if (1) the 'means justify the ends', i.e. if the research is important it excuses the methods that have to be used; (2) the participants are *debriefed* to give them the opportunity to withdraw their data and thus exercise their rights of *informed consent* post hoc; (3) the deception is relatively harmless, for example in some memory studies.

decision model: Latané and Darley's explanation for *psychological altruism* and *prosocial behaviour* generally that suggests *bystanders* consider a logical sequence of decisions when deciding whether or not to help in an emergency situation.

- The five steps are: (1) notice something is wrong; (2) interpret it as an emergency (informational influence); (3) decide whether to take personal responsibility (*diffusion of responsibility*); (4) decide what type of help to give;

(5) implement the decision. At any stage the decision may be to opt out, in which case no help is forthcoming. This model is a rather *mechanistic* approach to behaviour and people may not have the time for such apparently logical decisions.

declarative knowledge: a subdivision of *long-term memory*. Knowledge related to 'knowing that' as distinct from 'knowing how' (*procedural knowledge*).

■ Declarative knowledge includes *episodic* and *semantic* memory. Declarative memory is like *explicit memory* and is the kind of memory that is usually tested in psychological experiments.

■ ***e.g.*** A doctor knows that blood direct from the heart is bright red (declarative memory) and knows how to take a blood sample (procedural memory).

deductive reasoning: drawing a logical conclusion by applying a general law to a particular instance.

■ Going from the general to the particular. See *inductive reasoning.*

■ ***e.g.*** All humans are created equal, therefore you and I must be equal. Deducing that your girlfriend will like the dinner you cook because you heard that all women love anything that a man cooks for them.

deep processing: see *depth of processing.*

deep structure: see *transformational grammar.*

defence mechanism: see *ego defence.*

defensible space: semi-public areas that surround private dwellings which people can defend.

■ This is a secondary *territory* as distinct from your primary territory where you can control your social interactions. Research into the design of buildings has shown that people are more content living where they have a defensible space.

■ ***e.g.*** Newman studied two buildings in New York, the Van Dyke and the Brownsville project. Many more crimes were committed at the Van Dyke which lacked any secondary 'defensible' territories.

defensive attribution: seeking to explain the behaviour of others (attribution) in a way that increases one's own sense of safety or confidence.

■ When a crime has been committed or disaster occurs, people tend to seek some causal explanation for the event. This causal explanation tends to be *dispositional,* i.e. things only go wrong when it is someone's fault. Such explanations make us feel safer (i.e. it is a self-serving attribution). The end result is that we feel safer because things only go wrong when it is someone's fault (dispositional) rather than being an everyday possibility. Lerner called this a *just-world-hypothesis*.

■ ***e.g.*** In the case of a violent attack, people might prefer the explanation that the victim was foolish for walking down the street late at night, because this means we can avoid such negligence ourselves and thus avoid being attacked.

deindividuation: the loss of a sense of personal identity that can occur when, for example, in a crowd or wearing a mask.

- The effect of deindividuation is to free an individual from the constraints of normal behaviour. This may lead to increased *conformity* or *obedience*, such as when wearing a uniform people are more likely to conform to norms associated with the uniform. In a replication of Milgram's experiment where participants wore a hood, they gave more shocks to the learner. However, in another experiment where participants were given the opportunity to steal sweets, they stole more often if they were not asked to give their name. In this case deindividuation led to decreased conformity to social norms.

demand characteristic: feature of an experiment which helps participants work out what is expected of them and leads them to behave in certain predictable ways.

- In other words, these features 'demand' a certain response, and act as *confounding variables*. Participants, such as children, are most likely to be influenced by demand characteristics when they are least unsure of what to do. Then they search for cues about how to behave. Participants who most want to 'please the experimenter' are the ones most likely to be influenced by demand characteristics. Demand characteristics are an example of *participant reactivity*. They can be reduced by increasing *experimental realism* because the participant's attention is taken up by his/her interest in the experimental procedures rather than trying to figure out what to do.
- ***e.g.*** In conformity studies where the task is ambiguous, participants have to use available cues (demand characteristics) to determine their behaviour, such as the responses of other participants. Therefore the participants appear to be highly conformist, whereas they are actually responding to the demand characteristics of the experiment. In real life, there are other influences on our behaviour such as previous knowledge.

democratic style of leadership: see *leadership style*.

denial: in *psychoanalytic theory*, a form of *ego defence* whereby the ego simply denies the existence of something which is threatening.

- ***e.g.*** A fan of Elvis Presley who believes he did not really die, that in fact there is a conspiracy behind his apparent death. This prevents the fan from having to accept the truth.

density–intensity hypothesis: the view that *crowding* does not necessarily lead to aggression, because situations of high density intensify existing feelings — the result might be aggression (if the individual was initially feeling somewhat aggressive), but it might also result in euphoria.

- This explains why some crowd situations lead to aggression whereas others do not. When you are enjoying yourself, such as at a party, the feeling of arousal may increase your enjoyment, whereas in other situations it may lead to discomfort and aggression (see *arousal–aggression hypothesis*).

dependence: see *drug dependence*.

dependent variable (DV): the experimental *variable* that is measured by an experimenter, to assess the effect of the *independent variable (IV)*.

- ***e.g.*** In an experiment to find out if people who receive extra coaching are better at throwing a ball than those who did not receive help, the IV would be extra coaching and the DV would be the distance the ball is thrown.
- ***TIP*** Remember that the IV is the one that is manipulated, the DV is the one that is measured.

depression (bipolar): a mental illness which includes both manic and *depressive* episodes, two polar opposites.

- Mania is characterised by an elevated and expansive mood, rapid speech which may be hard to understand, delusions, overactivity and impulsive behaviour.

depression (unipolar): a mental illness characterised by a lowering of mood, often accompanied by disorders of thinking and concentration, feelings of anxiety, and disturbances of sleep and appetite.

- Other characteristics include increased or decreased activity, tiredness, feelings of worthlessness and hopelessness, and recurrent thoughts of death or suicide. Distinctions have been made between *endogenous* depression (caused from within, e.g. hormonal), and reactive (*exogenous*) depression (caused by an obvious stressor such as bereavement). A distinction is also made between major and minor depression. Suggested causes include *genetic* factors, hormones (e.g. *permissive amine theory of mood disorder*), and/or cognitive factors (e.g. irrational thoughts, see *cognitive triad*).

deprivation: the state of having lost or been dispossessed of something.

- ***e.g.*** (1) Attachment. To experience *bond disruption* as a consequence of separation from an attachment figure for a period of time (may be repeated short-term separations, or long-term separation). The distinction between deprivation and *privation* is that, in the former, the child has formed a bond with a caregiver and this bond is disrupted. If there is no bond disruption then it is 'separation' rather than 'deprivation' that has occurred. (2) Visual deprivation. The removal of visual stimuli during early development which results in permanent effects on the visual system. (3) Sleep deprivation. Studies are ambiguous about the effects of sleep deprivation. It may be that episodes of *microsleep* mean that individuals who stay awake for long periods actually have some sleep. Also: linguistic, social, sensory and physical deprivation.

deprivation dwarfism: physical underdevelopment found in children reared in isolation or in institutions.

- It is likely to be an effect of the *stress* associated with emotional *deprivation*.
- ***e.g.*** The 13-year-old called Genie, who had been locked up by her father throughout her childhood, looked like a child half her age when she first came to the attention of the social services department. She was physically, emotionally and cognitively underdeveloped.

depth of processing: in *levels of processing theory*, the amount of meaning that is extracted from data as opposed to how much processing is done.

- A kind of quality (meaning) versus quantity (repetition) of processing. The concept of depth has been criticised because it is potentially circular (something which requires deeper processing is better remembered and something that is better remembered was more deeply processed).

- ***e.g.*** Depth can be achieved through elaboration or organisation.

descriptive statistics: methods of organising and summarising research data in order to describe the findings.

- ***e.g.*** Methods of central tendency (*mean, median, mode*), measures of dispersion (*range, semi-interquartile range, variance, mean deviation, standard deviation, variation ratio*), and graphical measures (*frequency table, bar chart, histogram, frequency polygon, scattergram,* line graph, *stem and leaf diagram, box-plot*).

desensitisation: reducing one's sensitivity about a stimulus.

- In relation to *antisocial behaviour,* it is suggested that high levels of violence in the *media* reduce one's responsiveness to similar behaviour in the real world. This means that you might find such behaviour more acceptable and are therefore more likely to behave violently, or antisocially. Contrast this with *disinhibition,* another potential explanation for the effects of the media.
- ***e.g.*** You watch a fight between a father and his son, and this leads you to feel less anxiety about such arguments.

determinism/determinist: an argument or theory which proposes that behaviour is established by factors other than one's own will.

- *Free will* is not the opposite of determinism but it is the alternative. The opposite would be *randomly* determined behaviour. 'True' determinism has been called 'hard determinism', the view that free will is an illusion: you may think you have it whereas in fact your behaviour is totally predictable and determined. This was Skinner's view (*radical behaviourism*). 'Soft determinism' is the concept that each of us acts consistently within our own character. So our behaviour is determined by our character — a limited repertoire of behaviours and then different behaviours can be selected at different times from this repertoire, which brings in some element of free will. The concept of determinism causes a problem for the notion of *moral* responsibility. If all your behaviour is determined by something else then you have no responsibility for your actions. A non-determinist position causes a problem for the *scientific* approach which aims to identify *causal* relationships: how one thing causes a change in another (i.e. determines it).
- ***e.g.*** Environmental determinism (*behaviourism*), *physiological* determinism (hormones cause behaviour), *genetic* determinism (behaviour is determined by your genetic makeup), psychic determinism (the view from *psychoanalytic theory* that our behaviour is determined by early experience and conflicts).

developmental psychology: this is concerned with the changes that occur over a person's lifetime, starting from conception and infancy through to adolescence, adulthood, and finally old age.

- This approach has also been called *lifespan psychology*. Changes can be related to the interaction between *nature and nurture*.
- ***e.g.*** *Cognitive*, emotional (*attachment*), *gender, language, self*-development.

deviance amplification hypothesis: the view that the *media* over-report certain abnormal incidents, such as violent crime, thus altering our perceptions of the frequency of such incidents.

- This acts as a *filter* affecting our perception of social reality.

deviation: in statistics, the amount by which one thing differs from the *mean* or average.

- ***e.g.*** One way to attempt to define abnormality is in terms of deviation from a statistical norm. See also *standard deviation* and *mean deviation*.

diagnosis: the identification of a physical or psychological disorder by its symptoms, using a *classificatory system*.

- Diagnosis relies on the identification of a group of symptoms that have been associated with a particular disorder. The main purpose of diagnosis is to provide a suitable form of treatment. In the case of psychological disorders the process of diagnosis may be relatively unreliable and therefore an inappropriate treatment may be prescribed. This raises the question about whether diagnosis and classification is appropriate for psychological conditions.

Diagnostic and Statistical Manual of Mental Disorders: see *DSM-IV*.

diathesis–stress model: in *abnormal psychology*, the notion that psychological disorders occur when there is a *genetic vulnerability* (diathesis) which is triggered by environmental conditions (stressors).

- This would explain why *concordance* rates between twins for mental and even physical disorders are high but not 100%.
- ***e.g.*** Both schizophrenia and diabetes can be explained in terms of diathesis–stress.

dichotic listening task: an experimental technique used to investigate focused *attention* where participants are presented with two stimuli simultaneously and asked to attend to (shadow) only one of them. See also *dual-task performance*.

- ***e.g.*** Gray and Wedderburn (1960) asked participants to shadow one ear where 'dear, 5, jane' was presented. The other non-attended ear received '3, aunt, 4'. They found that participants recall by meaning rather than ear by ear ('dear aunt jane' rather than 'dear 5 jane 3 aunt 4'), refuting the *filter model*.

diffusion of responsibility: an explanation for *bystander behaviour*, that each individual feels less responsibility for an emergency situation when in a group because responsibility is shared and therefore spread out.

- This explains why people are less likely to help when they are in a group, whereas one might think that more help would be more forthcoming when there are more people around.
- ***e.g.*** When a thief steals a handbag in a crowded shopping centre.
- ***TIP*** This theory should be contrasted with Gregory's *constructivist theory*.

directional hypothesis (also called 'one-tailed hypothesis')**:** a statement of the direction of the difference or correlation in a *hypothesis*.

- ***e.g.*** A directional hypothesis: 'Participants remember more words from list A than list B' or 'There is a positive association between age and IQ test scores'.

A *non-directional hypothesis* (or 'two-tailed hypothesis'): 'Participants perform differently on test A and test B' or 'There is an association between age and IQ test scores'. The first two hypotheses give a direction ('more' or 'positive'). The second two hypotheses just state that a difference/association was expected but not whether it was more or less.

- ***TIP*** If you use a directional hypothesis you run the risk of obtaining a significant result, but one that is not in the direction predicted. In such cases you must still accept the *null hypothesis*, because you cannot accept the *alternative hypothesis*.

direct perception theory: Gibson's (1979) theory of *perception* based on *bottom–up processing*.

- Gibson argued that the information contains enough information to explain the process of perception. He said that the amount of data contained in the retinal image (the *optic array*) is often underestimated. For example, *optic flow patterns* and *texture gradients* produce perceptual information about depth and movement from the sensory data alone.

disclosure: revealing personal information about oneself.

- Mutual self-disclosure is an important part of relationship formation. By sharing information about yourself you demonstrate trust and that you are prepared to risk exposure. You encourage the other person to do the same and gradually an intimate and trusting relationship develops.

discounting principle: a concept in Kelley's *causal schemata* model of attribution, that people tend to attach less importance to one potential cause of behaviour when other more obvious potential causes are also present.

- This happens when information is limited. This principle is used in cases where there is only a single instance of behaviour on which to make an attribution, therefore an analysis of *covariation* is not possible.
- ***e.g.*** When a famous person is seen advertising soap powder we might attribute their behaviour to a number of things, such as a liking of the powder, a desire to be seen on TV, or the fee being paid. The discounting principle suggests that we discount all of those but the most simple or obvious cause, or the one that best fits in with our past experience.

discourse analysis (DA): a method of research that involves, rather obviously, the analysis of a discourse or conversation between two people.

- Such conversations may be spoken or written. The focus is on the language used. The main point is that such discourses can reveal a great deal about the behaviour, feelings, thoughts and *attitudes* of the individuals engaged in the discourse. Beyond this, the discourse can inform us about the culture in which it takes place because it reveals social attitudes and beliefs (*social representations*). The technique itself involves collecting data, coding it (putting it into manageable chunks) and then analysing. This process of analysis gains objectivity through being repeated (*replication*). There are no regular procedures for such analysis because then one might fall back into the trap of closed- rather than open-ended research and preclude finding the unexpected. There are two main phases of the analysis. (1) Patterns: reading and rereading the text to detect patterns and forming categories (see *content analysis*). A consideration of the variation between speakers in their dialogue, and within one speaker's conversation, to highlight specific meanings. (2) Function and consequence: forming hypotheses about the functions that are fulfilled by the discourse and its effects. The *validity* of the findings can be established, for example, by looking at coherence and fruitfulness of the data.

discovery learning: *Piaget* suggested that children learn best by constructing their own knowledge when placed in novel situations.

- The teacher should provide materials which moderately challenge current schemas, leading to disequilibrium and *accommodation*. However, the teacher does not make the discrepancies explicit, but stands back and allows the child to work it out for him or herself.

discrete: this is another word for discontinuous or distinct.

- The term is used in relation to data.
- ***e.g.*** Height is measured on a continuous scale but classifying people as dark-haired, blonde or ginger would be an example of discrete data.

discrimination: literally means to distinguish between. It is the behaviour that results from *prejudiced* attitudes.

- This unequal treatment of individuals or groups is based on *stereotypes*.
- ***TIP*** Theories of discrimination have an important practical application in terms of attempts to reduce discrimination (and prejudice). Such attempts include the *jigsaw method*, *superordinate goals*, increased social contact, challenging stereotypes, and the use of legislation.

disinhibition: lowering of inhibitions.

- In relation to *antisocial behaviour*, it is suggested that high levels of violence in the media promote the view that such behaviour is common and acceptable. Normally, we have inhibitions about behaving in a violent manner but such exposure to violent programmes reduces these normal inhibitions. Contrast this with *desensitisation*, another potential explanation for the effects of the media.
- ***e.g.*** You watch a fight between a father and his son and this decreases your normal inhibitions about behaving in such a way.

disinhibition hypothesis: the explanation for *bulimia nervosa* that a dieter's rigid cognitive style means that they respond to situations of overeating by going over the top (becoming disinhibited). Once they have overeaten they purge to rectify their mistake.

disorganised attachment (called 'type D')**:** a type of *attachment* behaviour where the infant shows no set pattern of behaviour at separation or reunion (thus 'disorganised').

- This kind of behaviour is associated with abused children or those whose mothers are chronically depressed.

displacement: in *psychoanalytic theory*, a form of *ego defence* where the individual unconsciously redirects the threatening emotion from the person or thing that has caused it onto a third party.

■ ***e.g.*** You might kick your dog after having a row with your boyfriend. Displacement can also be used to explain prejudiced behaviour (like *projection*) — redirecting feelings of frustration on to a scapegoat.

displacement activity: substitution of one response for another, which occurs when the original goal was blocked.

■ ***e.g.*** A cat which tries to leap on a table but finds the route blocked may start grooming itself.

displacement effect: the view that watching television is harmful because it displaces other, more beneficial activities such as doing your homework and also prevents interactions with the real world which would counterbalance the *stereotyped* view of the world presented by television programmes.

■ See also the *stimulation effect*.

display rules: the social rules we learn about how to show our feelings, and about what is acceptable in particular situations and cultures.

disposition: consistent patterns of behaviour in different situations.

dispositional explanation: this accounts for an individual's behaviour in terms of an individual's personality or disposition.

■ ***e.g.*** A dispositional explanation for the behaviour of prison guards would be that certain types of people are drawn to the job as they are aggressive by nature.

■ ***TIP*** Contrast this with *situational explanations*.

dissociative personality disorder: see *multiple personality disorder*.

dissolution of relationship: the breakdown or dissolving of a relationship.

■ Many theories of *interpersonal relationships* include suggestions of why this happens. For example, according to *equity theory* it is inequity which leads to dissolution and according to *reinforcement–affect* theory it is a lack of rewards. Duck described five stages in the dissolution of relationships. (1) Breakdown: dissatisfaction leads to breaking point. (2) Intra-psychic phase: brooding, private focus on the relationship. (3) Dyadic phase: talking with partner, deciding whether to break up or repair the relationship. (4) Social phase: including others in the debate. (5) Grave dressing phase: working out the public version of events and any future relationship between partners. At each stage there are recommendations for 'repair strategies', which is useful in marriage guidance settings where one might identify the stage a relationship is at and then offer appropriate advice for that stage. Other theories of dissolution include *fatal attraction theory* and *transactional analysis*. There are also a range of personal factors which may be important, such as distasteful personal habits, a change in interests, relocation, poor role models, or poor social skills.

distal stimulus: a physical object that gives rise to a *proximal stimulus*.

■ We may touch the distal stimulus to test our perceptual hypotheses.

distribution-free statistical test: a kind of inferential statistical test that makes no assumptions about the underlying population. *Non-parametric statistics* are 'distribution-free'.

divergent thinking: an approach to problem solving that aims to produce one or more novel solutions.

■ In divergent or *creative* thought there is no correct solution but correctness can be judged by others in terms of the appropriateness of the solution and its usefulness. See also *convergent thinking, lateral thinking* and *brainstorming*.

■ ***e.g.*** Trying to produce ten ideas for what to do with a brick. The 'convergent' solution would be to use it to build a house. A divergent response would be to use it as a table decoration.

divided attention: see *attention*.

dizygotic (DZ) twins: non-identical twins formed from two fertilised eggs (or *zygotes*).

■ Such twins are genetically as similar as any pair of siblings, i.e. share about 50% of the same *genes*. See *monozygotic twins* and *twin studies*.

DNA (deoxyribonucleic acid)**:** the *genetic* code.

■ The DNA molecule consists of a group of chemicals combined in a variety of ways. Each combination is an instruction code for the cell. Strands of *RNA* (ribonucleic acid) read off the chemical message from a segment of DNA and pass this on to other parts of the cell, so the cell knows what proteins to manufacture. A *chromosome* is made of two strands of DNA twisted round each other in the form of a double helix — akin to two spiral staircases intertwined.

dominant gene: see *chromosome*.

dopamine: a *neurotransmitter* of the monoamine (*catecholamine*) group that generally has an excitatory effect.

■ Low levels of dopamine are associated with Parkinson's disease which involves a degeneration of those neurones that produce dopamine. Cocaine and amphetamines are dopamine agonists (i.e. enhancing the natural effects).

dopamine hypothesis of schizophrenia: the suggestion that schizophrenia is caused by an excess of the *neurotransmitter dopamine*. Chlorpromazine blocks dopamine receptors (acts as an *antagonist*) and is used as a treatment for schizophrenia.

double-bind theory: this proposes that *schizophrenia* is a learned response to mutually exclusive demands being made on a child, which can be met or avoided (Bateson et al., 1956).

■ The contradictory messages received by the child leads to a sense of conflict, and difficulty interpreting other people's communications.

■ ***e.g.*** A child being asked to show affection to a parent and then being admonished for excessive displays of emotion.

double blind: a research procedure where neither the *participant* nor the *experimenter* knows the key details of the experiment.

■ This is done in order to reduce the effects of expectations on the *dependent variable*. The participant is prevented from knowing the actual aims of the experiment, using *deception*. The experimenter (as distinct from the *investigator* who has designed the study) also does not know the precise aims of the study so that *experimenter bias* is reduced. In addition, the experimenter may be prevented from knowing the treatments given to each condition (group) because otherwise he/she might treat participants in the experimental condition or control condition differently. See *single blind*.

Down's syndrome (or 'Down syndrome')**:** a mental and physical disorder caused by an *innate* but not inherited genetic condition. It is also referred to as 'Trisomy 21' and occurs as a result of the presence of a third *chromosome* in pair 21.

- Individuals with Down's syndrome have distinctive facial features, mental retardation and some physical defects, such as heart or gastrointestinal problems. Behaviourally, such children are thought to be very affectionate.

dream state: a series of visual images and events in the mind.

- Dreaming is associated with *REM* activity, though people awoken from REM sleep do not always report dreams and there is evidence that people dream during other sleep stages. There is a range of theories offered as explanations of why we dream/have REM sleep, including *neurobiological theories* (e.g. *activation–synthesis*), *psychoanalytic theory of dreams*, cognitive theories (e.g. *problem-solving theory*).

drive: the force that impels an animal to act. It is the result of a need (such as thirst) and being in a *motivational* state.

drive-reduction theory: both a physiological and psychological theory of *motivation*: an organism is motivated to act in order to satisfy biological needs, the satisfaction of such needs is *reinforcing* and this leads the organism to repeat the behaviour.

- This theory offers a useful distinction between physiological needs and psychological rewards. However, it cannot explain any behaviour that is not drive-reducing, because then there are no rewards, such as rats who eat saccharin even though it has no nutritional value.

drug: a substance used medically and recreationally for its presumed effects.

- All drugs have only partly predictable influences. Their effects are related to dosage (high or low); ongoing processes in each individual such as movement, arousal and diet; and the fact that all drugs (and *neurotransmitters*) have multiple effects. There are five main classes of drugs: sedative hypnotics (e.g. alcohol and *barbiturates*), stimulants (e.g. *antidepressants* and caffeine), opiate narcotics (e.g. heroin and morphine), hallucinogens (e.g. cannabis), and antipsychotics (e.g. chlorpromazine and lithium).

drug dependence: a reliance on a psychoactive drug.

- Physical dependence is evidenced by the fact that withdrawal after prolonged use leads to adverse physical symptoms. Psychological dependence results from a compulsion to take the drug, because of the pleasure derived from it.

- ***TIP*** Dependence is different from drug abuse, because dependence involves a compulsion. See also *tolerance*.

DSM-IV: the most recent version (1994) of the Diagnostic and Statistical Manual of Mental Disorders published by the American Psychiatric Association.

- It provides a means of classifying and diagnosing over 200 mental disorders. The key features of the system are that it is a multiaxial system, it focuses on symptoms and it aims to predict the course of the disorder. This is in contrast to the *ICD*, the classification system mainly used in Europe (including the UK). The multiaxial system consists of five axes that enable the *clinician* to describe an individual's condition in terms of key criteria. Axis I: Clinical disorders. A list of the symptoms so that a named condition can be identified. Axis II: Personality disorders may or may not be present in addition to clinical disorders. A personality disorder is a more enduring and ingrained group of maladaptive behaviours than the clinical disorders. Axis III: General medical conditions which may be relevant to diagnosis and treatment, such as diabetes. Axis IV: Psychosocial and environmental problems which may affect diagnosis and prognosis. Axis V: Global assessment of functioning on a 100-point scale which helps to predict the likely outcome of the disorder.
- ***TIP*** In order to assess the usefulness of this diagnostic tool it is important to consider issues such as *validity* (including cultural bias) and *reliability*, both of which tend to be low (e.g. Rosenhan's (1973) study). On the positive side we should recognise that treatment depends on *diagnosis* and therefore a classificatory system is a vital tool for *clinicians* and *psychotherapists*.

dualism: a philosophical debate about the relationship between mind and body.

- Parallel dualism takes the position that mind and body are separate and not interacting parts of the same organism. Interactive dualism proposes that mind and body are separate but interacting.

dual-process model: the view that *attitude* change can be described in terms of two processes: majority or *minority influence*.

- Moscovici claims that the two processes are different: majority influence is likely to result in a public change of behaviour (*compliance*), but no private change because majority views are accepted passively; minority influence produces conversion (*internalisation*), because deviant ideas produce cognitive conflict and a restructuring of thought.

dual-task performance: an experimental technique used to investigate divided *attention* where participants are presented with two or more stimuli and asked to attend or respond to all of them. See also the *dichotic listening task*.

DZ twins: see *dizygotic twins*.

eating disorder: any psychological illness where the symptoms are expressed in terms of harmful eating patterns.

■ ***e.g.*** *Anorexia nervosa, bulimia nervosa,* obesity, pica.

echolalia: a form of speech where the same sound or phrase is repeated.

■ The term is used to describe the first sounds produced by infants (e.g. 'dadada' or 'mamama'). This enables them to practise making *phonemes*. The term also describes one of the symptomatic behaviours of *schizophrenics*, who compulsively repeat senseless words or phrases that were spoken by someone else.

ecological theory of perception: see *direct perception theory*.

ecological theory of sleep: see *evolutionary theory of sleep*.

ecological validity: the extent to which a study can be *generalised* to real life, a type of *external validity*.

■ *Validity* means how true something is, and *ecology* refers to the study of things in the natural environment. Thus ecological validity is the concept of how true a study is to 'natural' (real) life.

■ ***e.g.*** An experiment conducted in a *laboratory* may not be very true to real life and therefore it may not be appropriate to draw conclusions about how people behave in the real world. However, some field studies, despite being conducted in a naturalistic setting, still lack ecological validity because they are related only to that setting (see example given for *external validity*).

■ ***TIP*** The more control an experiment has (high internal validity), the less ecological validity it may have.

ecology: the study of things in the natural environment.

ECT (electroconvulsive shock therapy): a *somatic* form of therapy for mental illness where brief electrical shocks are usually applied to a person's non-dominant *hemisphere*.

■ The electric shocks produce a convulsion which mimics an epileptic seizure and leads to a brief loss of *consciousness*. The therapy has been reasonably successful for depression and is not the barbaric treatment it once was. Some argue that it is more effective and preferable to the use of drugs. However, the reason it works is still not known and many people feel that it is an unethical form of treatment because it involves physical harm.

educational psychology: the branch of *applied psychology* that seeks to understand psychological influences on the process of education.

- Educational psychologists are employed to assess pupils with learning or other difficulties. They also formulate educational programmes for such pupils. Educational psychology is more widely concerned with, for example, *psychometric testing* and other forms of assessment, special educational needs, improving motivation and educational performance, considering the effectiveness of teaching programmes, understanding cognitive development, and ways of dealing with problem behaviour.

EE (expressed emotion) model: EE model of *schizophrenia* suggests the disorder is caused and/or exacerbated by a pattern of behaviours in the home.

- These behaviours include criticism received from family members, expressed resentment and emotional overprotectiveness.

EEG (electroencephalograph): a method of detecting activity in the living *brain* — *electrodes* are attached to a person's scalp to record general levels of electrical activity.

- When the nerves in the brain are active, a weak electrical current is produced. EEG can be used to detect differences between each *hemisphere* or to record *brainwaves*.
- ***TIP*** This technique can only record overall activity. *Microelectrodes* are used for finer detection of electrical activity.

efferent nerve: conveys impulses to sense organs from the spinal cord or brain, as distinct from an *afferent nerve*.

ego: a personality structure identified in *psychoanalytic theory*. It is the conscious, rational part of the mind.

- The ego develops during the first 2 years of life as a consequence of the infant's experiences of the world. The force which motivates the ego is the *reality principle*, which makes the child accommodate to the demands of the environment. The ego is equivalent to our rational mind. The ego must modify the demands of the *id*. The *superego*, which emerges later, influences the ego.
- ***TIP*** Freud used the term 'I' for the ego.

egocentric thought: seeing things from one's own viewpoint and being unaware that there might be other possibilities.

- *Piaget* claimed that this kind of thinking was typical of a child in the concrete pre-operational stage. He demonstrated this with the three mountains experiment, where children have to identify the scene as if they were seeing it from where a doll is standing. Younger children select a picture which represents their own view and not that of the doll. Other research has found egocentric thoughts in adolescents and older people.

ego defence: in *psychoanalytic theory*, the strategies used by the *ego* to defend itself against anxiety.

- ***e.g.*** *Denial, displacement, intellectualisation, projection* and *repression*.

egotistic altruism: see *altruism*.

eight ages of man: Erikson's *neo-Freudian* account of lifespan development in terms of eight stages, each of which is marked by a psychosocial (rather than Freud's psychosexual) crisis that needs to be resolved for healthy development.

■ The eight crises are: trust vs mistrust (age 1 year), autonomy vs shame (2–3), initiative vs guilt (4–5), industry vs integrity (6–11), identity vs role confusion (12–18), intimacy vs isolation (20–40), generativity vs stagnation (40–64), integrity vs despair (65+).

elaborated code: see *restricted code*.

Electra complex: the process by which girls resolve gender conflict by identifying with the same-sex parent, the equivalent of a boy's *Oedipus complex*.

■ *Jung*, a *neo-Freudian*, proposed that girls go through a similar process to boys during the *phallic stage* of *psychosexual development*. Electra was another Greek figure. In Jung's analysis, a young girl feels desire for her father and rejects her mother. Freud explained the resolution of the phallic stage in terms of *penis envy*.

electrical stimulation of the brain (ESB): the application of a weak electrical current to a specific area of the brain to determine the function of that region.

■ ***e.g.*** Olds (1958) used this technique to study the pleasure centre in rats, a region in the *limbic system*.

■ ***TIP*** This is not the same as the use of microelectrodes implanted in the brain to detect when particular regions are active.

electroconvulsive shock therapy: see *ECT*.

electrode: an electrical conductor.

electroencephalograph: see *EEG*.

emic: a culturally specific behaviour.

■ The focus is on how the same behaviour varies among different *cultures*, as distinct from an *etic*.

■ ***e.g.*** Phonemics is the study of universal sounds (*phonemes*) as they apply to a particular language.

emotion: a state of physiological *arousal* that has important motivational properties, in other words it drives an individual to behave in a particular way.

■ Emotion is an *affective* state, i.e. it produces a feeling which leads to a response. There are several strands to this affective state. (1) Physiological arousal (the *sympathetic branch* of the *autonomic nervous system* is activated) which leads to readiness for fight or flight. The seat of emotion in the brain is the *limbic system*. See also *Klüver–Bucy syndrome* and *sham rage* for further information on the brain and emotion.. (2) *Cognitive* experience of emotion — whether you feel happy or sad. This may be based on the physiological sensations or may be related to environmental cues. There are various theories to account for how this subjective state is determined. See the *James–Lange theory*, *Cannon–Bard theory*, *cognitive labelling theory*, *cognitive appraisal*. (3) Behaviour, including how you express an emotion, such as smiling when you feel happy. There are differing views about the extent to which this behaviour is *innate* or whether it is learned. See *primary* and *secondary emotions*, and *display rules*.

(4) Communication — an important element to emotion is that receivers are aware of our emotional state. For example, when you are angry this behaviour is 'read' by others as 'anger'. We often show our emotions without conscious awareness (see *nonverbal leakage*).

■ ***TIP*** The evidence appears to suggest that (1) physiological arousal alone can be sufficient, but (2) physiological arousal is not always necessary. This can be understood by regarding some emotions as being physiologically based (e.g. if a jet screams over your head, you duck and experience a tightness in your chest, then the basis of the emotional sensation is arousal), and some as psychologically based (e.g. you hear that you have passed your psychology exam and feel ecstatic, a cognitive state which may lead to physiological sensations).

empathy: being aware of and identifying with another person's feelings.

empathy–altruism hypothesis: Batson's explanation for *psychological altruism* and *prosocial behaviour* generally that suggests people are more motivated to help someone if they feel empathy for the victim rather than just because they can see that the victim is distressed.

■ It is claimed that empathy is an *innate* behaviour, like altruism. This model suggests that people are not always motivated to behave selfishly as would be suggested by the *arousal — cost–reward model.*

empirical: data that are collected through direct observation or experiment, rather than being generated from a theory.

■ The 'opposite' of empirical research is rational research, where theory is constructed from reasoned argument rather than direct observation.

■ ***e.g.*** If one wanted to decide whether the world would end in 20 days, the rational approach would be to argue that such a thing was unlikely. The empirical approach would be to wait and see what happened.

empiricism: the view that all behaviour is *learned* as opposed to being inherited.

■ In other words, direct experience is the mainspring of development. This was the view of many nineteenth-century philosophers and one of the influences on early *behaviourism*. The term 'empiricism' also applies to a method of conducting research, again through direct experience.

encoding specificity principle: an explanation for enhanced memory recall.

■ Memory is best when there is a large overlap between the information available at the time of retrieval and the information in the *memory trace*.

■ ***e.g.*** If you are given a list of words to remember and, when asked to recall them, given the hint that some of the words are animals, this would be less effective than a more specific clue, such as that some of the words are names of song birds and some are birds of prey.

endocrine system: a system of ductless glands in the body that produce *hormones*.

■ The endocrine system is governed by the *autonomic nervous system*.

■ ***e.g.*** The *pituitary gland* is called the 'master endocrine gland'. There are many other endocrine glands such as the *pineal, adrenal* and thyroid glands.

endogenous: internally caused, as distinct from externally caused (*exogenous*).

■ ***e.g.*** The *suprachiasmatic nucleus* is an internal or endogenous means of establishing our bodily rhythms. Endogenous depression is depression caused by internal factors, such as *hormones*.

endogenous depression: see *depression*.

endorphin: a *neurotransmitter* that acts as the body's natural painkiller by inhibiting the release of substance P, a *neurotransmitter* involved in the transmission of pain.

■ *Neurones* that release endorphins are activated by the perception of pain. Opium and morphine are endorphin *agonists* (i.e. they enhance natural action).

enkephalin: similar to *endorphin*.

enmeshment: a concept introduced in *family systems theory* to explain how certain families are likely to give rise to a child with an eating disorder.

■ Members of the family lack a clear sense of their own personal identity, i.e. they are enmeshed. This means that some individuals may feel 'forced' to assert their independence by controlling their intake of food.

environmental psychology: the branch of *applied psychology* that seeks to understand how the environment affects human behaviour.

■ The concerns of environmental psychology include the effects of noise, weather, pollution, crowding, technological disasters, urban renewal and housing design, as well as the study of personal space and territory, environmental cognition, and encouraging environmentally responsible behaviour.

EPI: see *Eysenck Personality Inventory*.

epilepsy: a *neurological* disorder which causes occasional storms of electrical activity in the brain leading to convulsions and loss of consciousness.

epinephrine: see *adrenaline*. ('Epi' = on top of, 'nephron' = kidneys.)

episodic memory: a subdivision of *long-term memory* which contains information about personal events, i.e. episodes of your life.

■ It is distinguished from *semantic memory* (memory for facts) in terms of the content. However, it may be more difficult to distinguish between episodic and semantic memory in terms of the processes involved because they depend heavily on each other.

■ ***e.g.*** If you remember what happened in class last Monday this is clearly episodic memory; however, semantic memory is also involved in so far as your knowledge of the education system is needed to identify features of the event.

equity theory: an explanation offered for the formation, maintenance and dissolution of *interpersonal relationships*. This view suggests that a sense of balance (or equity) is necessary in a relationship and this is achieved through perceived fairness of what each partner has.

■ Equity theory is a development of *social exchange theory*. In an equitable relationship what each partner gains from the relationship is equal to what he/she puts into it. Inequity results in a drive to restore balance by offering or taking things which will increase one's sense of reward. Otherwise the result will be *dissolution*.

- ***e.g.*** The *matching hypothesis* suggests that even if physical attractiveness is not matched, a balance can be maintained by other positive aspects of a person's character, such as intelligence or kindness.
- ***TIP*** It may be that equity is more important to some individuals than others, and the principle may apply less to romantic than other relationships because *romantic* relationships involve selflessness.

ERG theory (existence relatedness growth): Alderfer's psychological theory of *motivation* based on the *hierarchy of needs* model but suggesting that people also move downwards, using a lower need to substitute for a higher-order need when they are frustrated.

ESB: see *electrical stimulation of the brain*.

ethical guidelines: a set of rules which can be used to judge the acceptableness of behaviour.

- Professional bodies draw up such guidelines for all professions, such as doctors, solicitors and psychologists. In psychology, guidelines are needed in relation to human and non-human research, and for practising psychologists who treat patients.
- ***e.g.*** In the UK, the British Psychological Society (*BPS*) publishes guidelines. The same is true in many other countries.

ethics: concerns relating to what is regarded as acceptable human behaviour in pursuit of certain personal or scientific goals.

- Ethical issues relate to (1) how psychologists treat participants in research studies and (2) how psychologists treat patients with psychological disorders.
- ***e.g.*** The main ethical issues are *confidentiality, deception, informed consent, privacy*, protection from harm, the right to withhold data and the right to withdraw from any research study.
- ***TIP*** There is a distinction between morals and ethics. 'Morals' is used to refer to everyday standards of right and wrong, such as honesty and kindness. Ethics are determined by a balance between ends and means, or a *cost–benefit analysis*.

ethnocentric (ethnocentricism): believing that one's own *ingroup* (e.g. religious group, nation, gender) is superior to other cultures.

- This occurs as a result of *ingroup favouritism* and serves to increase personal *self-esteem*.

ethnography (also called 'ethnology')**:** the study of different cultures through the use of comparisons.

- By making comparisons between cultures we can learn more about a target culture, similar to the way that *comparative psychology* can enlighten us about human behaviour through comparisons with non-human animals.

ethnomethodology: the study of how we make sense of everyday social life.

- 'Ethno' means 'ordinary people'. Ordinary individuals act like scientists in discovering the rules embedded in their social world. Ethnomethodology studies how ordinary people discover and use these rules. It is similar to *discourse analysis* but does not rely on recorded conversation.

■ ***e.g.*** A traditional approach to explaining behaviour in an institution, such as a prison, might be to identify the implicit rules that operate there. Ethnomethodology goes further and suggests that the rules should become the object of study in themselves.

ethogenics: an alternative to those traditional forms of research that emphasise causal relationships, such as *experiments*.

■ The ethogenic perspective assumes that people are a store of social knowledge and the best way to access this is by analysing what they say. Observation alone cannot provide access to thoughts, whereas language and talk can provide this information. This is the distinction between social performance (behaviour) and social competence (talk). See also *discourse analysis*.

ethogram: a record of the behavioural repertoire of a particular species of animal.

■ This is used by researchers when conducting a naturalistic observation of that species.

ethology: the biological study of behaviour.

■ Ethologists promote the use of naturalistic observation, and focus on the importance of *innate* capacities and the functions of behaviours in making an individual better *adapted* to its environment. Ethologists ensure objectivity in their research by making repeated and lengthy observations of behaviour, often using *ethograms*.

etics: universals of behaviour.

■ The focus is to discover behaviours that are universal, in contrast with *emics*. See also *imposed etic*.

■ ***e.g.*** Phonetics is the study of universal sounds independent of meaning.

eugenics: a policy where individuals are selected for certain desirable characteristics and encouraged to breed, whereas those with undesirable characteristics are prevented from reproducing.

■ The aim is to produce a race of 'better' people through selective breeding.

Eurocentric: a special case of *ethnocentricism*, relating to Europeans.

evaluation: to determine the value of something.

■ ***e.g.*** When you describe a research study or a theory it is important to sit back and say 'So what? Is this a valuable study or explanation? In what way?'

evaluation apprehension: the concern or anxiety felt when being assessed by someone else.

■ In a research setting, this may *bias* the research findings because participants alter their behaviour in order to be positively evaluated. In terms of *bystander behaviour* this may explain why people sometimes avoid offering help, because they have a fear of being negatively evaluated.

event sampling: a method of collecting data in an *observational study* where a list of behaviours is drawn up and a record made every time the target behaviour(s) occurs.

■ See also *time sampling.*

evolution: see *theory of evolution.*

evolutionarily stable strategy (ESS): a behaviour or strategy that persists because it cannot be bettered.

■ Over the course of time, various new behaviours may appear as a part of an animal's repertoire. If and when they are not *naturally selected* this is because they do not offer any advantages over the existing ESSs. An ESS resists evolutionary pressure against it because it is the best compromise.

■ ***e.g.*** In the Coho salmon there are two male forms, a smaller and larger one. The smaller one matures early and lacks secondary sexual characteristics. They lurk behind rocks (being small helps this) and fertilise female eggs surreptitiously. The longer-maturing and larger, hook-nose male fights with other males for the opportunity to fertilise eggs. The fact that both forms persist shows that both strategies pay off; they form an evolutionarily stable strategy.

evolutionary psychology: an approach in psychology which aims to explain human behaviour in terms of the *theory of evolution* and the principles of *sociobiology.*

■ ***TIP*** It is a highly *determinist* approach to behaviour and may not be appropriate because it overlooks the influence of cognitive and cultural factors on human behaviour.

evolutionary theory of sleep: Meddis (1975) pointed out that *sleep* has an *adaptive* function.

■ Sleep may promote survival because it enables the animal to be immobile and safe from predators (*hibernation theory*) and/or it reduces energy expenditure. An alternative possibility is that different animals have evolved different patterns of sleep to fit their lifestyle — grazing animals sleep little whereas hunters sleep a lot. The main problem with the theory is that it is non-falsifiable because one could present an argument for the adaptive nature of any behaviour. Preyed-upon animals could be safer when asleep, but they could arguably be more vulnerable.

evolution of adult consciousness: Gould's (1980) extension of *psychoanalytic theory* to adulthood, suggesting that at different ages in adulthood there are false assumptions that have to be overcome in order to grow up.

■ ***e.g.*** Around the age of 20 one might think 'I will always belong to my parents and believe in their world'. If you maintain this false assumption it may lead to a romantic relationship based on a dependent rather than an independent relationship.

exchange theory: see *social exchange theory.*

exogenous: externally caused, as distinct from internally caused (*endogenous*).

■ ***e.g.*** A *zeitgeber* is an external or exogenous cue that resets our *biological rhythms.*

experiment: research undertaken to make a discovery about causal relationships.

■ The experimenter manipulates an *independent variable (IV)* to see its effect on the *dependent variable (DV)*. The two main features of an experiment are *control* and *replication*. These enable us to be confident that the IV did affect the DV in a consistent fashion.

- ***e.g.*** The *laboratory experiment* is the ideal form of experiment because of the potential for control. However, this is at a cost to *external (ecological) validity*. Other types of experiment are the *field experiment*, where the participants are unaware of being studied, and the *natural experiment*, where the IV varies naturally.
- ***TIP*** Not all experiments are artificial, though this is frequently given as a criticism of the experimental approach to research. Even laboratory experiments may be quite relevant to real life, e.g. studying exam anxiety.

experimental condition: in an experiment with a *repeated measures design* the condition with the *independent variable/experimental treatment*. See *control condition*.

experimental design: the plan used to conduct an experiment. In particular the method used to control the effects of *participant variables* on the *dependent variable* in an experiment.

- ***e.g.*** *Independent measures, repeated measures, matched pairs,* and *single participant designs*.

experimental group: in an experiment with an *independent measures design*, the group of participants who receive the *independent variable* or *experimental treatment*. See *control group*.

experimental hypothesis: the *hypothesis* written prior to conducting an experiment.

- The experimental hypothesis usually specifies the *independent* and *dependent variables* and the expected relationship between them. The experimental hypothesis is usually more specific and *operationalised* than the *research hypothesis*.
- ***e.g.*** 'The number of words recalled after 10 minutes is greater for younger participants than older participants.' This is a *directional* hypothesis.
- ***TIP*** It makes better sense to state the hypothesis in the present tense because it is a statement of what you believe to be true, not a statement of what will happen. Your aim is to prove or disprove the validity of the statement. It also makes better sense to exclude the word significant from the hypothesis since you may be testing *significance* later using an *inferential* test. This test is what determines the significance.

experimental realism: the extent to which an experiment is experienced as real by participants because it is interesting and/or attention-grabbing.

- If participants become so involved in an experimental set-up that they are fooled into thinking it is real rather than artificial, this helps to overcome problems of low *internal* and *external validity*. See also *mundane realism*.
- ***e.g.*** Milgram's study of obedience has been claimed to have high experimental realism, because otherwise participants would have refused to do such a thing.

They must have believed in the whole set-up in order to continue.

experimental treatment: the alteration of the *independent variable* for the *experimental group*.

experimental validity: see *internal validity*.

experimenter: the person conducting the experiment but not always the designer of the study. See *investigator*.

experimenter bias: the effect that the experimenter's expectations have on the participants and thus on the results of the experiment.

- Participants search for clues about how to behave in an experiment and thus are prone to be influenced by an experimenter's expectations. This may be especially true of child participants. It is not a problem in *field experiments* where a participant is usually not aware of participating in an experiment. It can be overcome by using a *double-blind design* where the experimenter is not aware of the experimental hypothesis and therefore cannot communicate expectations to the participants. (The experimenter is the person conducting the experiment as distinct from the *investigator* who organises the experiment.) See also *experimenter effects*.

experimenter effect: the effect of an experimenter's expectancy, personal characteristics (such as mood), treatment of the data and so on, on the findings of an experiment.

- **e.g.** *Experimenter bias*, experimenter loose procedure effect (experimenter may vary procedures), experimenter fudging effect (experimenter may fudge the findings to get better results).

explicit memory: a subdivision of *long-term memory*, memory that is based on conscious recollection as distinct from *implicit memory*.

- Explicit memory is similar to *declarative knowledge* (knowing that). One criticism of memory research is that it tends to test explicit rather than implicit memory, and therefore the findings from such research only apply to a limited kind of behaviour.

expressed emotion: see *EE model*.

external validity: the extent to which experimental findings can be applied to all situations.

- It is 'external' because it concerns issues outside the research situation itself. Ideally, we should feel confident that the experimental findings can be *generalised* to the total population from which the sample was drawn and to other populations (*population validity*), and to other settings (*ecological validity*). There are a number of things which may affect external validity, such as *demand characteristics* and *evaluation apprehension*.
- **e.g.** *Field experiments* are often seen as being high in external/ecological validity, because they take place in a more realistic setting, which therefore should relate more widely to other situations. However, this is not true of all field experiments. For instance, the obedience study of nurses by Hofling et al. (1966) may only apply to obedience between nurses and doctors, or other

people whose relationships are built on obedience. The study may tell us little about everyday obedience.

extinction: the disappearance of a learned response when stimuli stop being paired (*classical conditioning*) or no *reinforcement* occurs (*operant conditioning*).

- In classical conditioning if the *unconditioned stimulus* (UCS) and *conditioned stimulus* (CS) are no longer paired, then the *conditioned response* (CR) will cease to be associated with the CS. In operant conditioning if a behaviour is no longer rewarded, the probability of the behaviour being repeated is reduced, until the conditioned response is eventually extinguished.
- ***e.g.*** If your cat realised that the sound of a cupboard door was no longer accompanied by food (the tin was now in the fridge), it would soon stop running every time it heard the cupboard door open.

extraneous variable: any variable in a study except for the *independent* and *dependent variables*.

- Extraneous variables need to be *controlled*. If they are not controlled they may obscure the effect of the independent variable and turn into a *confounding variable*.
- ***e.g.*** Time of day, instructions to participants and *order effects*. These can all be controlled by good experimental design.
- ***TIP*** A confounding variable continues to confound the experimental finding (i.e. changes in the dependent variable). An extraneous variable is extra to the independent variable, but it has been controlled.

extravert: an individual who is outgoing and impulsive.

- Eysenck suggested that extraversion was one end of an extravert–*introvert* continuum. He suggested that extraverts seek greater excitement and more dangerous pastimes. This is because they have a lower level of *cortical* arousal and therefore need more stimulation to experience the same sense of excitement as introverts. Extroverts are also less easily *conditioned*, which may lead to a weaker conscience and an increased likelihood of *antisocial behaviour*.

eyewitness testimony (EWT): the descriptions given in a criminal trial by individuals who were present around the time of a crime.

- Such descriptions may include an identification of the criminals, important details of the sequence of events, who or what else was present and/or peripheral information, such as the weather that day. EWT is likely to rely on *reconstructive memory*, because memory is a reconstructive process, especially in eyewitnesses who may not have realised that they would need to remember the events, or in some cases, the stress of the occasion may have affected their ability to take in all the details. Such reconstructive recall is affected by expectations and *schema*, and is likely to be unreliable.

Eysenck personality inventory (EPI): a self-report test of *personality* developed by Eysenck.

face validity: a means of assessing the validity of a psychological test.
- The extent to which the items look as if they measure what the test claims to measure.
- ***e.g.*** On a creativity test, one would expect the items to look as if they are measuring creativity.
- ***TIP*** See other forms of establishing validity: *content, construct, concurrent, criterion,* and *predictive validity.*

false belief task: a method of research (*controlled observation*) used to see if a child has a *theory of mind.*
- ***e.g.*** The Sally Anne test, where children are introduced to two dolls: Sally and Anne. (1) Sally puts a marble in her basket. (2) Sally leaves the room. (3) Anne puts the same marble in her own box. (4) When Sally returns, the researcher asks the child, 'Where will Sally look for her marble?' If the child says (or points to) 'the basket' they demonstrate that they have a 'theory of mind' because they can perceive that Sally, who was out of the room, still believes the marble is in the basket (her belief is wrong or false). If the child indicates 'the box', then they have not got a theory of mind because they are assuming that Sally is thinking what they are thinking. The child is unable to accommodate Sally's false (wrong) belief.

false consensus effect: a mental shortcut (*heuristic*) that refers to the fact that individuals frequently overestimate the degree to which others think the same way as they do.
- This is a kind of *self-serving bias* because it supports your own behaviour and views. It is linked to the *availability heuristic* because individuals are more likely to remember cases where others agreed with them than when they disagreed.
- ***e.g.*** If people are asked to estimate the number of smokers in the adult population, smokers will provide a higher estimate than non-smokers.

false memory syndrome: a condition where an adult 'recovers' apparently *repressed memories.*
- It is possible that the memories are for events that did not happen and thus it is called 'false memory'. There is still some debate within psychology about the validity of such memories. However, the fact that memory relies to a large

extent on *reconstruction* suggests that it would be relatively easy consciously or unconsciously to plant false memories.

falsification: proving the truth of a research *hypothesis* by demonstrating that the null version is false.

■ Scientific theories cannot be proved to be true, they can only be subjected to attempts to prove them false. In everyday life we can often prove that a hypothesis is true through direct verification (I can test the hypothesis that the water in a river is cold by touching it). In research we simply do not have recourse to direct verification — you cannot tell that a child can or cannot *conserve* just by looking at them. The only way that you can prove that a child can conserve is by falsifying the *null hypothesis*. Some theories are impossible to falsify (they are non-falsifiable), such as the *evolutionary theory of sleep* or *psychoanalytic theory*.

family systems theory: see *enmeshment*.

fatal attraction theory: an explanation offered for the *dissolution of relationships* that the factors which created interpersonal attraction ultimately lead to relationship breakdown.

■ ***e.g.*** Behaviours that initially seem exciting, later may become quite wearing or even frightening.

feature detection model: a *bottom–up* explanation for pattern recognition in which individual features are recognised first and then the object is recognised.

■ There is neurophysiological support for this model, such as the different cells of the *visual cortex* which identify different line orientations. However, the theory cannot account for the effects of expectations and context.

■ ***e.g.*** The *pandemonium model*.

■ ***TIP*** Contrast with *template matching theory* and *prototypes*.

feminist psychology: an approach to psychological research that emphasises the importance and value of women, as well as issues related to power imbalance and minority groups.

■ In order to do this it is necessary to employ more *qualitative* research methods because traditional, *quantitative* research has such a potential for bias and thus tends to produce theories that are *gender biased*.

field experiment: an experiment conducted in a relatively naturalistic situation, where the participants are visually unaware that they are participating in a psychology experiment.

■ The *independent variable* (IV) is still manipulated, in contrast with a *natural experiment*. Field studies are usually high in *ecological validity* and avoid *experimenter bias* and *demand characteristics* when the participants are unaware of the experiment. On the other hand, in a field study it is much harder to control *confounding variables* and they are more time-consuming and expensive. In terms of ethical considerations, it is not possible to gain informed consent or usually to give *debriefing*. Participants may be distressed by the experience.

'fight or flight': the state of being ready to fight or take flight.

■ An environmental demand, such as a stressor, results in activation of the *sympathetic nervous system* and a state of physiological *arousal*. The individual's heart and breathing rates are increased, digestion is slowed down and sugar is released in readiness for intense activity — whether fighting or running away.

filial imprinting: a young animal learns to recognise a caregiver, most likely its mother, during a *sensitive period* of its early development as a consequence of its *innate* drive to *imprint* upon this caregiver (or object).

■ This is an *adaptive* behaviour because it leads to a *following response* which helps ensure feeding, protection and the opportunity to become independent by learning to fend for oneself through *imitation*.

filter: anything which screens out particular stimuli.

■ ***e.g.*** *Deviance amplification*.

filter model: Broadbent's (1958) explanation for focused auditory *attention* in terms of *serial processing*.

■ According to this model there is a 'bottleneck' early on in the selection process and therefore some selection must take place to reduce the incoming information. This is done by filtering messages on the basis of physical characteristics as demonstrated by the *cocktail party effect*. However, empirical studies have shown that far more processing of the non-attended message takes place than the filter model predicts and that the filter probably works on meaning as well as physical characteristics. See the *attenuator model*.

filter theories: these explain the formation of *interpersonal relationships* in terms of a series of stages during which choices are successively narrowed down.

■ Kerckhoff and Davis suggested that similar social variables (such as social class and education) act as an initial filter. As the relationship progresses the next filter is agreement on values and finally complementary personality traits.

fixation: in *psychoanalytic theory*, a focus on a particular stage of *psychosexual development* because of over- or under-gratification during that stage. The fixation is on the appropriate body organ for that stage.

■ If a child experiences severe problems or excessive pleasure at any stage of development, this leads to fixation on that stage. This means that the individual's *libido* becomes attached to that stage. Later in life, when in a stressful situation, an adult tends to regress (move back) to the psychosexual stage upon which they had previously fixated. The result would be that they behave as they would have done at that age.

■ ***e.g.*** In a stressful situation you might revert to sucking your thumb because that had previously given you much pleasure, such as sucking on a pencil.

fixed action pattern (FAP): an *ethological* concept, a unit of species-specific behaviour that is mainly *innate* but can be modified by experience, such as bird song.

■ FAPs are: (1) exhibited in a repertoire and thus more complex than reflexes; (2) independent of learning, but can be affected by experience; (3) inevitable, triggered by a specific stimulus (*sign stimulus*); (4) ballistic and inflexible —

once launched the rest is inevitable; (5) distinct — each serves one function and occurs in one circumstance.

■ ***e.g.*** In the greylag goose the mere sight of an egg outside the nest triggers a sequence of inevitable behaviours (the repertoire). The goose stands in the nest, faces the egg, extends its neck outwards until it is over the egg, puts the underside of the beak on the far side of the egg and starts to roll it back. If the egg does slip away (or is removed) the goose nonetheless continues back to the nest (ballistic and inflexible). Then, if it sees the egg again the sequence recommences until it is finally successful. Any goose that does not do this probably loses a lot of eggs and is likely to have little reproductive success (adaptive value).

flashbulb memory: accurate and long-lasting memories formed at times of intense emotion, such as significant public or personal events.

■ It is as if a flash photograph was taken at the moment of the event and every detail indelibly printed in memory. One suggestion is that the *hormones* released at a time of high emotion may enhance memory. However, it is also true that extreme emotion may lead to forgetting (e.g. *repressed memory*). It is also difficult to conduct research to demonstrate the accuracy of such memories.

■ ***e.g.*** Most people have a flashbulb memory of what they were doing at the time they heard about the death of Princess Diana. You may also have a clear memory of an early birthday.

flooding: a *behavioural therapy* that aims to present the patient with maximum exposure to a feared stimulus, exposure continuing until their fear subsides, thus extinguishing the conditioned response.

■ This can be done in one's imagination (*implosion therapy*) where the person imagines a very fearful situation. Flooding involves real-life exposure which may be more effective, but it does involve placing the patient in an intensely anxiety-provoking situation. Virtual reality may be a useful alternative with fewer anxieties.

■ ***e.g.*** Locking a claustrophic in a lift.

floor effect: occurs when a *psychometric test* or other measure of behaviour is too difficult and therefore nearly everyone gets a low score.

■ The end result is a failure to discriminate between individuals, which also occurs with the *ceiling effect*.

focal theory: Coleman's (1974) theory of adolescence that proposes that most adolescents cope with the changes which take place during adolescence by 'focusing on' and dealing with different issues at different times and therefore do not experience *'storm and stress'*.

focused attention: see *attention*.

following response: when a young animal follows a caregiver as a consequence of *imprinting*.

■ This is an *adaptive* behaviour because it helps ensure feeding and protection. The young animal also learns how to fend for itself through *imitation*.

food caching: part of *foraging* behaviour, where an animal stores food outside its body for later use.

- The advantage is that this may save energy because the animal can collect a lot of food at one time. It is also useful in times of scarcity. It does, however, depend on being able to prevent others from stealing the food and also on being able to relocate the food. Relocation involves *homing* behaviour and *cognitive maps*.
- **e.g.** A squirrel placing its nuts in a tree.

foraging: all the activities an animal engages in when satisfying its nutritional requirements.

- Herbivores have to spend a greater part of the day grazing to obtain sufficient food whereas carnivores can eat less often but when they do, it often involves a great expenditure of energy. There are omnivores, detrivores (consume dead organic matter) and parasites (eat but do not kill prey).

forced-choice question: on a *questionnaire* survey, a kind of question that has a limited range of answers.

- The respondent is forced into the given choices. See *closed question*.

forebrain: see the *brain*.

forensic psychology: see *criminal psychology*.

forgetting: the inability to recall or recognise information which was previously learned or placed in memory.

- The act of forgetting assumes that something was once stored in memory, and now has disappeared (is not available), or cannot be brought to mind (is not accessible).
- **e.g.** Lack of availability: encoding failure, *interference*, *trace decay*, brain damage. Lack of accessibility: *cue-dependent forgetting*, *repressed memory*.

formal operation: the final stage in *Piaget's theory of cognitive development*.

fovea: the central region of the *retina* which is densely packed with *photosensitive (photoreceptor) cells*, mainly *cones*. The fovea is used for detailed vision.

free association: a method used in *psychoanalysis* to access the unconscious mind and thus reveal repressed material and *ego defences* that are causing maladaptive behaviour.

- The psychoanalyst asks a question or introduces a topic, and the patient then says anything that comes into his or her head. It is important that neither psychoanalyst nor patient attempts to censure any thoughts.

free recall: in a *memory* experiment, participants are allowed to recall items in any order they please.

free will: the view that our behaviour is determined by our own will rather than by other forces (the *determinist* position).

- *Humanistic psychologists* emphasise the individual's capacity for self-determination (free will), in contrast to *behaviourists* and *psychoanalytic theorists*. We are each morally responsible for our own actions. The existentialist philosopher Sartre said that we each are 'condemned to be free', meaning that free will is a burden. The concept of free will causes a problem for the *scientific* approach, because it suggests that behaviour is not predictable and therefore no *causal* relationships can be identified in psychology.

frequency graph: any *graph* where the *y*-axis represents the number of observations (frequency).

■ ***e.g.*** *Bar chart, histogram, frequency polygon.*

frequency polygon: a kind of *graph* used to represent the frequency of data.

■ A frequency polygon is formed if you place a dot at the centre top of each column on a histogram and connect the dots. You end up with a many-sided shape (polygon).

■ ***TIP*** An important factor is the size of the intervals on the *x*-axis. If the intervals are too small, you will have a very up-and-down polygon. If the intervals are too large, you lose information.

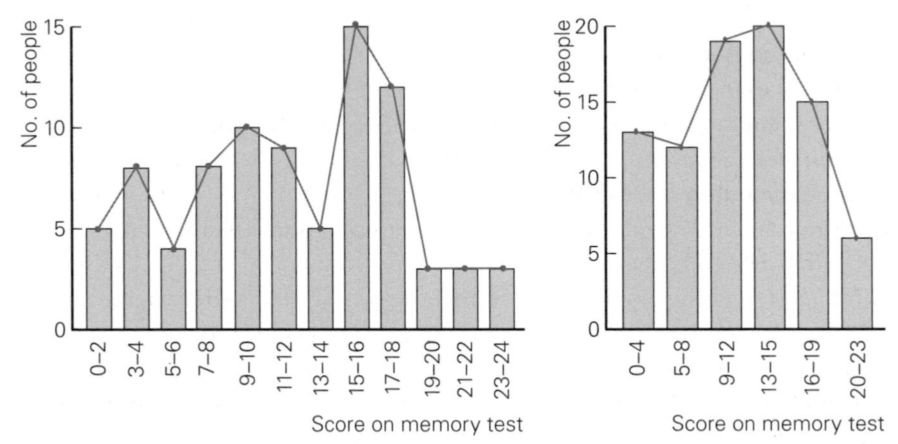

frequency table: a table of data which shows individual scores and the frequency of each, rather than listing each data item separately.

■ The scores may be grouped which makes it easier to see patterns. This is a form of *statistics* because it summarises the data.

Freudian: literally, anything related to the works of Sigmund Freud, or a follower of Freud.

■ The term has also come to mean 'unconscious' or having a 'sexual' innuendo.

■ ***e.g.*** 'Frank told a joke that was very Freudian', in other words the joke had some unconscious and/or sexual meaning.

Freudian slip: an unintentional error that reveals subconscious thoughts.

■ ***e.g.*** Freud gave the example of an MP who referred to his colleague as 'the honourable member from Hell' instead of from Hull.

frontal lobe: a region in each *hemisphere* of the forebrain (see the *brain*).

■ It is located in front of (anterior to) the *central sulcus* and above the lateral fissure. It contains the motor cortex (responsible for voluntary movement) and the prefrontal cortex which is involved with, for example, *working memory*. It also contains *Broca's area* (speech output).

frustration–aggression hypothesis: a *social-psychological* explanation for *aggressive* behaviour which states that frustration always leads to aggression and aggression is always caused by frustration.

- This explanation can be classed as social-psychological and *psychoanalytic*. Dollard et al. (1939) proposed that the pursuit of personal goals involves the arousal of psychic energy. When we attain those goals, the energy is released (*catharsis*). If the goals are blocked, then we experience pent-up psychic energy (frustration). This must be released and Dollard et al. suggested that it was via aggression. This has parallels with Freud's explanation of aggression. The frustration–aggression hypothesis can explain the *intergroup* aggression that arises from *prejudice* in terms of *scapegoat theory*. Lack of empirical support led to a modified version of the theory which claimed that frustration does not always lead to aggression and that there are other causes of aggression (such as pain or loud music, i.e. generalised arousal — see *arousal–aggression hypothesis*). See also *cue–arousal theory*.

F scale (fascism scale)**:** a test of tendencies towards fascism.

- High scorers tend also to be prejudiced and racist. The scale was used by Adorno in his research into the *authoritarian personality*. The scale has been criticised because there may have been a *response set* (agreement leads to authoritarian-type answers) and authoritarianism of the left was overlooked.
- ***e.g.*** Example items from the scale: Do you agree or disagree with the following: 'What youth needs most is strict discipline, rugged determination, and the will to work for family and country', 'Familiarity breeds contempt'.

functional fixedness: see *mental set*.

functionalism: any theory that stresses the analysis of behaviour in terms of its uses rather than its contents (i.e. structure, see *structuralism*).

- ***e.g.*** *Evolutionary* explanations.

functional theory of language acquisition: Halliday's (1975) view that language has a functional importance and that social interaction is a necessary ingredient to language acquisition, in addition to the *innate* and learned factors (*nativist theory* and *learning theory* respectively).

fundamental attribution error (FAE) or **bias:** in relation to *attribution theory*, the tendency to explain the causes of another person's behaviour in terms of *dispositional* rather than *situational* factors.

- This is an example of a *bias* in the attribution process. Other biases include the *self-serving bias* and *actor–observer effect*.
- ***e.g.*** When a friend is late to meet you, people tend to prefer to explain this as 'She is always late' (a *dispositional* explanation) rather than thinking that her bus might be late (a *situational* explanation).

GABA (gamma-amino butyric acid): a *neurotransmitter* that is produced at times of *stress* or anxiety, acting as the body's natural form of anxiety relief.

■ GABA is produced at times of anxiety and then inhibits the transmission of an *action potential* at a synapse, i.e. the *neuron* does not transmit a message to the next neuron. This has an inhibitory effect on the nervous system, i.e. it stops other neurones responding to anxiety. GABA is also related to *sleep* and *epilepsy*.

galvanic skin response (GSR): a method of detecting *emotion* or *stress*.

■ Moisture (sweating) increases electrical conductivity. People sweat when their *autonomic nervous system* is aroused, for example at times of high emotion or stress. If you place an *electrode* on a person's arm the electrical activity in the nervous system will be conducted to a machine that responds to electrical signals if the individual is sweating.

■ ***TIP*** This is the basis of *lie detectors*.

ganglion cell: see *retinal ganglion cell*.

GAS: see *general adaptation syndrome*.

gender: the psychological characteristics associated with being male or female.

gender bias: the differential treatment or representation of men and women based on stereotypes rather than real differences.

■ In psychology some theories are alpha-biased, that is they describe real and enduring gender differences but the result is a tendency to exaggerate these differences. Other theories may be beta-biased, that is they ignore or minimise gender differences and assume that what is true for one gender is true for all of human kind.

■ ***e.g.*** Evolutionary theory tends to be alpha-biased. Kohlberg's research on moral development is beta-biased.

gender identity: your concept of being male or female, a fundamental part of your self concept — 'I am a boy' or 'I am a girl'.

■ Gender identity generates gender behaviour — behaving like a boy or a girl. Such behaviour depends on a knowledge of *gender roles*.

gender role: a set of expectations that prescribe how males and females should think, act and feel.

- These expectations are embodied in cultural *stereotypes* about the behaviour of males and females.

gender schema theory: a *cognitive–developmental* approach to gender development, proposed by Martin and Halverson (1983), which suggests that gender *schema* help a child to organise and interpret their experience and it is this cognitive activity that drives gender development.

- Gender schema begin to form as soon as a child recognises that there is a difference between men and women. Children develop schema or 'theories' about gender-appropriate behaviour which affect the way they subsequently interpret new information about gender.
- ***TIP*** The key difference between gender schema theory and Kohlberg's cognitive–developmental theory of gender development lies in the stage at which the child is motivated to acquire knowledge about their gender. In Kohlberg's theory, a child must recognise the permanence of gender before they can begin to imitate same-gender models. In gender schema theory, gender schema form first.

gene: a unit of inheritance which forms part of a *chromosome*.

- Some characteristics are determined by one gene but most characteristics are caused by many genes (*polygenetic*).

gene-mapping: determining the effect of a particular *gene* on physical or psychological characteristics.

- ***e.g.*** Attempts have been made to identify the particular gene responsible for schizophrenia. One study found a possible site on chromosome 5, but this has not been replicated.

general adaptation syndrome (GAS): Selye's description of the *stress* response in terms of how an organism copes in an *adaptive* way (i.e. one that promotes survival).

- There are three stages to this adaptive response. (1) Alarm reaction. The *sympathetic branch* of the *autonomic nervous system* is aroused so that the animal can respond to the stressor. This is a healthy response which is important for survival. (2) Resistance. If the stressor persists, the body must adapt by trying to return to a normal level of functioning (*homeostasis*), i.e. reduce production of hormones which would otherwise become depleted. (3) Exhaustion. Eventually this low level of coping does deplete all resources. The *adrenal glands* cease to function properly and the *immune system* breaks down, leading to illness. This model has been very influential in identifying a link between stress and illness. It has been criticised because it is based on work with non-human animals and tends to overlook the influence of cognitive, social and emotional factors.

generalisability: the extent to which research findings can be applied from a particular research study to the population from which the sample was drawn, or to the world in general.

- In other words, moving from the particular to the more general. The generalisability of a set of findings depends on: (1) the success of the *sampling technique*

— was the sample representative of the population? (2) the representativeness of the population from which the sample was drawn — if the sample was drawn from a group of college students then, even if the sample is representative of the population, it is not reasonable to generalise the results to all people.

generalisation: in relation to *learning theory*, the tendency to transfer a response from one stimulus to another which is quite similar.

■ ***e.g.*** If a pigeon is trained to respond to a circle, this response will generalise to all round-shaped objects.

general problem solver (GPS): a computer program based on Newell and Simon's (1963) *means–end analysis*, an explanation of problem solving.

■ The program enabled them to demonstrate that their model does work by comparing the record of the computer's activity with a record of what a person did when solving the same problem.

genetic vulnerability: an inherited susceptibility to a particular condition or characteristic.

■ ***e.g.*** The *diathesis–stress model* suggests that individuals inherit a *gene* (or genes) that predispose the individual to become, say, schizophrenic or develop breast cancer. This is their genetic vulnerability. However, the condition will only develop when triggered by environmental events.

genital stage: in *psychoanalytic theory*, the final stage of *psychosexual development* when the organ-focus is again on the genitals (see *phallic stage*), but this time in relation to the onset of puberty and adult sexual relations.

■ The adolescent is concerned over issues of independence. If some issues remain unresolved from the earlier psychosexual stages, the individual cannot shift focus from their immediate needs to larger responsibilities involving others.

genotype: an individual's genetic constitution, as determined by the particular set of *genes* it possesses.

■ The actual observable characteristics are called the *phenotype*.

■ ***e.g.*** You inherit a genetic predisposition for height (your genotype) but your actual height is determined in relation to, for example, the diet you have (your actual height would be your phenotype).

geon: Biederman's (1987) more flexible alternative to the *template theory* of pattern recognition which suggests that there are a limited number of geometric shapes (geometric ions = geons) which can be used for pattern recognition.

■ Biederman has identified 24 geons — apparently three geons can be combined to produce 2.4 billion objects, so 24 geons could cope with an unimaginable number.

Gestalt psychology: a school of psychology which originated in Germany in the 1920s, based on *innate* and *holist* principles.

■ Gestalt psychologists believed that behaviour could only be understood in terms of the whole thing rather than being broken down into constituent parts. They also believed that we have an innate predisposition to organise information in particular ways. They applied this particularly to the study of perception, explaining how sensations give rise to *perceptions* according to the laws of meaning (Prägnanz). These laws allow us to give meaning to what we see. (The word 'Gestalt' means 'good form' or 'shape' in German.)

- ***e.g.*** Examples of the innate laws of meaning are given below. When you see the dots arranged as in the figure on the left, your natural inclination is to see them as groups (the rule of proximity). When you see a figure like the one on the right, you view it as a whole rather than an incomplete object (the rule of closure).

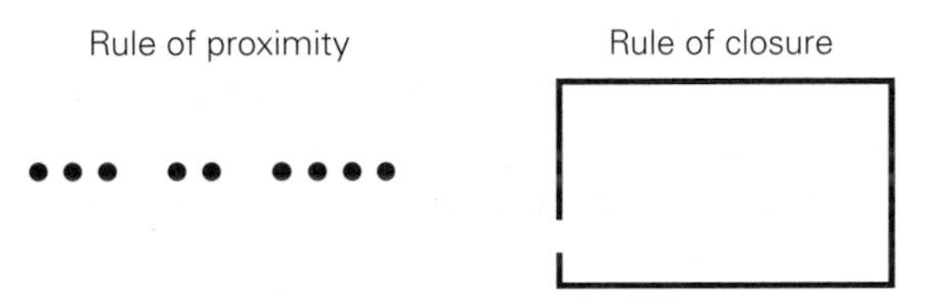

Gestalt therapy: a *humanistic* therapy developed by Perls (1969) which aims to develop a greater awareness of the *self* and a sense of wholeness ('gestalt').

- The focus is on the present rather than the past but the therapy is highly directive, unlike *client-centred therapy*. *Role play* is used where the client acts out both sides of a relationship in turn. This may involve the use of the 'empty chair technique' where the client addresses an imaginary person in a chair and then takes the part of the person sitting in the chair.

glucose: a form of sugar which is one of the main sources of energy for the brain and body.

glucostatic theory: an explanation for hunger *motivation* in terms of levels of blood *glucose*.

- There are glucoreceptors in the *ventromedial hypothalamus* which respond to alterations in levels of glucose and create a drive to eat.

good taste hypothesis: see *runaway process*.

grammar: the rules of how words are combined to provide meaning.

- An infinite number of meanings can be generated from a finite set of sounds. The rules of combination are called the 'grammar'. See *transformational grammar*.
- ***e.g.*** 'Shoe lace' means something different to 'lace shoe'.

graph: a visual representation of data that shows a relationship between variables and provides a form of summary.

- ***e.g.*** Suitable for all *levels of measurement* (*nominal, ordinal, interval*): pie chart, *bar chart*. Suitable for ordinal and interval level data: straight or curved line graph, *histogram, frequency polygon*, cumulative frequency graph (*ogive*). Suitable for correlational data: *scattergram*. Suitable for showing distribution: *stem and leaf diagrams, box-plots*.
- ***TIP*** Always use squared paper for drawing graphs and always ensure that the title of the graph and labels for axes are clear. The horizontal axis is called the *x*-axis, and the vertical axis is the *y*-axis.

great Eskimo vocabulary hoax: in relation to the *linguistic relativity hypothesis*, it has been suggested that many languages have a large vocabulary for certain concepts (e.g. the Eskimo words for snow) which enables native speakers to make cognitive distinctions not available to speakers of other languages.

- However, Pinker (1994) claims that the Eskimos actually only have around 12 words for snow rather than the 50 or so that has been claimed and that there are about the same number of 'snow words' in English (e.g. sleet, blizzard, powder). Even if Eskimos did have more words, it would not be surprising, because the more contact one has with a particular kind of thing the more one needs to represent finer distinctions. For example, people working in publishing have many words for printing fonts.

great man (or woman or person) theory: an explanation for the emergence and effectiveness of a leader in terms of the inherent characteristics of the individual.

- However, it is difficult to know to what extent such traits are developed by leaders and which ones give rise to their success.
- ***e.g.*** Height, intelligence, personality, physical attractiveness, dominance, sensitivity are all traits that might be associated with *leadership* success.

green beard effect: an explanation by Dawkins (1976) for the special characteristics possessed by kin that enable them to recognise each other.

Greenspoon effect: participants' behaviours are subtly reinforced by the experimenter's comments such as unconsciously nodding in agreement.

- This is one means by which an experimenter communicates his/her expectations (see *experimenter bias*).

grounded theory: a form of *qualitative analysis* where the text is used to develop theoretical accounts.

- What the researcher produces is 'grounded' in the text rather than based on prior theory (as in *thematic analysis*). The 'text' may come from, for example, an interview or a recorded conversation. The account is 'theoretical' in the sense that it is an attempt to produce a coherent account of the facts. You might identify certain themes which recur, or categorise types of behaviour.

group polarisation: see *risky shift*.

group socialisation (GS) theory: the view that children are *socialised* by groups outside the home, especially their peer groups, rather than the family.

groupthink: a term coined by Janis (1982) to describe and explain the fact that groups often make poor decisions as a result of group pressures.

- These pressures include *group polarisation*, *normative social influence*, decisional stress, biased leadership and the fact that groups may work in isolation.
- ***e.g.*** In 1961 the United States invaded the Bay of Pigs in Cuba, an action which almost escalated into a war with Russia. The decision to invade was taken by a group of presidential advisers who made a series of mistaken decisions best described as 'groupthink'.

GSR: see *galvanic skin response*.

hallucinations: the perception of things that are not real.

halo effect: in *impression formation*, the tendency for the total impression formed to be unduly influenced by one outstanding trait.

- One assumes that an individual who possesses one highly desirable trait will also possess a cluster of other desirable traits. The one desirable trait makes you see the individual as if they wore a halo.
- ***e.g.*** People who are beautiful are usually also judged to be friendly, humourous, honest, warm and so on.

handicapping theory: an explanation for elaborate sexual characteristics such as the peacock's tail, Zahavi (1975) proposed that females prefer mates with handicaps because this is evidence of their superior genetic quality.

- ***e.g.*** If a male peacock can survive despite his tail he must be good in other respects.
- ***TIP*** In this theory the 'good genes' are in terms of survival and reproduction as opposed to the suggestion by the *runaway process* theory that the good genes would be for producing attractive male offspring. Critics of handicapping theory say that the same might then apply to males who have been injured but survived, but this 'handicap' would not be heritable and in fact might act detrimentally because individuals who get injured tend to be weaker to begin with.

hard determinism: see *determinism*.

hardiness: a cluster of traits identified by Kobasa as being related to an ability to cope well with stress.

- The characteristics of a 'hardy' individual are a greater sense of commitment to work and personal relationships, seeing stressful situations as a challenge and an opportunity, and a stronger sense of personal control. Individuals who are 'hardy' have been found to cope well with stress and are less likely to become ill. This suggests that hardiness underlies better coping. An alternative interpretation is that people who are ill find it harder to be psychologically hardy.

hardiness training: a *stress management* technique based on Kobasa's concept of *hardiness*.

■ If hardy people are better able to cope with stress, then one way of coping with stress might be to learn hardiness. The suggested steps are focusing (becoming aware that you are feeling stressed so that you can deal with stress, rather than ignoring it), reconstructing stress situations (think about how a situation could have turned out better or worse and focus on the positive) and compensating through self-improvement (master tasks and reassure yourself that you can cope). The 'catch' is that the technique requires considerable effort and determination — the characteristics of a hardy personality.

hard-wired: the view that the connections in the nervous system, once determined, are fixed. See *plasticity*.

hassle: an ongoing stress and strain of daily living.

■ One explanation for *stress* is the effect of *life events*. DeLongis et al. (1982) noted that most people do not often experience major life events, therefore the strains of everyday life might be a better measure of stress and a better predictor of physical illness. The evidence suggests that there is a slightly better correlation between hassles and health than for life events and health. One problem, however, is the fact that the same thing is not always a hassle. For example, noisy neighbours would be annoying when you are trying to sleep but not if they were having a party and you enjoyed the music. This led DeLongis et al. to develop the *hassles and uplifts scale*.

■ ***e.g.*** Concerns about one's weight, rising prices, home maintenance, losing things, crime and physical appearance.

hassles and uplifts scale: a *questionnaire* to assess the number of stressful factors in your life.

■ Each event can be rated as a hassle and an uplift, which takes into account the fact that there are individual differences in the way hassles are perceived. Hassle vs uplift also varies for the same person on different days.

■ ***e.g.*** Example items: cooking, legal matters, exercise, your smoking, fellow workers, your work load. All are rated separately as both a hassle and an uplift.

hawk–dove strategy: an *evolutionarily stable strategy* for a species where there is the optimum balance between 'hawks' and 'doves'.

■ If there are too many 'hawks' (aggressive individuals) they will kill each other off until there are more 'doves' (non-aggressive animals). If there are too many 'doves' then a mutant or immigrant 'hawk' would win every fight and soon they would increase in number. Thus, there is an unbeatable, ideal mixture of hawks and doves forming an evolutionarily stable strategy (i.e. it cannot be bettered by any alternative).

Hawthorne effect: the change in a participant's behaviour that results from the knowledge that he/she is being observed.

■ A participant's performance in a research study may improve because of the extra attention he/she is receiving, not because of the experimental treatment. This acts as a *confounding variable*. It is named after the Hawthorne electrical factory in America where it was first observed.

Headstart: see *Operation Headstart.*

health belief model: an explanation of how health behaviour changes.

- An individual takes into account: (1) the perceived threats to one's health; and (2) the perceived possible effectiveness of actions that may reduce such threats.
- ***TIP*** The model can be applied to behaviour change in general.

health psychology: the branch of *applied psychology* that seeks to understand psychological influences on health and illness.

- Health psychologists are interested in topics such as stress, pain, the effect of lifestyles on health, psychosomatic health, patient–practitioner relationship, substance abuse, and theories related to changing health *attitudes* and behaviour. Health psychology is also interested in establishing health policy and interventions, as well as assessing their effectiveness.

hedonic relevance: see *correspondent inference theory.*

hello–goodbye effect: patients tend to exaggerate their unhappiness at the beginning of therapy to convince the therapist that they are in genuine need. At the end of therapy the reverse is true: in order to express thanks to the therapist, the patient exaggerates their well-being.

- ***TIP*** Using self-report methods to assess the effectiveness of therapies is likely to be unreliable because of this.

helping behaviour: providing assistance for someone in need.

- Unlike *altruism,* there is no personal cost involved. However, people may still desist from helping for reasons other than cost. See *bystander behaviour.*

hemisphere: the *cerebrum* is divided into two halves or hemispheres.

- Each half is largely the same, containing the same specialised regions with the exception of those functions that are lateralised, such as language.

hemispheric asymmetry: *lateralisation,* the fact that some functions are represented in one *hemisphere* and not the other.

hemispheric dominance: the condition for most people in which one *hemisphere* is dominant, making their motor control better for this side.

- For a right-handed person the left hemisphere is dominant.

heritability: the ratio between (a) genetic variability of the particular trait and (b) total variability in the whole *population.*

- This is expressed as a heritability ratio and calculated by dividing the genetic variability of a characteristic by the total variability plus the genetic variability. The genetic variance is calculated using, for example, *concordance* rates.
- ***e.g.*** Consider schizophrenia. One might find that 80% of such cases can be explained in terms of genetic factors. One can also observe the percentage of the population who exhibit schizophrenia, say this is 15%. Therefore the heritability ratio is $0.8/(0.15 + 0.8) = 0.84$. In a population with a lower rate of schizophrenia, the heritability ratio will be larger. For example, say the general occurrence in the population is 5%, then the heritability ratio will be $0.8/(0.05 + 0.8) = 0.94$.

heteronomous morality: see *autonomous morality.*

heuristic: a rule for doing something which serves the purpose of reducing the range of possible solutions to a problem.

- Heuristics are methods of solving a problem that make life easier for us. They are mental shortcuts. People tend to choose the approach that will allow them to reach their goal with the minimum of effort (i.e. they are *cognitive misers*). In social psychology, heuristics are used for making judgements about people. In cognitive psychology heuristics describe how we solve problems and make decisions. In both social and cognitive psychology *cognition* (thought) is involved. In order for a heuristic to be successful, it must be reasonably accurate most of the time, but heuristics inevitably lead to some *biases* and errors.
- ***e.g.*** *Stereotyping, availability heuristic, representativeness heuristic, false consensus effect.* A knitting pattern is also a heuristic.

hibernation theory: a variation of the *evolutionary theory of sleep*, that suggests that sleep serves a similarly *adaptive* purpose to hibernation.

- We sleep to keep ourselves quiet and safe at night.

hierarchy of needs: Maslow's (1954) explanation of what *drives* (motivates) behaviour.

- *Physiological* needs are at the bottom of the hierarchy and are 'prepotent' (more powerful when unfulfilled) to intermediate and meta needs. When lower needs are fulfilled, higher needs become motivators.

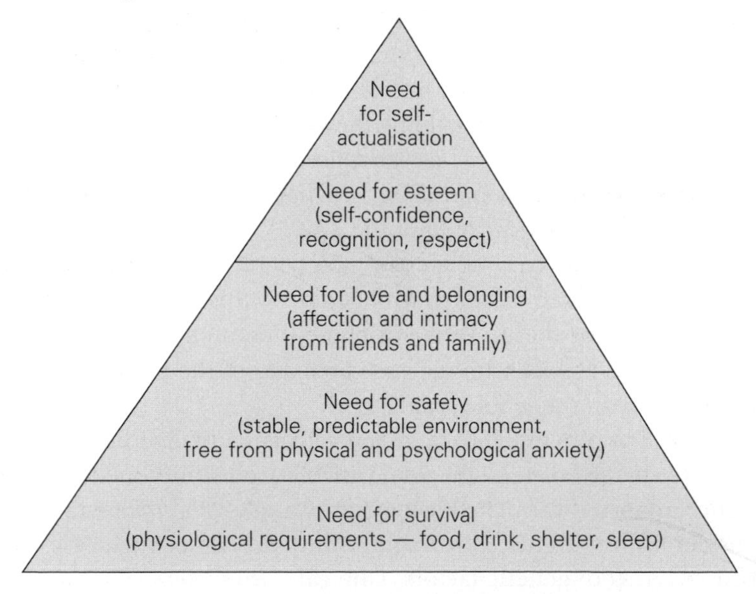

hindbrain: see *brain*.

hippocampus: a structure in the subcortical area of each *hemisphere* of the *forebrain*, associated with memory.

- Part of the *limbic system*, involved in motivation, emotion and learning.

histogram: a kind of *graph* used to represent the frequency of data. The height of the column represents frequency.

- The difference between a histogram and a *bar chart* is that the histogra only be used with *ordinal* or *interval* level data because the data on the must be continuous with a true zero. The *y*-axis represents frequency.
- **TIP** You must not miss out empty categories, or the *x*-axis would no longer be continuous. (See *bar chart*.)

holist: an argument or theory which proposes that it only makes sense to study a whole system rather than its constituent parts (which is the *reductionist* approach).

- This is based on the principle that the whole is greater than the sum of its parts. It is the approach taken by *Gestalt* psychologists.
- ***e.g.*** An appreciation of a work of art involves the whole picture rather than an analysis of the paint and techniques that might have been used. These might be relevant but they do not express the whole experience.

home field (ground) advantage: an *evolutionarily stable strategy* that describes the fact that individuals tend to win contests on their home ground.

- ***e.g.*** Football teams tend to win at home more often than when playing away matches.

homeostasis: the process of maintaining a reasonably constant environment or steady state.

- The term literally means 'same state'.
- ***e.g.*** Homeostatic control can be seen in the thermostat that governs a central heating system to maintain a constant temperature. In the body it is also important to maintain a steady temperature, as well as maintaining, for example, constant levels of glucose. In terms of *stress*, homeostasis results in a return to the normal, unstressed state.

homeostatic drive theory: a physiological theory of *motivation*, that an organism has a drive to return to a steady state (*homeostasis*).

- Therefore motivation is due to situations where basic needs, such as hunger and thirst, are not fulfilled. This creates a *drive* which causes the organism to act. However, this cannot explain higher-order needs.

homing: behaviour used by an animal to locate its home (nest, burrow), origin or food store.

- Animals use various methods such as local landmarks, temperature, day length, the position of the sun, smell and magnetic information. There are elements of both *nature* and *nurture* in this clearly *adaptive* behaviour. Homing involves both 'orientation' and 'navigation'. At the beginning an animal must point themselves in the right direction (orientation) and then the rest of the journey requires 'navigation'.
- ***e.g.*** The homing pigeon starts in unfamiliar terrain and uses the sun, smell, or magnetic information to orientate itself until it is within familiar terrain; then it uses familiar local landmarks to locate its target destination.

horizontal décalage: the concept in *Piaget's theory of cognitive development* that not all aspects of the same stage appear at the same time.

- Piaget suggested that uneven cognitive performance is probably due to different learning experiences.
- ***e.g.*** The ability to conserve number and volume may not appear at the same time, but one after the other.

hormone: chemical substance produced by an *endocrine* gland.

- Hormones are circulated in the blood and only affect target organs. They are produced in large quantities but disappear very quickly. Their effects are slow in comparison with the nervous system, but very powerful. See also *pheromones*.
- ***e.g.*** *Adrenaline, melatonin, testosterone, oestrogen.*

hostile aggression: see *aggression*.

hothousing: the belief that very early enrichment will have positive long-term effects on a child's intellectual development.

- Hothousing may involve *prenatal* stimulation (using music or speaking to the child), or intensive educational programmes in infancy and early childhood (e.g. training in reading). The term was 'invented' to suggest that children could be matured in the same way that tomatoes are grown in a hothouse.
- ***TIP*** Such early gains are unlikely to be very long-lasting, though a consuming desire to succeed may be what is learned.

humanistic psychology: an approach in psychology that emphasises the uniqueness of each individual, one's capacity for self-determination (*free will*), one's drive for *self-actualisation* and the importance of subjective experience.

- Humanistic psychology is a relatively recent development in psychology (post-1950). It is derived from the wider principles of humanism, a belief system that emphasises the personal worth of each individual but does not involve a divine being. Humanistic psychology is also derived from nineteenth-century philosophers such as Kierkegaard who founded the existentialist movement, arguing that subjectivity is truth. Humanistic psychology is a contrast to the more *deterministic* and *reductionist* approaches like *behaviourism* and *psychoanalysis*. Maslow called humanistic psychology the third force in psychology. Humanistic psychologists prefer an *idiographic* approach and emphasise the importance of *free will*. They believe that psychological theories should be humanly, rather than statistically, significant, claiming that objective data can tell us little about subjective experience. Humanistic psychologists believe that research should ideally be conducted using methods such as *ethogenics* and *ethnomethodology*.
- ***e.g.*** Rogers's *client-centred therapy*, Maslow's *hierarchy of needs*, Kelley's *personal construct theory*.

hydraulic model of motivation: *ethologists* suggested that behaviour is driven by action-specific energy (ASE).

- This energy is stored between demand and if there is no demand, it will build up and finally overflow like a cistern waiting to be flushed. This overflowing triggers certain *fixed action patterns* (FAPs) which occur in the absence of any stimulus. Freud's model of aggression is also a hydraulic model.

hypertension: a condition associated with very high blood pressure.

- It is a major risk factor for coronary heart disease (CHD) when experienced for a prolonged time (more than a few weeks). Hypertension is caused by a variety of factors such as obesity, drinking too much coffee (caffeine) or alcohol, lack of exercise, *genetic vulnerability* and high levels of stress.

hypothalamic–pituitary–adrenal axis: the three major components of the *stress* response: the *hypothalamus*, the *pituitary gland* and the *adrenal glands*.

- The *hypothalamus* produces hormones in response to stress, e.g. *corticotropin-release factor* (CRF) which stimulates the anterior pituitary gland to secrete its hormones. The anterior *pituitary gland* releases *adrenocorticotropic hormone* (ACTH) which stimulates the adrenal glands. The *adrenal glands* secrete *adrenaline* and *noradrenaline*, which are associated with arousal of the *sympathetic branch* of the *autonomic nervous system*.

hypothalamus: a structure in the subcortical area of each *hemisphere* of the *forebrain*, responsible for integrating the activity of the *autonomic nervous system* and thus behaviours such as *stress*, *emotion* and *motivation*.

- It is located underneath the *thalamus* and each hypothalamus is about the size of a baked bean. It has widespread connections with the rest of the forebrain and the midbrain as well. The hypothalamus is part of the *limbic system*. The hypothalamus is associated with the regulation of *homeostasis* in eating and drinking, and arousal of the autonomic nervous system (*'fight or flight'* response and emotion generally). See also *lateral hypothalamus* and *ventromedial hypothalamus*.

hypothesis: a testable, predictive statement of what you believe to be true.

- It is a proposition made so that it can be tested to see if it is true. A hypothesis is not much use unless it is stated in a form which can be tested (i.e. unambiguous and *operationalised*). The hypothesis either states a predicted difference between an independent and dependent variable (an *experimental hypothesis*), or it states a predicted relationship (in the case of a *correlational study*).
- **e.g.** *Research hypothesis, experimental hypothesis, null hypothesis, alternative hypothesis, directional hypothesis, non-directional hypothesis.*

ICD-10: the most recent version (1993) of the International Classification of Disorders published by the World Health Organisation.

■ It provides a means of classifying mental disorders and providing basic health statistics, as distinct from being primarily a *diagnostic* tool which is the aim of *DSM-IV*. Mental disorders were not originally included in ICD. The ICD now identifies 11 major categories of mental disorder and provides examples in each category: (1) organic; (2) mental and behavioural disorders due to psychoactive substance abuse; (3) schizophrenia; (4) mood (affective) disorders; (5) neurotic, stress-related and somatoform disorders; (6) behavioural syndromes associated with physiological and physical disturbances; (7) disorders of adult personality; (8) mental retardation; (9) disorders of psychological development; (10) behavioural and emotional disorders with onset in early childhood and adolescence; (11) unspecified mental disorder.

■ ***TIP*** The most recent version of DSM was written with the requirement that it was better coordinated with ICD.

id: a personality structure identified in *psychoanalytic theory*. It is the primitive, instinctive part of the personality which demands immediate satisfaction.

■ The id is motivated by the *pleasure principle*, driving the individual to do things for pleasure or gratification and also to avoid pain. In the early months of life, an infant's behaviour is driven by the id until its demands are modified by the appearance of the *ego*. Throughout life the id, ego and *superego* are in conflict, which produces anxiety and *ego defences*. During development, the id seeks gratification through different organs of the body: the mouth *(oral stage)*, anus (*anal stage*), the genitals (*phallic stage*) and later in adolescence through the genitals again (*genital stage*).

■ ***TIP*** Freud referred to the id as the 'it'. It wants to be satisfied.

ideal self: the person you would like to be.

■ If there is a large difference between your ideal *self* and your *self-concept*, this results in maladjustment, according to Roger's *self theory*. The individual has to strive to become something else and this prevents *self-actualisation*.

identification: to become associated with a person or a thing.

■ In relation to *conformity*, it describes conforming to the demands of a given role because of a desire to be like a particular person in that role. For example, a policeman conforms to the role of being a policeman because of a desire to do the job. Kelman identified this as one of three types of conformity (the other two are *compliance* and *internalisation*). In relation to *psychoanalytic theory*, it is a key part of the *phallic stage* where the child resolves the psychosexual crisis (*Oedipus conflict* or *penis envy*) by identifying with his/her same-sex parent. This results in the child taking on the attitudes, especially moral ones, of the parent. In relation to *social learning theory*, learning is more likely if the individual identifies with the model.

identity crisis: the difficulty experienced when establishing one's sense of independence and thus identity.

- Freud (*psychoanalytic theory*) suggested that adolescence (genital stage) is a time of becoming independent, i.e. identity formation. Drawing on this, Erikson (see *eight ages of man*) suggested the adolescent crisis is identity vs role confusion. Failure to resolve this psychosocial crisis will result in a lack of personal identity (i.e. role confusion). Marcia (1966) reformulated Erikson's account of the adolescent crisis, suggesting that there were four possibilities. An individual may pass through all or some of them and may never reach the end. (1) 'Identity diffusion or confusion'. The individual has not even started to think about the issues. (2) 'Identity foreclosure'. The individual has prematurely formed an opinion which is not based on individual consideration. (3) 'Identity moratorium'. Decisions about identity are put on hold while the adolescent may 'try on' various possibilities. (4) 'Identity achievement' occurs when an adolescent has been through the period of confusion or crisis and achieved their own identity.

idiographic approach: an approach to research that focuses more on the individual case as a means of understanding behaviour, rather than aiming to formulate general laws of behaviour (the *nomothetic approach*).

- The idiographic approach is favoured by *humanistic* psychology and also the approach taken by Freud in his case histories.
- ***e.g.*** Case studies focus on individuals, such as the study of Jenny undertaken by Allport (1965). He analysed 300 letters written by Jenny, arguing that this idiographic perspective could tell us more about human behaviour and personality than could the use of personality tests, which provide statistical information.

illusion of outgroup homogeneity: the tendency to perceive all members of an *outgroup* as being very similar, whereas more differentiation is made between members of the *ingroup*.

- In other words, outgroup members are perceived in terms of their *stereotypes*. The illusion of outgroup homogeneity serves to maintain in/outgroup distinctions because stereotypes are *self-fulfilling*.
- ***e.g.*** The saying, with regard to outgroup members, that 'They all look the same to me'.

imitation: behaving in the same way as something or someone else, i.e. copying.

■ This is the central concept in *social learning theory*. See also *modelling* and *observational learning*.

immune system: a system of cells within the body that is concerned with fighting against intruders such as viruses and bacteria.

■ This system acts like an army; white blood cells (*leucocytes*) identify and kill foreign bodies (called *antigens*). There are several kinds of leucocytes, including T-cells, B-cells and natural killer cells. T-cells destroy invaders, T-helper cells increase immunological activity, and natural killer cells destroy certain kinds of tumour cells and cells infected with viruses. *Antibodies* also attack antigens to fight off infection. It is thought that *stress* interferes with the immune system in various ways (e.g. it reduces T-cell activity) so that it is less effective, and this explains why high levels of stress may predispose an individual to illness.

implicit memory: a subdivision of *long-term memory*, it is memory that is not based on conscious recollection, as distinct from *explicit memory*.

■ Implicit memory is similar to *procedural knowledge* (knowing how) and involves *incidental learning*. Memory tests involve explicit rather than implicit memory and therefore cannot tell us much about the characteristics of implicit memory. Research has shown that people suffering from *amnesia* tend to retain their implicit memories, but have difficulty with explicit memory.

implosion therapy: a form of *behavioural therapy* where the patient is asked to imagine maximum exposure to a feared stimulus, with the intention of extinguishing a learned response. See *flooding*.

■ ***e.g.*** An arachnophobic imagining they are in a room full of spiders.

imposed etic: a technique or theory that is developed in one culture and then used to study the behaviour of people in other cultures.

■ The difficulty is that the technique is likely to be based on cultural assumptions and not to have the same meaning in another culture.

■ ***e.g.*** Intelligence tests (and *culture bias*), treatments used for abnormal behaviours and the *strange situation*.

impression formation: forming a global impression of another person on the basis of limited information.

■ Such impressions are then used to generate expectations about the individual. This is part of the process of *interpersonal perception* and is likely to be influenced by *stereotypes*. It can also be explained in terms of the *halo, primacy* and *recency effects*.

impression management: the way you manage the impression you make on others.

■ Individuals who are high in *self-monitoring* skills are better at creating a good impression. This would be useful in certain jobs, such as working as a salesperson or a politician.

imprinting: an *innate* readiness to acquire certain behaviours during a *critical* or *sensitive period* of development.

■ Imprinting involves both *nature* and *nurture*. The drive to imprint is innate, i.e. a young animal is 'genetically programmed' to imprint on an object with certain characteristics, such as movement. The actual change in behaviour is *learning*. The young animal learns to identify certain characteristics of an imprint object, such as a visual characteristic, a smell, or a sound. Imprinting is seen as an *adaptive* behaviour with important short-term effects (e.g. *filial imprinting*) and long-term effects (e.g. *sexual imprinting*). Imprinting is claimed to be irreversible, or at least difficult to change.

■ ***e.g.*** Filial imprinting, sexual imprinting, visual imprinting (sight), aural imprinting (hearing), olfactory imprinting (smell).

■ ***TIP*** Imprinting may simply be a special form of learning in so far as it takes place more rapidly and easily during certain developmental windows (critical or sensitive period).

incidental learning: *learning* that occurs without any intention to learn, such as in the absence of any instructions that there will subsequently be a memory test. Also called *implicit memory*.

inclusive fitness: a central concept in *sociobiological theory*, that *natural selection* includes the survival of any relatives sharing your genes.

■ The principle of the theory of evolution is that any characteristic which increases an individual's reproductive success will be naturally selected. Such characteristics increase individual fitness. Sociobiologists suggest that in fact any characteristic that increases the continuance of your gene pool will also be naturally selected (= *kin selection*). Inclusive fitness is measured in terms of the number of surviving descendants and relatives.

independent behaviour: resisting the pressures to *conform* or to *obey*.

■ True independence means behaviour that does not respond to group norms. It involves following one's conscience rather than being disobedient or non-conformist. Apparent non-conformity (*counter-conformity*) occurs when an individual is apparently not conforming to group norms, but is in fact conforming to a different set of group norms.

■ ***e.g.*** Resisting authority is not independent behaviour if everyone else in your class is doing it, because you are conforming to the norms of your class. Belonging to the resistance movement during the Second World War was also probably independent behaviour, even though there was an element of following others.

independent measures design: an *experimental design* where different participants are used for each condition in the experiment. Compare with *repeated measures design* and *matched pairs*.

■ One group receives the *experimental treatment* (or *independent variable*). The other (the *control group*) does not receive the experimental treatment, or receives a different experimental treatment. Performance on the *dependent variable* is compared between the two groups. Independent measures design is used when repeated measures are not possible, for example to avoid *order effects*, or because otherwise participants would realise the purpose of the experiment. The limitations of this design are that one lacks *control* of *participant variables*, though this potentially confounding factor can be overcome to some extent by using *random allocation* of participants to groups. A further limitation is that the independent measures experiments usually need more participants. In terms of *inferential statistics*, unrelated tests of difference are less *powerful* in detecting relationships.

■ ***e.g.*** Group A, the experimental group, has to follow a moving target with a pen, while at the same time listening to rock music. Group B, the control condition, does the same task without any music. The independent variable is music. Both groups are tested on the dependent variable (performance with moving target). If the same experiment was done using a repeated measures design, each participant would be exposed to both conditions: music and no music. It would necessary to use *counterbalancing* to avoid order effects.

■ ***TIP*** In some experiments there are more than two groups of participant. For example, there might be a rock music group, a classical music group and a no music group.

independent variable (IV): a feature of the experiment that is manipulated by the researcher in order to observe whether a change occurs in the *dependent variable (DV)*.

■ ***e.g.*** An experiment to see whether photographs of physically attractive individuals are rated as more likeable than those of physically unattractive individuals. The IV would be the attractiveness of a person's photograph and the DV would be the rating of how 'likeable' they were. A *confounding variable* may act as an additional independent variable if it varies constantly with the IV. It might be that all the 'attractive' photographs were of blondes whereas the unattractive ones had dark hair. Hair colour would be acting as a second IV.

■ ***TIP*** Remember that the IV is the one that is manipulated, the DV is the one that is measured.

individual differences: the characteristics that vary from one individual to another.

■ This is a key issue in psychological research because many theories assume that people are all the same (the *nomothetic approach*): all men are the same, all Americans are the same and so on.

■ ***e.g.*** People vary in terms of their IQ, personality, *temperament, attachment* types, responses to the same *stressors*.

■ ***TIP*** If you want to comment on any psychological research (a theory or study), it is likely that you can say something positive or negative in terms of individual differences. You can also consider situational differences.

individualist: a culture which values the rights and interests of the individual.

■ This results in a concern, for example, for independence and self-assertiveness. People tend to live in small, *nuclear families* unlike *collectivist* societies.

■ ***e.g.*** American and British culture.

inductive reasoning: drawing a logical conclusion by using particular instances to infer a general law.

■ Going from the particular to the general. See *deductive reasoning.*

■ ***e.g.*** Reasoning that all people in the world laugh when a baby smiles because that is how you behave.

industrial psychology: see *organisational psychology.*

inferential statistics: a type of *statistical* analysis that permits one to make inferences about an underlying *population* from a *sample* of data.

■ This contrasts with *descriptive statistics* which aim to describe the data. Inferential statistics allow us to decide whether a research finding is simply due to chance, in which case we should accept our *null hypothesis.* Or the finding is due to the *experimental treatment* and then we should accept our *alternate hypothesis.* Then we can draw a conclusion from our sample of data about the population in general. The procedure is to select an appropriate inferential test and calculate an *observed value* for the data. This value is then compared with the appropriate *critical value,* found in a table of critical values. If the observed value is not at the required level then the finding must be due to chance.

■ ***e.g.*** There are *parametric* and *non-parametric* inferential tests. There are tests of difference (for related or unrelated samples) and of *correlation.* The main tests used at A-level are summarised below.

		Test of difference		Test of correlation
		Related samples	Unrelated samples	
Parametric tests		*t*-test for related samples	*t*-test for unrelated samples	Pearson's product–moment correlation coefficient
Non-parametric tests	Ordinal data	Wilcoxon (*T*) signed ranks test	Mann–Whitney (*U*) test	Spearman's rho
	Nominal data	Sign test	Chi-squared (χ^2) test	Chi-squared (χ^2) test

informational social influence: when an individual *conforms* because others are thought to possess more knowledge. See *normative social influence.*

■ ***e.g.*** If you are dining out and do not know what knife to use, you may rely on informational social influence. In Sherif's study of the autokinetic effect there was no right answer and therefore individuals looked to each other for some idea about what might be correct.

information processing approach: an approach in psychology that is based on a computer analogy, i.e. the concept that mental processes are similar to computer processes.

■ The advent of the 'computer revolution' in the 1950s provided *cognitive psychologists* with a new way to describe and explain behaviour. They realised that mental processing could be described using the same terms as information processing: data are input, stored in networks, processed serially or in parallel, output and so on.

information processing theories of cognitive development: see *neo-Piagetian*.

informed consent (voluntary informed consent): the permission provided by participants in a research study.

■ It is considered to be an ethical obligation on the part of a researcher to provide participants with the opportunity to give their informed consent prior to taking part in any research. The use of the term 'informed' suggests that the participant should be informed of key details before giving their consent, such as being informed about what will be required, being informed about the purpose of the research and being informed of their rights (e.g. the right to confidentiality, the right to leave the research at any time). There are many situations where this is not possible, such as with child participants or individuals who have impairments that limit understanding and/or communication. It is also not possible to obtain informed consent in *field experiments* and some *observational* studies and when *deception* needs to be used. It is possible to compensate for these problems by various means: using the consent of a parent or guardian, careful post-research debriefing offering the opportunity to withhold data and asking for *presumptive consent* or *prior general consent*.

infradian rhythm: a *biological rhythm* that occurs or recurs in a cycle of more than 24 hours ('infra' and 'dies' = below or lower frequency than a day).

■ ***e.g.*** Human female monthly menstrual cycle. See also *circannual, circadian* and *ultradian rhythms*.

ingroup: any social group to which you belong, as distinct from the *outgroup*.

■ Group membership is determined by shared characteristics such as the school you go to, the football team you support, your gender or race. Psychological research has shown that ingroups are formed on the basis of *minimal group* membership.

ingroup favouritism: the tendency for individuals to show a positive *bias* to members of their own group (the *ingroup*).

■ *Social identity theory* predicts that this increases one's sense of personal self-esteem by making comparisons between groups. Ingroup favouritism and *outgroup negative bias* both enhance social and personal esteem and lead to biased perceptions of in- and outgroup members.

inherited: see *innate* and *chromosomes*.

innate: literally means 'inborn', a product of *genetic* factors.

■ The term 'inherited' means the same as innate. Innate behaviours may be present at birth, or may appear later as a result of *maturation*. The word *congenital* describes behaviours present at birth which are not genetic.

■ ***e.g.*** The onset of menstruation is an innate behaviour which is not present at birth.

innate learning: see *preparedness.*

innovation: a form of *social influence* suggested to be the result of *minority influence,* whereby a group is converted to a new point of view or new practices.

■ This is in contrast with *conformity* which is the result of majority influence which tends to maintain the status quo. Minority influence also results in a change of private opinion, whereas majority influence may only affect public behaviour.

insecure attachment: a form of *attachment* between an infant and caregiver which is not optimal for healthy development.

■ It may be associated with poor cognitive and/or emotional development.

■ ***e.g.*** *Avoidant attachment, resistant attachment.*

insight learning: a new behaviour is acquired (i.e. learned) simply through the process of insight rather than *trial and error.*

■ This cannot be explained by *learning theory* because the latter suggests that learning involves no *cognitive* activity. Insight, on the other hand, is entirely cognitive (mental).

■ ***e.g.*** Archimedes is said to have 'discovered' the concept that a body (such as a ship) displaces its own volume in water in a flash of insight — as he got into the bath. Köhler observed that chimpanzees often appeared to solve problems in the same way (such as how to reach a banana with a stick), without testing out possible solutions.

insignificant: a statistical outcome that has no value. The correct term is *non-significant.* Insignificant means of no importance whereas a nonsignificant result is as important as a significant one.

instinct: an *innate* drive that is characteristic of members of a species.

■ An instinct is notable for the fact that it can be found in individuals reared in isolation, such as bird song.

■ ***e.g.*** Freud referred to the instincts of eros and *thanatos;* ethologists wrote about aggressive instincts.

■ ***TIP*** The concept of instincts has gone out of fashion more recently because it involves making a distinction between learned and *innate* behaviours, whereas current thinking acknowledges the inseparability of these factors.

instrumental aggression: see *aggression.*

instrumental learning: see *operant conditioning.*

intellectualisation: in *psychoanalytic theory,* a form of *ego defence* that copes with a threatening event by removing the emotion from it.

■ ***e.g.*** Dealing with the diagnosis of a terminal illness by reading all the books on the disorder. This may well be a useful response, but the individual has not dealt with the related emotional issues which may be *displaced* elsewhere.

intelligence: the ability to acquire information, to think and reason well, and to deal effectively and adaptively with the environment.

■ There are many different definitions, including the idea of a general intelligence (*g*) and also of different kinds of intelligences (such as mathematical, spatial, personal). A more practical though circular definition is that intelligence is what intelligence tests measure (see *IQ*). The question of *nature* or *nurture* in relation to intelligence remains open to debate. A significant proportion of a person's IQ appears to be due to inherited factors (possibly as much as 80%), but environment can have a major influence on the extent to which one's innate potential is developed.

intelligence quotient: see *IQ*.

intelligence test: see *psychometric test*.

interference: a cause of *forgetting* whereby one set of information competes with another, causing it to be 'overwritten' or physically destroyed.

■ This kind of forgetting is due to a lack of availability rather than accessibility, because the *memory trace* has been deleted. There are two kinds of interference: *proactive* and *retroactive interference*. Interference is most likely to occur when two sets of data are similar and this is not a common aspect of real-world memory. Therefore interference tends to offer a rather poor explanation for forgetting except in certain circumstances.

■ ***e.g.*** When you put on the windscreen wipers instead of indicating when driving someone else's car. Your usual memory for the location of the wipers interferes with the new memory (proactive interference). If, after using your friend's car for a while, you make a similar mistake in your own car that would be retroactive interference.

interference task: in a memory experiment participants are given a task to perform between exposure to stimulus and recall of information.

■ This is used to prevent rehearsal between exposure and recall so that data cannot be transferred from *short-term* to *long-term memory*, nor can the participant process the data in any way to improve recall in a way not intended by the experimenter.

■ ***e.g.*** Participants are given a list of words to learn and then are asked to count backwards in threes from 100, before being tested on recall.

intergroup: behaviour between groups as distinct from behaviour within a group (*intragroup*).

■ ***e.g.*** *Social identity theory* is an intergroup approach to explaining behaviour.

inter-interviewer/judge/observer reliability: see *inter-rater reliability*.

internalisation: incorporating the attitudes and beliefs of others into one's own *cognitions*.

■ Kelman identified this as one of three types of conformity (the other two are *identification* and *compliance*). Internalisation is 'true' conformity because it continues even when there is no external pressure to conform. The group norms have become personal norms.

internal validity: the extent to which something measures what it was intended to measure.

- (1) In terms of psychological tests, it is the extent to which the test is 'true'. Does it measure what it says it measures? For example, in the case of a test of anxiety — does it actually measure anxiety?
- **e.g.** *Content, construct, concurrent, criterion, face, predictive validity.*
- (2) In terms of an experiment, it is the extent to which the results of an experiment are actually due to the manipulation of the *independent variable*. Internal validity concerns what goes on within the experiment, as distinct from *external validity*. It is sometimes called experimental validity because it is a measure of the extent to which the *experimental design* actually did the job it set out to do. There are a number of things which may affect internal validity, such as the *reliability* of the measures used, *random errors*, lack of *standardised procedures*, lack of *experimental realism*. The end result is that the findings are rendered meaningless.
- **e.g.** A well-controlled experiment using standardised tests and procedures would be said to have high internal validity. Low internal validity might be exemplified by an experiment with *order effects* — we could not be certain whether changes in the dependent variable were due to the order effect or to the independent variable.

internal working model: a mental model of the world (or *schema*) which enables individuals to predict and control their environment.

- An individual has numerous internal working models, but the phrase is most closely associated with Bowlby's theory of *attachment*. He proposed that the intense emotional relationship between a primary caregiver and infant (*monotropy*) leads to the formation of an internal working model for relationships. This has several consequences: (1) In the short term it gives the child insight into the caregiver's behaviour and this opens up a whole new relationship where the infant can influence consciously what the caregiver does. (2) The internal working model influences the child's self-concept. Securely attached children develop a positive working model of themselves, based on their feelings of security derived from having an emotionally responsive primary caregiver. This then helps them to form secure relationships later in life. Insecurely ambivalent children have a primary caregiver who is inconsistent and consequently the children tend to have a negative self-image and exaggerate their emotional responses as a way to obtain attention. (3) The first relationship acts as a template for all future relationships because it generates expectations about how people behave.
- ***TIP*** There are criticisms of this model, mainly based on the evidence of low correlations between an infant's various relationships, which means that the monotropic relationship cannot provide a single template or internal working model for relationships in general. There is a different model for each different relationship.

International Classification of Disorders: see *ICD-10*.

interpersonal attraction: the initial stage of relationship formation.

■ This area of psychology is concerned with the factors that lead one to become involved with another person — for love or friendship. Subsequent developments are considered in terms of theories of the maintenance and/or dissolution of relationships.

interpersonal perception: the process of perceiving the characteristics of other people.

■ This includes: *impression formation, stereotyping, prejudice*. See also *social perception*.

interpersonal relationship: a relationship between people.

■ The study of relationships involves various stages: formation (e.g. factors such as proximity or attractiveness, or theories such as *social exchange theory, sociobiological theory*), maintenance (e.g. *equity theory, filter theories*), and dissolution (e.g. Duck's model of *relationship dissolution*). Two main difficulties for theories of relationships are that there are many different kinds of relationship (*love*, friendship, voluntary and involuntary relationships, parents, pen pals at a distance and so on) and there are important cultural differences in relationships (related to *individualist* vs *collectivist* societies). This means that it is unlikely that any one theory can account for all interpersonal relationships.

inter-rater reliability: the extent to which two raters provide consistent or similar responses.

■ The ratings from each person are correlated to check for agreement. It is a method of assessing the external *reliability* of a set of measurements or ratings, such as in an *observational study* or an *interview*.

interval scale: a *level of measurement*. Data are measured using units of equal intervals.

■ The intervals reflect a real difference. This scale is used with any 'public' unit of measurement, such as measuring height or distance. Many psychological studies use *plastic interval scales* where the intervals are arbitrarily determined; therefore we cannot know for certain that there are equal intervals between the numbers, but we assume that the intervals are equal. Psychological tests, such as IQ tests, also have apparent interval scales but they only appear that way because they are *standardised*. These are sometimes called *quasi-interval scales*.

■ ***e.g.*** Measurement of temperature is on a true interval scale, whereas height is on the *ratio scale* because it has a true zero.

interview: a method of spoken data collection that may form the basis of a research study.

■ See *survey* for a general discussion.

interviewer bias: where the interviewer affects the kind of responses given in an *interview*.

■ The interviewer may subtly communicate expectations in the same way as an experimenter might (see *experimenter bias*). This is especially likely in an unstructured interview.

intragroup: behaviour within a group, i.e. interactions between group members, as distinct from behaviour between groups (*intergroup*).

- ***e.g.*** *Conformity* is an intragroup behaviour.

introspection: studying and reporting one's own thought processes in order to understand how they work.

- Early psychologists used introspection as a method of investigating mental states. The method has been criticised as being subjective. However, Wundt's use of introspection involved highly trained individuals who learned to make observations of their own thoughts, which were claimed not to be biased by interpretations or previous experience. The advantage is that this makes it possible to access conscious thought.

introvert: an individual who is more inward-focused and thoughtful than an *extravert*.

- Eysenck suggested that introversion was one end of an extravert–introvert continuum. He suggested that introverts are more easily conditioned, more socially conforming, able to concentrate longer and have lower sensory thresholds, which would make them more sensitive to pain.

investigative psychology: see *criminal psychology*.

investigator: the person directing the research, as distinct from the *experimenter* or researcher, who is the person actually carrying out the study.

- Sometimes the investigator, experimenter and researcher are all the same person, but often an academic psychologist is the investigator and graduate students are the experimenters.

investigator effect: see *experimenter effects*. (See also *experimenter bias*.)

ipsilateral: a description for behavioural functions that are controlled by the same side of the cerebral *hemisphere*.

- ***e.g.*** Vision is both ipsilateral (there are connections from the right visual field to the right visual cortex) and *contralateral* (connections from the right visual field cross over to the left visual cortex).

IQ (intelligence quotient): a measure of *intelligence*, an IQ test produces a score that represents a person's mental age (MA). This is divided by their chronological age (CA) to adjust for the fact that children of the same intelligence but different ages will not achieve the same score on the test. Finally, the quotient is multiplied by 100 to remove any fractions.

- The average IQ is 100. The scores are standardised so that about 64% of the population have a score between 85 and 115.
- ***TIP*** There are many criticisms of the concept of IQ tests, such as the fact that the number obtained gives the semblance of being something real, whereas in fact it represents the test designer's notion of intelligence. The tests themselves are prone to *culture bias*.

item analysis: a method of assessing the internal *reliability* of a psychological test, i.e. the extent to which the test measure is consistent within itself.

- A test will have high reliability if each item on the test discriminates well between individuals, i.e. those people who do well on the test overall tend to do well on each item and those people who do poorly on the test tend to do less well on each item. If all participants do well on an item, then the item does not discriminate and cannot contribute to the effectiveness of the test. One way to conduct an item analysis is to compare performance on each test item with the overall score. Good correlation between all items and the overall scores suggests the test will have high internal reliability because each item is a good discriminator.

James–Lange theory: a theory of *emotion* proposed independently by James (1884) and Lange (1887), that *physiological* changes come first and form the basis of an emotional experience.

- This theory is the reverse of the commonsense view that it is one's cognitive state that causes behaviour. James said: 'You are frightened when you see a bear because you run, not the reverse, that you run because you are frightened'. The theory cannot account for emotional experiences before or without any arousal (e.g. the *Valins effect*), nor can it explain the role of learning in emotion.

jigsaw method: an approach to reduce *prejudice* which involves working together towards *superordinate goals*.

- Aronson et al. (1978) pioneered this method, arranging for multi-ethnic groups to research a topic. Each topic was divided into six parts so that each group member could be given a piece of the puzzle to research. Individual members reported back to the group about what they found out and then they were all tested on the total knowledge. Thus they had to cooperate in pursuit of group goals rather than compete against each other. The benefits did not generalise especially outside the school situation.

Jungian: views that are related to the work of Jung, a *neo-Freudian*.

- Jung emphasised psychosocial rather than psychosexual influences on development and behaviour and used the concept of the 'collective unconscious' (a part of our unconscious which we share with other members of our culture and which is an innate remnant of our ancestral past).

just-world hypothesis: the belief that this is a just and predictable world, i.e. if you behave well you get treated well and vice versa.

- This applies to *attribution theory*. We make attributions about the behaviour of others in a way that maintains our sense of a just world. It is a form of *defensive attribution* which makes us feel safer.
- ***e.g.*** If someone loses their job we would tend to explain this in terms of their competence rather than acknowledging the fact that some people lose their job unfairly. This makes us feel it is a just world and everyone gets what they deserve. So long as you try hard you should be OK.

Kennard principle: Kennard (1938) stated that it is easier to recover from brain damage earlier rather than later in life.

■ However, sometimes damage in younger children is more serious, as when a neonate suffers brain damage through oxygen deprivation.

kibbutz: in Israel, a *collectivist* farming community where everything is shared including the child care arrangements.

kin selection: a means by which individuals and their *genes* are selected for survival.

■ The process of *natural selection* functions at the level of an individual's genes. Any gene that promotes the survival of all 'kin' (genetic relatives) will also be selected. This is kin selection.

■ ***e.g.*** Altruism does not make sense in terms of Darwin's concept of individual fitness because it may result in the individual's death. However, if this death promotes the survival of a genetic relative (such as an offspring) then we can see how altruism is an *adaptive* behaviour.

Klüver–Bucy syndrome: the consequences of *bilateral* removal of the *temporal lobe* of the *cerebral cortex*.

■ In an experiment conducted by Klüver and Bucy (1938) *ablated* monkeys were found to exhibit profound changes in their social and emotional behaviour, suggesting that such behaviours are directed by the temporal lobe.

Korsakoff's syndrome: a form of *amnesia* found in alcoholics where they experience *short-term memory* losses yet their *long-term memory* remains intact.

■ This is support for the *multi-store model* of memory.

K-strategy: an *adaptive* reproductive behaviour where the individual protects its genetic line by having few offspring but then devoting a lot of energy to caring for them, thus ensuring the survival of the offspring (and the individual's genes).

■ ***e.g.*** Mammals, females.

■ ***TIP*** The *r-strategy* is a contrasting approach which is also adaptive.

labelling: the effect of attaching a 'label' to a psychological condition.

- The associated problems are that such labels may tend to be enduring and *self-fulfilling*.
- ***e.g.*** An individual who has had measles is not subsequently referred to as a 'measley' person whereas someone who has experienced clinical depression may forever be associated with that label. It may also lead the individual to develop certain expectations about themselves.

laboratory: any environment where *variables* can be well controlled.

laboratory experiment: an *experiment* conducted under highly controlled and often artificial conditions.

- The participant is aware of being studied and therefore may be affected by *experimenter bias, evaluation apprehension* and *demand characteristics*. The advantages are the effective *control* of all variables, especially extraneous ones (high *internal validity*), and *replication* is good. On the other hand, total control is never possible and other problems include *sampling bias*. Perhaps most importantly, the laboratory experiment is an artificial situation (low *ecological/external validity*). In terms of ethical considerations it may be necessary to deceive participants and therefore *informed consent* is not always possible.
- ***TIP*** There are advantages and disadvantages to laboratory vs *field experiments*. Field experiments tend to have higher external validity, whereas laboratory experiments have higher internal validity because of the greater control.

Lack's hypothesis: the explanation that shared parental care increases reproductive success, proposed by Lack (1968).

- ***TIP*** This was meant to explain why many songbirds are monogamous. However, it has been found that when resources are plentiful male songbirds become *polygynous*.

LAD: see *language acquisition device*.

laissez-faire style of leadership: see *leadership styles*.

language: a set of arbitrary conventional symbols through which meaning is conveyed.

- It is possibly specific to humans. Aitchison (1983) suggested that there are four criteria which, taken jointly, enable us to make a qualitative distinction between human and non-human animal language: semanticity (the use of arbitrary symbols to communicate meaning), displacement (reference to things not present in time or space), structure-dependence (meaning communicated through order, i.e. *grammar*) and creativity (potential for infinite generation of novel utterances).

- ***TIP*** There is considerable debate about the extent to which language is uniquely human and any definition which excludes non-human animals is self-defeating. Therefore a list of criteria is a useful guide rather than just saying 'language is a human form of communication'. There is evidence that some non-human animals are able to use human language and many of them certainly have natural animal language systems of their own (for example, dolphins, bees and primates). The key difference may lie in the ability to use a grammar which is enabled by an *innate LAD*.

language acquisition: the process by which language is acquired.

- This process can be explained in terms of *learning theory* (Skinner): children make random sounds (mands) and these are positively *reinforced* and 'shaped'. '*Motherese*' helps this process. This contrasts with the *nativist theory* (Chomsky) view that we are born with an *innate* drive to acquire language. A third view (*functional theory of language acquisition*) emphasises the social importance of language. It is likely that all three ingredients are necessary: an *innate* ability, learning and social interactions.

language acquisition device (LAD): the biological system proposed by Chomsky which enables a child to acquire language *innately*.

- The device produces universal linguistic rules (*grammar*) which transform the native linguistic input into language.
- ***TIP*** LAD has also been called language acquisition system, or LAS (a linguistic input device) — just to balance the gender bias. There is also LASS, a linguistic acquisition support system (see *functional theory of language acquisition*).

language centres: the *localised* areas of the brain which control language, usually *lateralised* (left *hemisphere* only).

- ***e.g.*** *Broca's area* and *Wernicke's areas.*

latency stage: in *psychoanalytic theory*, the fourth stage of *psychosexual development* which occurs between the age of 6 and the onset of puberty.

- During this stage little psychosexual development takes place. The focus is mainly on social development through peer interactions.

latent content: see *psychoanalytic theory of dreams*.

latent learning: *learning* that takes place in the absence of any observable behaviour, or with no apparent *reinforcement*.

- Such learning cannot be explained within *learning theory* because of the *cognitive* component.
- ***e.g.*** A rat may spend time exploring a maze without any reward. If, later on, a reward is placed in one arm of the maze, the rat with previous experience will learn the route to the reward more quickly than rats with no prior

experience. This demonstrates latent learning and the existence of *cognitive maps* formed during the initial, unrewarded exploration period. Operant conditioning theory states that learning cannot take place without rewards.

lateral hypothalamus (LH): thought to be a hunger centre in the brain.

- Animals who have *lesions* to the LH undereat. The LH acts in a *homeostatic* fashion in conjunction with the *ventromedial hypothalamus*.

lateralisation/laterality: the uneven division of labour between the cerebral *hemispheres*.

- Lateral means 'side'. Any behavioural function that is found on one side of the brain only is called a lateralised function. Functions that are represented equally on both sides of the brain are *bilateral*.
- ***e.g.*** The *language* centres are usually lateralised, being found in the left hemisphere only. Sometimes individuals have language centres in both hemispheres, which may be linked with stuttering. It is suggested that this is the reason for laterality — for some behaviours the existence of competing centres would be unhelpful.
- ***TIP*** Some functions in the brain are *localised*. In fact language is both lateralised and localised.

lateral thinking: thinking sideways or *divergently*.

- It is a term 'invented' by Edward de Bono to describe a way of tackling problems so as to avoid fixed thinking and thus generate novel solutions.

law of effect: Thorndike's concept that positive effects (rewards) lead to the stamping in of a behaviour, whereas negative effects (punishments) lead to the stamping out of behaviour.

- This is the basis of *operant conditioning*.

law of equipotentiality: Lashley's suggestion that the *brain* has some capacity to take over the functions of any parts that are damaged.

- Certain areas of the brain are capable of generating new *neurones*, even after maturity; dendritic branches can grow or retract, thus forming new connections. See *plasticity*.

law of social impact: see *social impact theory*.

leadership: a form of *social influence*, essentially *minority influence*.

- There are various theories offered to account for why certain individuals become leaders (e.g. *great man theory* or *situational explanations*) and why some leaders are more effective than others (e.g. *leadership style* and *contingency theory*).

leadership style: the relationship between leaders and followers determines the effectiveness of the leadership.

- ***e.g.*** *Authoritarian style* (the leader tells everyone what to do), *democratic style* (decisions are made after consultation), *laissez-faire style* (the leader plays a passive role). In research studies it has been found that the democratic style produces better quality work, whereas the authoritarian style produces more quantity. The laissez-faire style encourages a more friendly atmosphere.
- ***TIP*** It may be that each style is appropriate for different kinds of task.

learned helplessness: if an animal finds that its responses are ineffective, then it *learns* that there is no point in responding and behaves passively.

■ ***e.g.*** A dog placed in a cage with an electrified floor from which there is no escape will soon stop trying to escape, even when later given an opportunity.

■ ***TIP*** This has been used to explain *depression* in humans.

learning: a relatively permanent change in behaviour as a result of experience and which is not due to biological maturation.

■ ***e.g.*** The human eye cannot focus at birth, but this changes as a result of maturation. Other changes in the visual/perceptual system are a consequence of learning, such as two-dimensional depth perception.

learning style: the effectiveness of a *teaching style* may be related to the preferred style of the student.

■ ***e.g.*** Some individuals prefer a highly structured, formal style (teacher-centred) whereas others prefer informal, pupil-centred styles.

learning theory: the explanation of behaviour using the principles of *classical* and *operant conditioning*.

■ The view that all behaviour is learned, a position held by some *behaviourists*.

■ ***TIP*** The following examples of learning are all evidence of the relevance of *cognitive factors* and thus can be used as arguments against learning theory: *innate learning, insight learning, latent learning, learned helplessness, one trial learning, transfer of learning*.

least preferred co-worker (LPC): see *contingency theory*.

legitimate aggression: see *aggression*.

lesion: severing connections in the brain as a method of investigating *cortical* functioning.

■ This may be the result of an accident, or it may be done deliberately, either in order to isolate a section of the brain (which is equivalent to *ablation*) or to treat a disorder. Temporary lesions can be achieved using anaesthetics.

■ ***e.g.*** Lesions to the *ventromedial hypothalamus* in rats have been used to study eating behaviour. The *split-brain procedure* involves cutting the *corpus callosum* as a treatment for epilepsy.

■ ***TIP*** The danger with lesion studies is that one might assume that any deficit is due to the region that is disconnected, whereas it may be that the lesion has disrupted the flow of information from one region to another.

leucocyte: part of the *immune* system, a type of white blood cell that finds and destroys *antigens*.

level of measurement: variables can be measured at different levels of detail.

■ Each level expresses a different amount of information about what we are measuring.

■ ***e.g.*** *Nominal, ordinal, interval, ratio* (in ascending order of increased information).

level of significance: this indicates the extent to which a set of results are due to chance factors alone rather than the *independent variable*.

- The level of significance is equivalent to the *probability* (p) of a result being due to chance. When an *inferential test* is used, a statistic is calculated leading to an *observed value*. This value is checked against *critical values* at various levels of significance.
- ***e.g.*** A 5% level of significance ($p < 0.05$) means that there is less than a 5% chance that the obtained results are in fact due to chance, or less than a 5% chance that the *null hypothesis* is correct. There is more than a 95% chance that the null hypothesis is wrong. This level of significance would make us feel fairly confident about rejecting the null hypothesis and accepting the *alternate hypothesis*. Common levels of significance are given in the table below.

Low (stringent) significance level	0.1% level	(p = 0.001)	Very highly significant	Used in life-and-death research, where chances should be minimised	*Type II error* more likely ↑
	1% level	(p = 0.01)	Highly significant	Ideal when challenging previously accepted research	
	5% level	(p = 0.05)	Significant	Usual level for psychological research	
High (lenient) significance level	10% level	(p = 0.1)	Indicates a trend	Follow-up studies might prove worthwhile	↓ *Type I error* more likely

levels of processing theory: the view put forward by Craik and Lockhart (1972) that enduring *memories* are created through *depth of processing* rather than a repeated number of analyses (rehearsal).

- Depth is determined in terms of the meaning extracted rather than by repetition, the view espoused by the *multi-store model* of memory. The levels of processing model proposes that at the shallowest level, processing involves only physical characteristics (such as whether a letter is in capital letters or not) and this would not create much memory for the word. An intermediate level would be phonemic processing (e.g. considering whether two words rhyme with each other) which leads to an increased *memory trace* and finally the deepest level is semantic processing (considering the meaning of a word). The theory has been criticised because it ignores the evidence that supports the distinction between *short-term memory* and *long-term memory*; however, other evidence supports the importance of depth (which includes elaboration, organisation and distinctiveness).

libido: psychological energy that is especially associated with sexual drives.

- In *psychoanalytic theory*, the libido is the *id*'s sexual (biological) drive. At each stage of *psychosexual development*, the libido becomes focused on a part of the body.

lie detector: a machine that claims to be able to detect when someone is lying, by employing the *galvanic skin response*.

■ Someone who is telling a lie is presumed to be in a state of *autonomic nervous system* (ANS) arousal. The problem is that being given the lie detector test may create anxiety which in itself increases ANS arousal. A further problem is that some people are 'good liars' and do not exhibit arousal when lying.

lie scale: a set of questions in a *survey* to determine the extent to which the participant's answers are truthful.

■ A survey would contain certain questions to 'trap' the respondent, such as 'Do you always tell the truth?' An individual whose answers are affected by a *social desirability bias* is likely to say 'Yes'. If a respondent scores high on a set of lie scale questions, their data may be rejected. Other techniques for detecting social desirability bias include the *bogus pipeline* technique.

life event: a commonplace experience that involves change from a steady state and a means of explaining why some people become ill.

■ Such events can be good or bad, but they all absorb 'psychic energy', leaving less available for other matters such as physical defence against illness. Life events are commonplace but not everyday, unlike *hassles*. They are measured using the *social readjustment rating scale* (SRRS) which has been used to show a weak but *positive correlation* between life events and illness.

■ ***e.g.*** The top five life events on the SRRS are death of spouse, divorce, marital separation, jail term and death of close family member. Though one should remember that this list was compiled over 30 years ago.

lifespan psychology: another term for *developmental psychology* that emphasises the fact that development continues throughout one's lifespan.

■ In the past there was a tendency to think that development stopped after adolescence whereas psychologists now recognise that people change throughout their lifetimes — in terms of, for example, cognitive abilities and personality.

■ ***e.g.*** Erikson's *eight ages of man*.

Likert scale: probably the most widely used method of assessing *attitudes*.

■ Typically about 30 statements are prepared on a topic, representing both pro- and anti-views on it. The respondent then rates each statement on a five-point or seven-point scale. A score is calculated by reversing the numerical value for anti-statements and then adding the values up.

■ ***e.g.*** Respondents are given a statement such as 'Men should never wear make-up', and asked if they: strongly agree (1), agree (2), are uncertain (3), disagree (4), or strongly disagree (5).

limbic system: a group of mainly *subcortical* structures which form a border around the *brainstem* ('limbus' means 'border' in Latin). The structures are important in motivation and emotional behaviours, such as feeding, drinking, sexual behaviour, anxiety and aggression.

■ The limbic system consists of the olfactory bulb, the *hypothalamus*, the *hippocampus*, the *amygdala* and the cingulate gyrus.

linguistic determinism: see *linguistic relativity hypothesis.*

linguistic relativity hypothesis: the view that one's native *language* influences the way you think about the world.

- The extreme view (linguistic determinism) is that language actually alters the way you think. The linguistic relativity hypothesis suggests that the language you speak provides categories which may shape your thinking. This may be true in so far as language affects your *perception* and influences *stereotypes.*
- ***e.g.*** It has been claimed that the fact that Eskimos have 20 words for snow enables them to make finer distinctions between kinds of snow (i.e. their language shapes their ability to categorise). However, it may be that it is hard to know whether the categories come first (thought before language) and this creates the need for new words. See also the *great Eskimo vocabulary hoax.*

linguistic universals: those features of *grammar* that appear in all languages.

- The existence of such universals is evidence in support of the *nativist theory.*
- ***e.g.*** All languages have nouns.

lipostatic theory: an explanation for hunger *motivation* in terms of a set-point for body fat.

- Body fat is normally maintained at a steady level and therefore fat levels are monitored and affect sensations of hunger.

lobotomy: a form of *psychosurgery* in which fibres running from the frontal lobes to other parts of the brain are cut.

- Lobotomies typically make patients calmer. However, the side-effects include apathy, diminished intellectual powers, impaired judgements and even coma and death.
- ***TIP*** A prefrontal lobotomy only involves the prefrontal cortex.

localisation: certain areas of the *cerebral cortex* are associated with specific behavioural functions.

- Localisation allows for more specialised behavioural development because certain areas of the brain are 'pre-wired' for their function. Functions that are localised are not necessarily *lateralised.*
- ***e.g.*** The *suprachiasmatic nucleus* acts as the body clock. There is only one of these which is located centrally (i.e. it is not lateralised).
- ***TIP*** Behaviours which are governed by many different areas of the brain, such as memory and language, are generally not considered to be localised functions because they involve a vast array of different functions. One could say that procedural memory is localised, as this is more specific.

locus coeruleus: a small area of cells in the *pons* that is related to the sleep–wake cycle and memory.

- The locus coeruleus (LC) is inactive during *REM sleep*. It releases *noradrenaline* which may act as an REM-off switch in conjunction with the *raphe nucleus* and in opposition to the pons (which operates the REM-on switch). The LC is also inactive during most awake activity except, for example, during periods of learning associated with high arousal. It may be that the fact that the LC is switched off during REM sleep explains why we often forget dreams.

longitudinal study: a research method that enables comparisons over time.

- The same individuals are studied over a long period of time. Such studies may involve working out a *correlation* between age and a named variable, or determining the effect of age on some behaviour. In the latter case age is the *independent variable* and since this is not actually manipulated by the experimenter and participants are not *randomly allocated* to conditions, this is a *quasi-experiment*. Longitudinal studies have the advantage of being a *repeated measures design* and therefore offering good control for *participant variables*. However, such studies take a very long time which involves expense (in comparison with *cross-sectional studies*), and replication is difficult. They also may suffer from the *cross-generational effect* and from participant drop-out — participants cannot always be recontacted and the remaining group becomes less representative.
- ***e.g.*** Much research in developmental psychology has followed a *cohort* of individuals, such as Tizard and Hodge's (1978) study of institutionalised children.

long-term memory (LTM): relatively permanent storage which has unlimited capacity and duration.

- The *multi-store model* proposes that there are three *memory* stores: *sensory memory* (SM), *short-term memory* (STM) and long-term memory. Data are passed from one to the other as a consequence of verbal rehearsal. Four different kinds of LTM have been identified: *procedural* memory (knowing how), *declarative* memory (knowing that), *semantic memory* (facts) and *episodic memory* (events). There is also a distinction made between *explicit* and *implicit memory*. Six kinds of evidence are provided to distinguish between STM and LTM: capacity, duration, coding differences (semantic coding in LTM and more acoustic in STM), *serial position effect* (*primacy effect* related to LTM), evidence from studies of brain damage (*anterograde amnesia* affects LTM), and differences in forgetting (e.g. *cue-dependent forgetting* in LTM).

looking-glass self: the idea that our *self-concept* is derived from how others see us.

- Cooley (1902) suggested that our self-image is largely determined from the reactions of others, i.e. as if looking in a mirror.

love: an intense feeling of deep affection for another.

- Psychologists distinguish between liking and loving and between different kinds of love, most importantly *companionate* and *passionate* (romantic) love. Sternberg suggested that love involves three components: an emotional component (intimacy), a motivational component (passion and sexual desire) and a cognitive component (commitment). See also *attachment*.

Machiavellian intelligence: a means of demonstrating animal intelligence in terms of the ability to deceive another animal.

maladaptive: the extent to which a behaviour is not *adaptive*.

- The concept of adaptiveness comes from the *theory of evolution*. Any behaviour which is adaptive increases the reproduction potential of an individual and survival of its genes. In terms of mental disorders, the concept of maladaptiveness implies that a behaviour interferes with normal living.
- ***e.g.*** Being afraid to go outside (agoraphobia) interferes with normal functioning, such as being able to go to work or go shopping.

mania/manic depression: see *depression (bipolar)*.

manifest content: see *psychoanalytic theory of dreams*.

Mann–Whitney U test: an *inferential* and *non-parametric test* of the difference between unrelated samples.

- The reasons for selecting this test are: (1) a test of difference is required, (2) the samples are unrelated, (3) the data do not fit *parametric* assumptions (e.g. the distribution is not *normal* and the *level of measurement* is ordinal).

matched pairs design: an *experimental design* where different participants are used for each condition in the experiment, but *participant variables* are controlled by matching pairs of participants on key attributes.

- One partner is exposed to the *independent variable* and both are compared in terms of their performance on the *dependent variable*. This avoids *order effects* and other problems of *repeated measures design* and also offers some control of participant variables, which is not usually the case with two groups of participants (*independent measures designs*). On the other hand, matching is difficult, time-consuming, may waste participants and is inevitably inexact.

matching hypothesis: an explanation for the formation of relationships whereby individuals choose a partner who 'matches' them in terms of certain criteria.

- The criteria for matching may be in terms of physical attractiveness, but education and background can also be factors in matching. Matching may be explained in terms of *balance theory*, or it may be due to fear of rejection so that you choose someone who is not likely to turn you down.
- ***e.g.*** People tend to select a partner who is of a similar kind of physical

attractiveness, as assessed by an objective observer.

■ ***TIP*** The 'computer dance' experiment is often (mistakenly) said to be evidence supporting the matching hypothesis whereas the opposite was found. Male participants rated the most attractive dates as being most desirable, not the ones who were a better physical match. However, this may be because they were rating desirability rather than asking someone to go out with them.

maternal deprivation hypothesis: the view that separation from a *primary caregiver* (maternal deprivation) leads to the breaking of *attachment* bonds and long-term effects on emotional development.

■ Bowlby (1953) likened maternal deprivation to physical deprivation, suggesting that maternal care was as necessary for healthy development as vitamins. Bowlby later revised his maternal deprivation hypothesis, formulating a more complex theory of *attachment*.

■ ***TIP*** Note that the term 'maternal' refers to 'mothering', not 'women'.

maturation: the process of ripening. A change that is due to *innate* factors rather than learning.

■ ***e.g.*** The onset of puberty is due to maturation. Piaget suggested that cognitive development is largely due to maturation, i.e. certain key developments such as the use of symbols can only occur when the individual is biologically ready.

■ ***TIP*** The process of maturation is no longer regarded as a purely biological unfolding. Instead it is clear that environmental input is needed for normal development to proceed within inherited boundary conditions.

mean ($\bar{x}$): a measure of *central tendency*. The mean is calculated by adding up all values, and dividing by the total number of values (N).

■ In any set of data the *mode* and *median* may bear no relation to the mean. The mean takes all values into account, which is an advantage, except that when there are extreme values the mean may be unduly affected by one extreme value. For example, if the scores on a test were 3, 5, 6, 7, 8, 9, 45, the mean would be 11.6 — hardly a typical or representative value of the data. In this case the median would be more representative.

mean deviation: a *measure of dispersion* which expresses the 'average' deviation from the *mean* for each score in a set of data.

■ It is calculated by working out the deviation between each score and the mean and then calculating the mean of these deviations (ignoring any minus signs). This is simpler to calculate than the *standard deviation* but does not provide an estimate of the population parameters (i.e. we cannot claim the same deviation for the entire population from which the sample was drawn).

means-end analysis: see *problem-space theory*.

measure of dispersion: a *descriptive statistic* showing the spread of a set of data.

■ ***e.g.*** This may be expressed as the *range* of scores from top to bottom, or the extent to which the data are clustered around the mean (*variance* and *standard deviation*). *Variation ratio* analyses the spread of nominal data.

mechanistic: explanations which liken animal behaviour to that of a machine.

■ Such explanations tend to overlook the influence of emotional and social factors and are also highly *determinist* and *reductionist*. On the positive side, metaphors are commonly used in science to advance our understanding of systems.

■ **e.g.** *Information processing approaches* use the analogy of a computer or a telephone exchange.

media: methods of mass communication.

■ **e.g.** Television, video, books, magazines.

median: a measure of *central tendency*. It is the middle or central value in an ordered list.

■ The median is calculated by placing all the values in order and finding the mid-point. If the mid-point lies between two numbers, you must work out the mean of these values. The median should be used for ordinal level data and in cases where extreme values would unduly affect the *mean*. See also the *mode*.

medical model: an explanation for illness based on the assumption that all illnesses (physical and psychological) have an underlying *physiological* basis.

■ The actual cause may not be known but the assumption implies that physical (*somatic*) treatments are appropriate. In order to prescribe a suitable treatment it is necessary to identify the illness and this is done by describing symptoms. Symptoms lead to a *diagnosis*, and this leads to appropriate treatment.

medulla oblongata (or just 'medulla')**:** a structure in the *hindbrain* that is located just above the spinal cord and as such is more or less an extension of it. The medulla controls many vital functions, such as heart rate and breathing as well as important reflexes such as salivation and sneezing.

melatonin: a hormone produced by the *pineal gland*, which increases sleepiness.

■ ***TIP*** Artificial doses of melatonin have been used to help cope with sleep problems and jet lag, though it is not clear how beneficial it is.

memory: the encoding, storage and retrieval of experience.

■ ***TIP*** What is the difference between *learning* and memory? Perhaps the key difference is that learning is a concept used by behaviourists — they cannot use 'memory' because it involves relying on internal processes as a means of explaining behaviour. 'Learning' is the observable part of memory.

memory trace: the physical record or 'trace' of a memory.

mental set: the readiness to solve problems or think in a particular manner.

■ People tend to reuse the same strategies in all situations, which restricts their ability to think creatively when the situation demands it.

■ **e.g.** In one experiment participants were given candles, drawing pins and a box of matches and asked to mount the candle on the wall. Their problem-solving was blocked because they thought in terms of the box as a container. When they were given an empty box, they found the solution more easily.

meta-analysis: a form of analysis in which the data from several related studies are combined to obtain an overall estimate.

■ **e.g.** Bouchard and McGue (1981) performed a meta-analysis on familial studies of IQ.

■ ***TIP*** One problem with this approach is that the different studies use different methodologies and therefore comparisons may not be appropriate.

metabolism: the chemical processes within the living organism that produce energy.

methodological behaviourism: the view that all approaches in psychology use *behaviourist* concepts to some extent.

■ ***e.g.*** *Cognitive* and *psychodynamic theories* all refer to *reinforcement* and *learning*.

microelectrode: a very small *electrode* which can record the activity from one *neurone*.

■ ***e.g.*** Hubel and Weisel (1962) placed microelectrodes in the *visual cortex* to record which neurones were active when a line of a particular orientation was shown to the eye.

microsleep: small periods of rest during the day which are functionally equivalent to sleep. The individual is not aware that they have been asleep.

■ Such periods of relaxation may permit the body to replenish certain chemicals that have become depleted, and this explains why sleep deprivation does not always have noticeable consequences. It also means that people who claim to be having no sleep may actually be sleeping in very short bursts.

midbrain: see the *brain*.

mimicry: the resemblance of one animal to another.

■ There are several forms of mimicry. (1) Aggressive mimicry where the mimic lures its prey because it looks like a harmless animal. For example, the angler fish dangles a worm-like bait on the end of a rod-like appendage, attracting worm-eating animals, which it then eats. (2) Batesian mimicry: a prey species has the same markings as some other poisonous or distasteful animal. For example, one kind of harmless coral snake has the same colouring as its poisonous relative. (3) Mullerian mimicry is based on universal indicators of poisonous prey. A number of species, all of which are noxious, share the same warning signals which trigger an innate response in the predator.

■ ***TIP*** There are distinct benefits to the mimic in terms of safety from predation, though it is difficult to explain how such colourings might have gradually evolved because there is a period during which the mimicry is not yet fully developed and the bright coloration must act as a positive disadvantage.

mind–body problem: the philosophical debate over the distinction between the mind and the body. (See *dualism*.)

minimal group: group identification based on almost nothing.

■ ***e.g.*** In Tajfel's (1970) 'minimal group experiment' group membership was determined by whether the boys were designated over- or under-estimators. The boys were randomly allocated to these groups but despite such minimal and meaningless identity, the group identity created was sufficient to arouse *ingroup favouritism* and *discrimination*.

minority influence: the influence of the majority by the minority.

■ Moscovici (1980) proposed that minority influence occurs for different reasons to majority influence (*dual-process* theory). In order to exert an influence the minority must be consistent, show some flexibility rather than being dogmatic, hold relevant views in relation to social trends, and be committed. The result is conversion instead of *compliance*. See *innovation*.

mnemonic: a technique used to improve memory.

■ ***e.g.*** The loci system (method of locations) where objects are 'placed' by forming strong visual images.

mode: a measure of *central tendency*. It is the most common value.

■ To calculate the mode one places all the values in some order and finds the value or values which occur most frequently. If all the data values are equal in frequency then there is no mode. If two values share the highest frequency then the data are *bimodal*, or it may even be multi-modal if there are more than two modes. For nominal data you must use the mode.

■ ***TIP*** The other two measures of central tendency are the *median* and the *mean*.

model: less complex than a theory, usually comprising a single idea.

■ ***e.g.*** *Internal working model, cost–reward model.*

modelling: the process of *imitating* the behaviour of a model.

■ ***e.g.*** Social learning theory: an aggressive individual watches someone else deal with another person's threatening behaviour. Modelling therapy: an arachnophobic watches someone else calmly handling a spider and this enables them to behave in the same way.

modules: a model for divided *attention*, proposed by Allport (1993), suggesting that attention consists of a number of independent units (modules), each of which deals with a different skill.

■ This can explain why task similarity decreases *dual-task performance* because similar tasks use the same module. This model is also supported by neurophysiological research which has identified discrete areas of the brain that can be linked to particular functions.

monoamines: a group of neurotransmitters that are chemically similar.

■ ***e.g.*** *Serotonin, dopamine* and *noradrenaline*.

monoamine theory of depression: depression is the result of depletion of monoamine (*catecholamine*), neurotransmitters such as serotonin and noradrenaline. *Antidepressant drugs* aim to increase these neurotransmitters.

monogamy: having one mate ('mono' means 'one' and 'gamy' refers to mating).

■ Some animals are monogamous for one mating season only.

■ ***TIP*** Monogamy is associated with shared *parental investment*.

monotropy: Bowlby's concept that the infant has an *innate* tendency to form a strong, qualitatively different attachment to one person.

■ The child has many attachments, each serving different purposes, and these form a hierarchy, at the top of which is the *primary* caregiver. Bowlby proposed that this primary relationship was distinguished by its emotional intensity and was critical in the development of the *internal working model*.

monozygotic (MZ) twins: identical twins formed from the same fertilised cell (*zygote*). See *dizygotic twins* and *twin studies*.

mood-dependent recall: a form of *cue-dependent forgetting*, things are recalled better when you are in the same mood as when they were initially learned.

■ ***e.g.*** You tell someone an innermost secret when feeling very unhappy. This memory comes back to you the next time you feel deeply depressed.

moral dilemma: an investigative technique used by Kohlberg and by Gilligan.

■ These differed from Piaget's *moral stories* in that the dilemmas were more complex and reflected the fact that in real life there is often no single 'correct' answer. The key factor is how people explain their decision rather than the decision itself.

moral panic: the view that the *media* exaggerate the danger present in the real world. See *deviance amplification*.

moral realism: a stage of moral development described by Piaget where a young child (under the age of 8) regards morals as absolute rules. See *heteronomous morality*.

moral relativity: a later stage of moral development described by Piaget where a child (over the age of 8) has come to understand that morals are rules that are mutually agreed and can be changed by mutual consent. See *autonomous morality*.

moral story: a description of an event, such as a child breaking some dishes, where the child's intentions were either good or bad.

■ Piaget used these stories to investigate the role of intention and consequence in judging moral behaviour.

morpheme: the minimal unit of language that has a meaning, as distinct from a *phoneme*.

■ ***e.g.*** In the word 'manhunt' there are two morphemes, 'man' and 'hunt'. In the word 'names' there are two morphemes, 'name' and 's'.

motherese: the special form of language that adults use when talking to children.

■ The *learning theory* account of *language acquisition* suggests that this simplified form of speaking aids the infant in imitating adult speech.

■ ***TIP*** The term 'motherese' is rather gender biased and so alternative terms have been used: parentese or 'Baby Talk Register'.

motion parallax: things that are closer appear to move faster, a phenomenon used in depth perception.

motivation: the internal state that *drives* or encourages an organism to act.

■ This internal state is also affected by external factors (see *needs theories*). There are three main classes of explanation for motivation: *physiological* explanations (e.g. *homeostatic drive theory*, *drive-reduction theory*, *psychoanalytic theory*), *behavioural* explanations (e.g. *learning theory* and rewards), psychological explanations (e.g. *needs theories*, *hierarchy of needs*).

MRI scan (magnetic resonance imaging): a method of detecting activity in the living *brain* to determine the function of different regions.

■ Participants are asked to engage in an activity, such as reading. The MRI uses magnetic fields instead of the X-rays used by *CAT scans*. See *brain scans*.

Mullerian mimicry: see *mimicry*.

Müller–Lyer illusion: see *visual illusion*.

multiple personality disorder (MPD): a type of mental disorder where two or more relatively independent personalities exist in one person.

- The disorder is also called 'dissociative personality disorder' because the separate personalities have become 'dissociated' from each other. Dissociation may occur as a consequence of stress. The personalities may or may not be aware of each 'other's' existence and are usually quite different.
- ***e.g.*** The case of the 'three faces of Eve' studied by Thigpen and Cleckley (1954).
- ***TIP*** There is some debate about how rare this disorder is. Some researchers feel it is overdiagnosed, whereas others feel it has been underdiagnosed and that individuals with MPD may be wrongly diagnosed as schizophrenics or manic depressives.

multi-store model: the concept that memory is divided into several kinds of store (*sensory memory (SM)*, *short-term memory (STM)* and *long-term memory (LTM)*) and data are passed from one to the other because of verbal rehearsal.

- The best support for this model comes from empirical evidence indicating STM/LTM differences (in terms of capacity, duration, *serial position effect*, coding, effects of brain damage, explanations of forgetting). However, some of these differences can be explained using the alternative *levels of processing theory*. The multi-store model is probably an over-simplification and moreover it presents a passive view of memory and cannot account for active processes such as reconstruction. Furthermore, the relevance of rehearsal may be an artefact of memory experiments where participants are tested on *explicit memory*.

mundane realism: the extent to which an experiment is experienced as real because it appears real (mundane) rather than artificial to the participants.

- If an experiment lacks mundane realism this may be compensated for by *experimental realism*.

mutation: a *genetic* change which can then be inherited by any offspring.

- This is one of the key factors in the process of *evolution* because it enables genetic variation. Most mutations result in disadvantageous characteristics but occasionally a mutation produces a better *adapted* individual. The other source of genetic variation is sexual reproduction.
- ***e.g.*** *Down's syndrome* is the result of a mutation on chromosome 21.

mutualism: two or more individuals may cooperate because there is a net gain in terms of survival and reproductive benefit.

- ***e.g.*** Non-relatives may collect food together because they offer increased protection from predation (as in geese grazing) or more effective capture techniques (as in lions hunting).
- ***TIP*** This is not true *altruism* because both individuals benefit.

myelin sheath: a white fatty substance that protects the *neurone* and speeds up the transmission of messages along the length of the axon.

MZ twins: see *monozygotic twins*.

nativist theory of language acquisition: Chomsky's (1959) view that humans acquire language because they have an *innate* ability to generate the grammatical rules (provided by *LAD*) and apply these to their native vocabulary.

- The reason we learn to speak is the same as the reason we learn to walk upright. Both are *hard-wired* into our biological systems. The existence of *linguistic universals* suggests that there are innate rules. Chomsky's concept of *transformational grammar* can explain the generativity of language and the way that children acquire language (e.g. *overgeneralisations*).
- ***TIP*** If non-human animals can be taught to use human language this suggests that a LAD is not an *innate* prerequisite to *language acquisition* and this would then support the *learning theory* view of language acquisition.

natural experiment: a type of *experiment* where use is made of some naturally occurring *independent variable (IV)*.

- A natural experiment is a *quasi-experiment* because the IV is not directly manipulated (and therefore one cannot be certain that the IV is the cause of any observed effect) and the participants are not randomly allocated to conditions (therefore participants in different conditions may not be comparable). Natural experiments have the advantage of greater *ecological validity* and they may also be the only way to study certain behaviours, such as early childhood deprivation. The disadvantages include the problems with replicating such studies. Ethical considerations, such as invasion of privacy, are also important.
- ***e.g.*** A number of studies have looked at the effects of television viewing on aggression by observing societies where television has recently been introduced. In this case the IV (television viewing) varies naturally. The *dependent variable* (aggression levels) is measured by the researchers.

naturalistic observation: a kind of *observational study* where behaviour is recorded in the natural environment.

- All variables are free to alter and interference is kept to a minimum. Such studies are high in *ecological (external) validity* because they relate to real life, but low in *internal validity* because they lack control.

natural selection: the process by which individuals are selected because they are best *adapted* to their environment.

- Any behaviour which promotes survival and reproduction will be naturally selected just because an individual with that characteristic is more likely to survive. In fact it is the *genes* that are selected rather than the individual. It is a passive process which occurs through *selective pressure,* i.e. the pressure is exerted in terms of what works and what does not work. No one decides that one characteristic is better than another. See *theory of evolution*.
- ***TIP*** Reproduction is the key as distinct from survival. As long as your genes are reproduced that is all that matters.

nature and nurture: nature is that which is inherited and *genetic*, as distinct from *nurture* which refers to all influences after conception, i.e. experience.

- At one time this was referred to as the 'nature vs nurture debate'. It is now recognised that both contribute and interact in such a way that it is not a simple matter of saying that one **or** the other causes behaviour.
- ***e.g.*** There are important, ongoing debates about whether IQ and mental illnesses, such as schizophrenia, can be explained most in terms of inherited factors (nature) or experience (nurture).

need satisfaction theory of interpersonal relationships: a suggestion by Argyle (1994) that we have relationships because they satisfy our basic needs.

- He listed seven needs, each of which can be satisfied in part by relationships: biological (e.g. eating together), dependency (e.g. comforting each other), affiliation (e.g. the company of others), dominance (establishing social order), sex (reproduction), aggression (e.g. interpersonal hostility) and self-esteem needs (being valued by another).

needs theories: psychological theories of *motivation* that emphasise external (extrinsic) rather than internal (intrinsic) motives.

- ***e.g.*** The need for achievement (nAch). Murray (1938) described 20 different human motives such as a need for understanding, affiliation and aggression.
- ***TIP*** Psychological theories can explain higher-order motives which cannot be accounted for in terms of internal, *physiological* needs.

negative correlation: as one *covariable* increases the other decreases.

- The covariables vary in a constant relationship. The perfect negative correlation coeffcient is –1.0, and on a *scattergram* the dots would range from top left to bottom right.

negative-state relief model: Cialdini's explanation for *prosocial behaviour* that suggests people are motivated to help in order to reduce their own negative state of distress which has been created through *empathy* with the victim.

- This model suggests that helping or altruism is ultimately a selfish act, like the *arousal — cost–reward model* but different from the *empathy–arousal hypothesis*.

neo-behaviourism: literally 'new behaviourism'. This view combines traditional *learning theory* with *cognitive* explanations.

- ***e.g.*** *Social learning theory*.

neo-Freudian: *psychoanalytic theorists* who modified the theories of Freud.

- The main change was a shift from biological to more social influences.

■ ***e.g.*** Horney or Fromm. Some people do not class *Jung* or Erikson as neo-Freudian because their theories were more than a slight modification.

neonate: a newborn mammal.

neo-Piagetian: theories of *cognitive development* that use *information processing* concepts to reinterpret aspects of Piaget's stage theory.

■ ***e.g.*** Case's theory, which suggests that cognitive development is the result of cognitive strategies becoming more automatic.

nerve: a bundle of *neurones*.

nervous system: see *central nervous system* and *neurone*.

neurobiological theory of dreams: a group of explanations for dreaming (*REM sleep*) based on the activity of the *brain* during sleep.

■ ***e.g.*** *Activation–synthesis model* (Hobson and McCarley), *restoration theory of dreaming* (Oswald), *reverse learning* (Crick and Mitchison).

neuroleptic drug: another word for *antipsychotic drug*.

neurone: a cell that receives information and conducts it to others by electro-chemical means.

■ The neurone consists of a cell body, which has a number of projections called dendrites. Extending from the cell body is an *axon* which is covered along most of its length by a protective *myelin sheath*. There are regular breaks in the myelin sheath where there are nodes of Ranvier. At the end of an axon is a *terminal bouton* containing vesicles which store and release *neurotransmitters*. Information is received via dendrites and transmitted via the axon and terminal boutons. Some neurones are only minute whereas others are as long as several feet.

neurosis: a personality or mental disturbance characterised by anxiety but where the patient has not lost touch with reality, as distinct from *psychosis*.

■ ***e.g.*** *Phobia*.

■ ***TIP*** The distinction between neurosis and psychosis is no longer recognised in the classification systems (e.g. *DSM*) but the terms continue to be used.

neurotransmitter: a chemical substance that is released at *synapses*.

■ Neurotransmitters either facilitate (excitatory) or block (inhibitory) communication between nerves.

■ ***e.g.*** *Acetylcholine, dopamine, noradrenaline* and *serotonin* are excitatory neurotransmitters. *GABA* is an inhibitory neurotransmitter.

NMR (nuclear magnetic resonance): see *MRI scan*.

nominal scale: the lowest *level of measurement*. Data are in discrete categories.

■ ***e.g.*** Grouping people according to their favourite TV programmes.

nomothetic approach: an approach to research that focuses more on general laws of behaviour than on the individual, possibly unique, case (the *idiographic approach*).

■ The nomothetic approach involves the study of a large number of people and then seeks to make generalisations about them.

■ ***e.g.*** Research on gender differences highlights the way that men on the whole and women on the whole differ from one another.

non-directional hypothesis (also called 'two-tailed hypothesis')**:** a prediction of a difference or correlation between two variables but no statement about the direction of this difference.

- This is contrasted with a *directional hypothesis* (see entry for examples and 'tip').

non-parametric tests/statistics: a group of *inferential statistics* that are less powerful than *parametric statistics* and are distribution-free (i.e. the tests make no assumption about the distribution of the population from which the data are drawn).

nonsense syllable: information devoid of meaning and used in memory experiments.

- ***e.g.*** Trigrams (such as BDT), consonant-vowel-consonants (such as HIG).

nonsignificant: not statistically *significant*. See *level of significance*.

nonverbal communication (NVC): communication which is not linguistic.

- NVC tends to communicate emotion in both humans and non-human animals.
- ***e.g.*** It may be vocal (such as crying) or nonvocal (such as screwing up your face to show disgust).

nonverbal leakage: the tendency to express one's emotions unconsciously, through *nonverbal communication*.

- Most people find it quite difficult to control their nonverbal signals.
- ***e.g.*** People who are trying to smuggle things past customs are often detected because of nonverbal leakage — customs officers are sensitive to subtle cues relating to deception and nervousness.

noradrenaline (norepinephrine): a biochemical substance that acts as both a *hormone* and a *neurotransmitter*.

- (1) Noradrenaline is a hormone produced by the *adrenal gland* which usually increases physiological *arousal*; similar to the hormone *adrenaline*. (2) Noradrenaline is also a neurotransmitter produced at synapses. It is a *monoamine* which usually inhibits *postsynaptic* transmission. Noradrenaline stimulates many of the *synapses* of the *sympathetic nervous system*. It is also produced in the *locus coeruleus* and is involved in *REM sleep*.
- ***TIP*** The adjective is 'noradrenergic'.

norm: something that is standard, usual or typical of a group.

- The term appears in two areas of psychology. (1) *Conformity*: individuals conform to a group norm, i.e. majority influence, though *minority influence* is also possible. (2) *Abnormal behaviour*: in order to define what is abnormal we need to identify a norm or desirable standard of behaviour. Such norms can be set by, for example, statistical frequency, social acceptability, the adaptiveness of behaviour, or the idea of what is mentally healthy.

normal distribution: the bell-shaped frequency distribution in which most of the scores are close to the mean.

- This distribution occurs when certain variables are measured, such as IQ or the life of a light bulb. Such 'events' are distributed in such a way that most of the scores are clustered close to the mean. The ends of the curve are called the 'tails'. The key characteristics are: (1) the mean, median and mode are all the same in a normal distribution; (2) in every normal distribution the area between each *standard deviation* represents exactly the same percentage of cases. Thus the curve is defined by the mean and standard deviation of the sample.

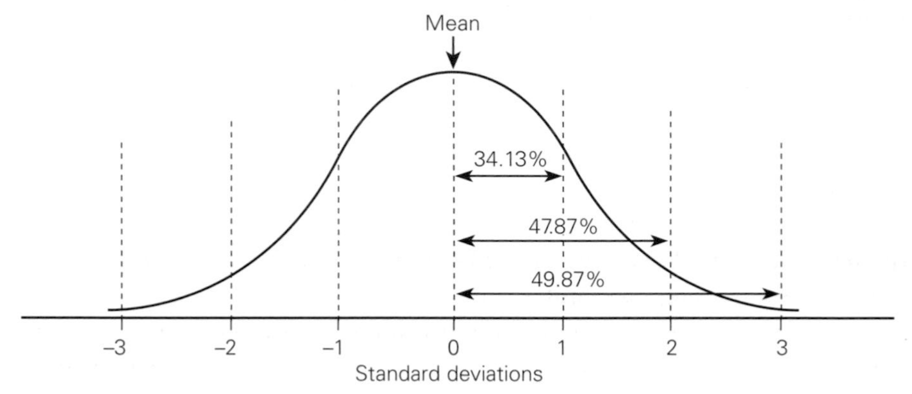

Number of standard deviations from the mean. 34.13% of any population will lie between the mean and 1 SD above the mean. For example, if the mean IQ score is 100 and the SD is 15, 34% of people will have an IQ between 100 and 115.

normative social influence: when an individual *conforms* in order to gain liking or respect from others.

- ***e.g.*** In Asch's study, the participants gave a clearly wrong answer and must have been conforming in order to be accepted within the group.

NREM sleep: all *sleep stages* excluding *REM sleep*.

null hypothesis: the statement of no difference between the *independent variable* and *dependent variable*, or no relationship between the *covariables*.

- It is the hypothesis which represents the assumption that all the data are drawn from the same population. The null hypothesis accounts for the results by attributing them to chance. The null hypothesis is needed to bring precision to hypothesis testing. 'There is no difference between performance in condition A and condition B' is precise because it leads to a prediction that the single most likely outcome is that performance will be equal in both conditions (or there will be a small difference). In contrast, the *alternative hypothesis* 'Participants do better in condition A than condition B' is imprecise, because it does not indicate how much better. This lack of precision makes it impossible to decide the exact extent to which the findings do or do not support the experimental hypothesis.
- ***e.g.*** 'There is no difference in performance on test A and test B' or 'Any difference in performance on test A and test B is due to chance factors alone'.
- ***TIP*** The abbreviation for the null hypothesis is H_0.

nurture: all environmental influences such as *learning*, diet and experience generally.

- Everything bar heredity. This also excludes any *maturational* influences, which are biologically determined, such as changes around puberty or those suggested by Piaget for cognitive development. See *nature and nurture*.

obedience: a form of *social influence* where one behaves as instructed but not necessarily changing one's opinions.

- Usually obedience is in response to individual rather than group pressure. Obedience happens when you are told to do something, whereas *conformity* is affected by example. Obedience is a generally desirable and *adaptive* behaviour. However, when obedience is to unjust authority the outcome may be disastrous, as in the case of Nazi Germany. Obedience can be explained in terms of the *agentic state, deindividuation*, graduated commitment, and *informational social influence*.
- ***TIP*** Resisting obedience is called *independent behaviour*. To disobey is to continue to respond to social influence.

objective: an unbiased view, gained from outside the individual perspective.

- There is a debate in psychology over whether objectivity is ever obtainable or desirable. Even in the natural sciences it may not be possible ever to be truly objective. In psychology there has been a shift in research orientation. *Introspection* was favoured in the nineteenth century and recently there has been a return to more '*subjective*' methods such as *discourse analysis*. Such methods may, in fact, be as objective as the *experimental* approach.

object permanence: the understanding that objects that are no longer visible continue to exist.

- *Piaget* claimed that this kind of thinking develops around the age of 9 months.

observational learning: learning through *imitation*. See *social learning theory*.

observational study: a form of research where data are collected through observation of participants. No *independent variable* is manipulated but a *dependent variable* may be measured.

- It is both a technique for gathering data (as in all research) and a method of study. Observational studies are conducted systematically (for example, the use of *ethograms, observation grids*, and point or *time sampling*). Observational studies generally do not have any hypotheses because the aims tend to be more open-ended, but one can state research questions. Observational studies are useful when studying behaviour for the first time and offer a way to study behaviour where there are ethical objections to manipulating variables.

Observations have high *ecological validity*. Furthermore, if the observer(s) remain undetected, the method avoids many problems, such as *experimenter bias*. In terms of limitations, observational studies generally lack *control* (except for *controlled observations*) which reduces their *internal validity*. Another challenge to their *validity* is the fact that such studies are difficult to *replicate*. Observations may also lack *reliability* because of *observer bias*. Finally, when participants know they are being watched (disclosed observations) they may behave unnaturally and be affected by *evaluation apprehension*. Even non-participant observers, by their mere presence, can alter a situation. An important ethical consideration concerns invasion of privacy. It is assumed to be acceptable to observe someone without their permission in any public area.

■ ***e.g.*** *Naturalistic, controlled, participant* and *undisclosed observation*, and *content analysis*.

observed value: the numerical value calculated when using a test of *inferential statistics* with a set of data.

■ ***TIP*** When reporting the significance of your observed value it is usual to make a statement such as: 'The observed value was less than the critical value ($p < 0.05$ one-tailed). Therefore we can reject the null hypothesis and accept the alternate hypothesis.'

observer bias: the effect that the observer's expectations have on what they observe and thus on the findings of the study.

■ An observer is unlikely to be able to record behaviour objectively. Evidence on perception shows that what we see is influenced by our expectations. Expectations also influence the categories that are selected.

observer reliability: a measure of the consistency (*reliability*) between the observations made by two or more observers.

■ An observational study that employs more than one observer increases the *validity* of the findings because *observer bias* can be controlled for.

obsessive–compulsive disorder: a mental illness characterised by obsessional experiences and compulsive acts.

■ The obsessions are thoughts which are recognised as one's own but are beyond the individual's control. The thoughts are usually undesirable or unpleasant. The individual uses rituals (compulsions) as a means of briefly relieving the anxiety associated with the obsessions. Compulsions are often concerned with personal hygiene and many involve repeating the same action for several hours each day. *Cognitive–behavioural* therapies have offered some success.

occipital lobe: a region in each *hemisphere* of the forebrain (see the *brain*).

■ This region is located at the back of the brain and is almost entirely devoted to visual processing (see the *visual cortex*).

occupational psychology: another term for *organisational psychology*.

Oedipus complex: Freud's explanation of how a boy resolves his love for his mother and feelings of rivalry towards his father by identifying with his father.

■ During the *phallic stage* of *psychosexual development*, around the age of 3, a boy first becomes sexually aware. This results in an unconscious desire for his mother and means that the boy sees his father as a rival for the mother's love. This leads the boy to wish to get rid of his father. He then fears that his father will discover his true feelings and this leads to feelings of anxiety. Eventually the complex is resolved when the boy comes to identify with his father. Identification is important for both moral and gender development.

- ***TIP*** *Jung* proposed the idea of an equivalent *Electra complex* in girls, whereas Freud used the concept of *penis envy*.

oestrogen: a female sex hormone.

- Oestrogen promotes the development of some female secondary sexual characteristics (such as breast growth) and governs the menstrual cycle.

ogive: a kind of *graph* used to represent cumulative frequency.

- The frequency of data in one class is the sum of that class and all classes below it. You can easily mark the 25th, 50th and 75th percentiles on an ogive (see *semi-interquartile range*).

one-tailed hypothesis: see *directional hypothesis*.

one-tailed test: used when carrying out a test of significance on a *directional hypothesis*.

one trial learning: when *conditioning* occurs immediately, after one trial only.

- This is especially *adaptive* in situations where danger is involved.
- ***e.g.*** When a child is bitten by a dog, the child learns a fear response after the one episode.
- ***TIP*** It is possible that some cases of such rapid learning can be explained in terms of biological *preparedness*.

ontogeny: the evolution of a single individual from conception to death, in contrast to *phylogeny*.

open-ended question: on a *questionnaire survey*, a kind of question that does not restrict the range of possible answers.

- The advantage is that one may get unexpected answers that would have been excluded if using a *closed question* or *forced-choice question*. The disadvantage is that it is harder to score/summarise the answers to open-ended questions.
- ***e.g.*** 'What do you like about smoking?' In a closed question a range of answers would be provided.

operant conditioning: learning due to the consequences of a behaviour, through reinforcement and punishment.

- Thorndike first described *instrumental learning*. An animal naturally produces many 'random' behaviours. Those that happen to result in a positive state of affairs are 'stamped in' whereas those that result in a negative state of affairs are stamped out. He called this the *law of effect*. Skinner extended the principles of instrumental learning. He chose the phrase 'operant conditioning' to represent the fact that the animal 'operates' on its environment and this results in rewards (*reinforcement*) or *punishments*. Both positive and negative reinforcement increase the probability of a behaviour being repeated, whereas any punishment decreases the probability. It is unlikely that an animal will learn something straight away and therefore the process of *shaping* is important in understanding operant conditioning. Operant conditioning has many important applications, such as in *programmed learning* and *behaviour modification therapies*.

■ ***e.g.*** A rat is placed in a 'Skinner box' where there is a lever. At some point the rat accidentally presses the lever and food appears. The food acts as a reward and makes it more likely that the rat will repeat this behaviour. A new *stimulus–response link* has been learned. The stimulus is the lever and the response is to press it.

■ ***TIP*** Classical conditioning focuses on the behaviours themselves whereas operant conditioning is concerned with the effects of behaviour. However, in reality this distinction is not so clear. It is possible that reinforcement is not really instrumental in forming learning responses.

operational definition/operationalisation: defining all *variables* in terms of their constituent operations.

■ This makes it easier to measure them and makes any statement less ambiguous.

■ ***e.g.*** One can operationalise 'hunger' by stating the exact hours since a participant last had food.

Operation Headstart: an enrichment programme begun in 1965 in the USA.

■ The rationale was that some children begin school at a disadvantage and therefore are destined for failure. If they were given an early boost through intensive preschool care, involving both health and education, this might break the cycle of failure. When the Headstart children did start school, they showed IQ gains in comparison with those disadvantaged children who had not attended day care programmes, but these differences soon disappeared. However, follow-up studies have found many general gains, such as lower delinquency rates, less need for welfare and continuance in further education.

operations: the term used in *Piaget's theory of cognitive development* for internally consistent, logical mental rules, such as rules of arithmetic.

■ Pre-operational thought is guided more by external appearances than internal consistency or logic. This is not to say that children of a younger (pre-operational) age are not using rules but that their rules lack internal logic.

opponent–process theory: this suggests that the perception of colour is made possible by three pairs of receptor systems — red–green, blue–yellow and black–white — which work in opposition. Stimulation of one of the pair results in inhibition of the other.

■ ***TIP*** It is probable that this explains colour perception at the level of the *retinal ganglion cells* but that initial colour detection is explained by the *trichromatic theory*.

opportunity sample: a *sampling technique* where participants are selected because they are available (opportune).

■ This method is sometimes mistakenly regarded as *random* whereas it is invariably biased. It is the most commonly used method because it is easy in terms of time and therefore money.

- ***e.g.*** Selecting participants by asking passers-by in the street or people in your class in school.
- ***TIP*** Sometimes potential participants decline to take part so that, in effect, your opportunity sample may turn into a *volunteer sample*.

optic array: a concept in *direct perception theory*, expressing the richness of data presented to the retina which contains all the information needed for perception.

optic chiasma: the point at which the optic nerves from each eye cross over to the opposite side of the brain.

- Each side of the brain receives information from both eyes. Nerves from the side of the *retina* closest to the nose cross over to the other side of the brain (contralateral). Those from the outer side of the retina carry on. Data from the right visual field of both eyes travel to the right *visual cortex* and the same occurs for the left visual field (ipsilateral).

optic flow patterns: a concept in *direct perception theory*, describing how the environment seems to flow past a moving observer and the point to which we are moving stays still.

optimal foraging strategy (OFT): an 'economic' explanation for *foraging* behaviour in terms of a balance between costs and benefits: balancing the amount of food gathered against the energy expenditure in gathering it.

- Stephens and Krebs (1986) identified three considerations: (1) decisions (what to eat, where to find it, how to get there); (2) currencies (short-term benefits and long-term ones in terms of reproduction success); (3) constraints (anything that prevents the animal foraging optimally, e.g. limited memory for food sites, predation risks). OFT has been criticised because it is hard to know what is actually optimal for any one animal. Suboptimal strategies are probably selected most of the time because they are good enough.

oral stage: in *psychoanalytic theory*, the first stage (0–18 months) of *psychosexual development* when the organ-focus is on the mouth.

- The *id* experiences pleasures related to the mouth, for example eating and sucking. Under- or over-gratification at this stage results in certain enduring *fixations* and personality characteristics. The oral receptive personality (over-gratification) is very trusting and dependent on others whereas the oral aggressive personality (under-gratification) is dominating.

order effects: in a *repeated measures* experiment, participants may perform differently on two conditions because of the order in which the conditions are performed.

- In the second condition performance may be enhanced, for example as in the *practice effect*. Or performance may be depressed, as in the *boredom effect*.
- ***TIP*** Order effects act as *confounding variables*. They can be dealt with by using *counterbalancing* or an *independent measures design*. A further possibility is to leave a time gap between conditions so that participants have time to recover.

order of gamete release hypothesis: an explanation offered for *parental investment* suggested by Dawkins and Carlisle (1976) that both sexes prefer not to be left 'holding the baby' because this decreases their own reproductive potential.

■ Internal fertilisation allows the male to get away first. Where there is external fertilisation the female can leave first.

ordinal scale: a *level of measurement*. Data are ordered in some way but the intervals between each item are unequal.

■ ***e.g.*** Asking people to put their favourite TV programmes in order of liking: *EastEnders* could be first, followed by *Top of the Pops* and *Blind Date*. The 'difference' between each item is not the same, i.e. the individual may like the first item a lot more than the second one, but there might only be a small difference between the items ranked as second and third.

organic disorder: any disorder which is proposed to have a physical cause (i.e. based on the body organs), as distinct from *psychogenic illness*.

■ ***e.g.*** Physical illnesses, such as chicken pox and pneumonia, are organic. Some mental illnesses are proposed to be organic, such as *schizophrenia*.

organisational psychology: the branch of *applied psychology* that aims to explain and guide personal interactions in the workplace.

■ The area of interest includes large and small companies, and voluntary and paid employment. Organisational psychologists consider *motivation*, procedures involved in selection and assessment of employees, *psychometric testing*, *leadership* and group behaviour, managing change and redundancy.

organism: a whole, living thing.

■ The term was preferred by *behaviourists* and lacks the emotiveness of 'animal'.

outcome study: research which examines the potential benefits of a therapeutic intervention.

■ ***e.g.*** A study might consider the effects of a particular drug by comparing a group of *schizophrenics* who received the drug with a group who were given a *placebo*. Another study might compare therapies.

■ ***TIP*** Outcome studies are different from 'process studies' which focus on how a therapy works.

outgroup: any social group to which you do not belong; not the *ingroup*.

outgroup bias: the negative *bias* shown to members of an *outgroup*.

■ *Social identity theory* predicts that this increases one's sense of personal self-esteem, as does *ingroup favouritism*. If the outgroup is seen in a poor light, the ingroup appears more desirable as a result of social comparison.

overgeneralisation: applying grammatical rules to irregular instances.

■ It is a characteristic behaviour of children when acquiring language, which demonstrates their application of the rules of *grammar*.

■ ***e.g.*** 'I goed to school' instead of using 'went'.

owner wins strategy: see *home field (ground) advantage*.

paired associate learning: participants are given a pair of stimuli, such as a syllable and a digit, and then recall is tested by presenting the participant with a member of the pair and recording if its partner can be remembered.

pandemonium model: a *feature detection model* of pattern recognition proposed by Selfridge (1959) that suggests there are four stages in the process: (1) image recorded by image demons; (2) features analysed by feature demons; (3) this information passed on to the cognitive demons, each of which detects one pattern and then 'shouts' out 'my pattern' for the (4) decision demons, who decide which pattern demon is shouting loudest.

paradigm: a representative example of a theory or methodology.

- ***e.g.*** Pavlov's experiment on salivation in dogs is the paradigm example of classical conditioning.
- ***TIP*** The concept 'paradigm' was given a special meaning by Kuhn and this is the meaning sometimes attached to the word — namely, that a paradigm is a set of attitudes and procedures attached to a particular perspective at a specific time in the development of that perspective.

paradoxical sleep: a term for *REM sleep* because of the behavioural contradictions (paradoxes): eye movement, breathing, etc. are increased but the body is in a state of near paralysis and it is difficult to wake a person up.

parallel processing: an *information processing* concept that means dealing with several pieces of information at one time, as distinct from *serial processing*.

- ***e.g.*** Divided *attention* assumes that processing is being done in parallel.

parametric tests/statistics: a group of *inferential statistics* that make certain assumptions about the parameters of the population from which the sample is drawn.

- An example of a 'population parameter' would be the *mean* or *standard deviation*. Parametric statistics are more powerful than *non-parametric statistics*. This means that they are more likely to detect statistically *significant* effects, which is due to the fact that parametric statistics use all of the data whereas non-parametric statistics use comparative data, such as ranks. There are certain criteria that must be fulfilled in order to use a parametric statistic. (1) The sample is drawn from a *normal population*. (2) The samples must have equal or known *variances*. (3) The data were measured at an *interval* level. *Quasi-interval* data are acceptable.

■ **e.g.** *t-tests* (related and unrelated), *Pearson's product–moment test of correlation*.

parasympathetic nervous system (parasympathetic branch): a division of the *autonomic nervous system* which controls the relaxed state, conserving resources and promoting digestion and metabolism.

■ It consists of nerves that control, for example, decreased heart rate and breathing, and increased digestive activity. The parasympathetic branch works in opposition to the *sympathetic* branch of the ANS.

parental investment: Trivers (1972) introduced this term to describe how any animal parent aims to achieve a balance between effort (time and resources) and reproductive success.

■ Mating reduces the parent's future reproductive potential and therefore it is important to offset this by increased success.

■ ***TIP*** The question of which parent ends up doing the caring may be related to the mode of fertilisation. See *paternity certainty hypothesis, order of gamete release hypothesis* and *association hypothesis*.

parent–offspring conflict: the conflict between a parent's interest in all of its offspring plus its own future reproductive success and the offspring's interest in its own survival.

■ Trivers (1974) predicted that parent–offspring conflict should occur because each offspring has a greater interest in their parent's care than parents have for each individual offspring. Parents have an equal interest in all offspring and want to distribute their investment evenly.

■ **e.g.** *Weaning conflict.*

parietal lobe: a region in each *hemisphere* of the forebrain (see the *brain*).

■ It is located just behind (posterior to) the *central sulcus* and above the lateral fissure. It contains the somatosensory cortex which is concerned with sensory information. The parietal lobe also contains part of the *association cortex*.

partial reinforcement: when *reinforcement* is not received on every occasion that the right response is made.

■ There are vaious partial reinforcement schedules. (1) A fixed ratio *reinforcement schedule*: reinforcement after a regular number of correct responses, e.g. every fifth correct response. (2) A variable ratio reinforcement schedule: reinforcement after a variable number of correct responses, e.g. after the second, then the sixth, then the fourth, etc. correct response. (3) A fixed interval reinforcement schedule: reinforcement after a fixed time interval provided a response occurs within that time period, e.g. every 10 seconds. (4) A variable interval reinforcement schedule: reinforcement after a variable time interval.

■ **e.g.** The classic example of the success of partial reinforcement schedules can be seen in the appeal of fruit machines and gambling. It is the fact that you do not always win that keeps you coming back for more.

participant: an individual who takes part in an experiment and provides data for analysis.

- The term 'participant' has come into use as a replacement for '*subject*' because the former reflects more accurately the active nature of participation. In the past, researchers regarded subjects as rather passive contributors to the research process. In reality, participants actively engage in, for example, searching for cues about how to behave and trying to work out the research aims. The term 'participant' encourages the researcher to take account of the effects the participant may have on the research process, for example in terms of *demand characteristics* and *experimenter bias*.

participant observation: a kind of *observational study* where the observer is also a participant in the activity being observed.

- In most observational studies the observer is a non-participant. One advantage to participant observation is that it gives the observer a greater understanding of what is going on. However, such observers are likely to be *biased* and their involvement may affect the behaviour of other participants.

participant reactivity: the tendency for participants to react to cues from the researcher or the research environment.

- This will affect their behaviour and may act as a *confounding variable*, thus threatening the *validity* of the research findings.
- **e.g.** *Demand characteristics, evaluation apprehension, Hawthorne effect.*

participant variables: characteristics of *participants* such as their abilities, gender, age, social class and education.

- These characteristics are important: (1) when assessing the extent to which a *sample* is *representative*; and (2) if acting as a *confounding variable* in an *independent measures* experiment because one group may be, for example, more able or older than the other group. If an independent measures design is used, participant variables can be controlled using *random allocation* to conditions/groups. The advantage of *repeated measures* or *matched pairs designs* is that they control for participant variables.

passionate love: *love* which is a powerful emotional state involving many contrasting feelings: tenderness and sexual desire, joy and anxiety, excitement and deep despair.

- Passionate love is distinguished from the more steady *companionate love*.

paternity certainty hypothesis: an explanation offered for *parental investment* by males.

- Males are more likely to care for young when fertilisation is external because, having guarded the eggs against fertilisation by other males, they can be sure the offspring are theirs. Therefore it is worth investing further time in ensuring the offspring's survival. In the case of internal fertilisation the female cannot desert, but the male can desert, thinking that the offspring are his. In fact the male may be wrong (see *sneak copulation*).

Pearson's product–moment test of correlation: an *inferential* and *parametric* *test* of the *correlation* between covariables.

■ The reasons for selecting this test are: (1) a test of correlation is required; (2) the data fit *parametric* assumptions (e.g. the distribution is *normal* and the *level of measurement* is at the interval or ratio level).

peer tutoring: an effective form of learning, recommended by *Vygotsky's theory of cognitive development* because peers are potential 'experts' (individuals with greater knowledge).

■ Vygotsky saw learning as a collaborative process, all children working together for the general good rather than competing against each other for individual gain (a Marxist view).

penis envy: a girl's recognition of not having a penis and desire to have one.

■ Freud suggested that, in girls, penis envy is the conflict that is experienced during the *phallic stage* of *psychosexual development* (boys experience the *Oedipus* conflict). A girl around the age of 3 comes to realise that she does not have a penis and she blames her mother for this. The girl's father now becomes her love-object and she substitutes her 'penis envy' with a wish to have a child. This leads to a kind of resolution and ultimate identification with her same-gender parent. *Jung* proposed a different version of the resolution of this stage in females, called the *Electra complex*.

■ ***TIP*** It has been suggested that penis envy is actually an envy of male power.

perception: an active searching for the best interpretation of available sensory data.

■ It is the process by which we turn sensory data (visual, auditory, touch, taste) into recognisable objects. The process can be explained in terms of *bottom–up processing* (e.g. *direct perception theory*) or *top–down processing* (e.g. *constructivist theory*) or a combination of both (e.g. *analysis-by-synthesis model*).

perceptual constancy: several sensory inputs result in one perception of an object with constant size and shape.

■ This is the reverse of an ambiguous figure where the same sensory input can result in several different perceptions. Constancy depends on knowledge of the real object. We persist in seeing it in line with our expectations despite changed *retinal* images which may distort the image.

■ ***e.g.*** As you move a book around, you still 'see' the same three-dimensional rectangular object despite the fact that the retinal image is not that shape.

perceptual defence: words that are emotionally threatening are recognised less easily than words which do not have emotional significance.

■ ***e.g.*** Research has shown that the time taken to recognise words such as 'belly' and 'filth' is longer than 'music' and 'trade'.

perceptual set: a tendency to respond in a certain manner to a sensory stimulus, in line with expectations built on past experience.

■ ***e.g.*** If participants are shown one of the following two displays: 'TA13LE' or '12 13 14', they 'see' the '13' as a B or 13 depending on the *set* created by the other figures.

permissive amine theory of mood disorder: Kety's (1975) explanation for depression to account for the role of both *serotonin* and *noradrenaline*, which are both *neurotransmitters* in the amine group.

- Serotonin moderates levels of noradrenaline. In depressed individuals serotonin levels are low and this results in some extreme lows and highs of noradrenaline, leading to depression and mania.

personal construct therapy: a *cognitive* and *humanistic* therapy devised by Kelly.

- Personal constructs refer to an individual's view of the world. The therapist identifies these constructs by compiling a repertory grid. The individual lists significant people and then is asked to consider three of these people at a time and state the ways that two are the same and differ from the third person (or event). This gives the therapist access to the individual's personal constructs — the way the patient distinguishes between things in their world.

personality: an individual's characteristic, coherent and relatively stable set of behaviours, *attitudes*, interests and capabilities.

- Theories of personality include social–psychological approaches — *psychoanalytic theory*, *social learning theory* and *situationalism* — and *biological* approaches — Eysenck's *type theory* (which is also psychological) and Cattell's *trait theory*. Personality tests include *projective tests* and Eysenck's Personality Questionnaire (EPQ).
- ***TIP*** Mischel's *situationalist* theory contradicts all other approaches in suggesting that there is no such thing as a consistent personality.

personal space: that area of space immediately around you.

- Inappropriate intrusions lead to a sense of discomfort. Inappropriateness is culturally determined.

pertinence model: a model of focused auditory *attention* proposed by Deutsch and Deutsch (1963) that is based on late selection and *serial processing*.

- This is in contrast with the *filter model* which involves early selection. According to the pertinence model, all information is initially analysed in the memory system and only then does selection take place on the basis of how important (pertinent) the information is. Pertinence is determined by factors such as previous experience and *situational* cues. The main problem is that this model is uneconomical because much unnecessary information appears to be analysed. Such a system would require a large processing capacity.

PET scan (positron emission tomography): a method of detecting activity in the living *brain* to determine the function of different regions.

- Participants are asked to engage in an activity, such as reading. The participant is given an injection of a mildly radioactive form of glucose and then put in a scanner. Active regions of the brain use the glucose and its radioactivity is detected by the scanner. See *brain scans*.

phallic stage: in *psychoanalytic theory*, the third stage of *psychosexual development* when the organ-focus is on the genitals.

- The child aged 3–6 years becomes aware of gender issues and gender conflicts.

The resolution of this conflict results in the development of a *superego* (see *Oedipus complex, penis envy, Electra complex*). Unresolved conflicts may result in a poorly developed conscience, homosexuality, authority problems and rejection of appropriate gender roles. A fixation at this stage results in the phallic personality type who is self-assured, vain and impulsive.

phenotype: the observable characteristics of an individual, which result from interaction between the genes he/she possesses (i.e. the individual's *genotype*) and the environment.

phenylalanine: an amino acid which is needed to produce *dopamine, adrenaline* and *noradrenaline*.

phenylketonuria (PKU): an inherited disorder that prevents metabolism of *phenylalanine*, resulting in a build-up of poisonous substances that cause brain damage. If the disorder is detected at birth, the individual can be given a diet that avoids phenylalanine and thus prevents the potential brain damage.

- ***TIP*** This is an example of an interaction between *nature* and *nurture*.

pheromone: a chemical substance produced by the body and secreted into the air, whence it is transmitted to other animals of the same species and absorbed into their bloodstream. The pheromone then works like a hormone and influences the behaviour of the receiver.

- ***e.g.*** Women who are menstruating emit pheromones which may affect the menstrual cycles of other women so that their menstrual cycles come into phase at the same time.

phobia (phobic disorder): an excessive fear of a specific object or situation which is irrational and disproportionate.

- *Behavioural therapy* has proved successful in treating phobias.
- ***e.g.*** *Agoraphobia*, social phobia (fears about interacting with people or being in public places), arachnophobia (fear of spiders).

phoneme: the minimal unit of speech that makes a difference to the listener.

- ***e.g.*** In the words 'man', 'mat' and 'match', the phonemes /n/ and /t/ and /ch/ make a difference. (/ / is used to delineate a phoneme.) See also *morpheme*.

phonemic processing: *processing* words according to their sounds.

- This is a more *shallow* level of processing than *semantic processing*.
- ***e.g.*** 'Does hat rhyme with cat?' requires phonemic processing.
- ***TIP*** *Levels of processing theory* suggests that semantic processing is best for creating an enduring memory trace. However, if recall is based on a rhyming recognition test, then phonemic processing comes out better than semantic processing.

photosensitive (photoreceptor) cell: a specialised cell that converts light into an *action potential*.

- ***e.g.*** *Rods* and *cones*.

phylogeny: the evolution of a species, in contrast to *ontogeny*.

physiology: the study of the functions of the constituent parts of living organisms.

Piaget's theory of cognitive development: Piaget proposed that *cognitive development* occurs as a consequence of *maturation* and *adaptation*.

- The infant starts life with a set of *innate reflexes* or schemata (*schema*). Experience causes the infant to adapt these schema to fit reality. This adaptation occurs through the twin processes of *assimilation* and *accommodation*, driven by the desire for equilibrium (balance). Piaget suggested that a child moves from one qualitatively different stage to another when he/she is ready to progress. Stage (1), sensorimotor (0–2 years), is characterised by *circular reactions* and behaviours such as *object permanence*. Stage (2), pre-operational (2–7 years), is when the child can cope with symbols (such as using language) but cannot cope with adult logic (*operations*). The child exhibits *animism*, *egocentricity* and *moral realism* in his/her thinking. Stage (3), concrete operations (7–11 years), is when the child can now use adult logic but not for abstract problems. Characteristic modes of thought now include the ability to cope with *conservation*, *seriation* and *moral relativity*. Stage (4), formal operations (11 onwards), includes formal adult logic and abstract thinking. The two main criticisms of the theory are that Piaget undervalued the role of language in development and also the role of practice. See *neo-Piagetians*, *horizontal décalage*.
- ***TIP*** Some people see Piaget's theory simply in terms of the stages, whereas there is a lot more to the theory than that. The other main theory is *Vygotsky's*, which explains cognitive development in terms of external influences, whereas Piaget thought that the main causes of change were internal.

pilot study: a smaller-scale, preliminary study conducted prior to a research study.

- This makes it possible to check out and adjust standardised procedures and general design before investing time and money in the major study.

pineal gland: a very small *endocrine* gland located in the brain that produces *melatonin*.

pituitary gland: the master gland of the *endocrine system* because it directs much of the activity of the endocrine system.

- Some of the hormones produced by the pituitary: *adrenocorticotropic hormone* (ACTH), follicle-stimulating hormone (FSH) which leads to production of *testosterone* and *oestrogen*, and prolactin which promotes milk.

placebo: a substance prescribed for psychological reasons but having no physiological effects.

- In psychological research, a placebo condition is used to *control* for the effects of expectations because it means that all participants think they are receiving the *experimental treatment* when in fact only the experimental group are.
- ***e.g.*** A study that investigated the effects of caffeine on memory would have an experimental condition where participants were given caffeine and a control condition with no caffeine. However, it would be important to give participants in the control condition a substitute substance (placebo) so that they thought they were receiving caffeine. In addition it might be important that the experimenter was not aware of which participants were getting the real thing because otherwise the experimenter's expectations might affect performance.

plastic interval scale: a kind of *interval scale*, where the intervals between units are numerically equal but they are not, in reality, the same size.

■ ***e.g.*** Any psychological scale that has not been *standardised*, such as asking people to score their liking for TV programmes on a scale of 1 to 10. The difference between 9 and 10 is not necessarily the same as between 5 and 6.

plasticity: the view that after a *critical* or *sensitive period* in the development of the nervous system it is still possible to recover or regenerate specialised functions. See *hard-wired*.

play therapy: a form of *psychotherapy* developed for children.

■ The child is able to demonstrate his/her feelings through play and then the therapist can help the child to resolve his/her conflicts.

pleasure principle: in *psychoanalytic theory*, the drive to do things which produce pleasure or gratification and to avoid pain.

■ The *id* is motivated by the pleasure principle.

pluralistic ignorance: an explanation for *bystander behaviour*, that help is less forthcoming when an individual is in a group because many emergency situations are ambiguous and therefore we seek clues about how to behave from those around us. Each non-acting person sends out the message 'It's OK, no help is needed'.

■ Therefore everyone continues to do nothing.

point sampling: method of collecting data in an *observational study* where one observes an individual for a fixed period of time, such as 5 minutes, and then moves on to the next individual. See also *time* and *event sampling*.

polyandry: a mating strategy where one female mates with many males ('poly' means 'many' and 'andry' refers to males).

■ ***e.g.*** Spotted sandpiper, and reported among people in Tibet where brothers may marry one woman.

■ ***TIP*** Polyandry tends to result in female parental care because the male investment is made by fertilising many females.

polygamy: having more than one mate. See *polyandry* and *polygyny*.

polygenetic: the description of a characteristic that is caused by an interaction of *genes* rather than a single pair of genes.

■ ***e.g.*** IQ is polygenetically determined whereas eye colour is determined by one pair of genes.

polygynandry: both males and females mate with many members of the opposite sex.

■ ***e.g.*** The dunnock.

polygyny: a mating strategy where one male mates with many females ('poly' means 'many' and 'gyny' refers to females).

■ There is simultaneous polygyny (as in a harem where many females live with one male at the same time) and serial polygyny (males bond with one female at a time but, over a breeding season, have several females).

- ***TIP*** Polygyny tends to result in female parental care because the male investment is made by fertilising many females.

pons: a structure in the *hindbrain* that contains the *reticular formation* and is associated with arousal and sleep.

ponzo illusion: see *visual illusion*.

population: the group of people from whom a *sample* is drawn for a study.

- The findings of the study can only apply to this population. The population is likely to be *biased* (unrepresentative).
- ***e.g.*** In a study where the sample of participants is drawn from schools in Bristol, the population is 'school students in Bristol'. The findings only apply to that group of people, not all school children in Britain, and certainly not children all over the world.

population validity: the extent to which experimental findings can be *generalised* to the total population from which the sample was drawn and to other populations.

- This is a type of *external validity*, and is related to the representativeness of the sample (generalising to the *population*) and to the representativeness of the sampling population (generalising to other populations).
- ***e.g.*** A considerable amount of psychological research involves American student participants who are on a psychology course. This sample is not representative of all students, nor of all Americans.

positive correlation: as one *covariable* increases the other also increases.

- They vary in a constant relationship. The perfect positive correlation coefficient is +1.0, and on a *scattergram* the dots would range from bottom left to top right.

postsynaptic membrane: the covering of the *neurone* that is receiving the information at the *synapse*.

post-traumatic stress disorder (PTSD): a disabling reaction to stress following a traumatic event.

- The traumatic event acts as a *stressor*, and like many stressors, is in some way life-threatening. The response does not always appear immediately after the event but may be delayed. The reactions are long-lasting, and include: reliving the event recurrently in flashbacks and dreams, emotional numbness and avoidance of things which serve as a reminder, general anxiety which may result in lack of concentration and guilt about surviving.

powerful: used to describe *inferential statistical tests*.

- A test that is 'powerful' is one that is better able to detect small differences or correlations. This means that you will be more likely to reject the *null hypothesis* when it is false and avoid making a *type II error*. *Parametric tests* have greater power at detecting relationships than *non-parametric tests*.

practice effect: performance is improved as a result of doing the task previously.

- This may occur in an experiment with a *repeated measures design* (an *order effect*), or may apply to psychological testing. Practice effects can be overcome by using *counterbalancing* or leaving a time gap between conditions/testings. It is also possible to use two different but comparable tests (see *test–retest*).

precocial species: an animal whose young are relatively mature at birth and can feed themselves as soon as they are born/hatched.

- The key importance of this concept is in terms of *imprinting*, which is more critical for precocial young who need to follow a caregiver for safety and to learn about food-gathering and so on. *Altricial* young are immobile and therefore easier to look after in terms of safety.
- ***TIP*** The word 'precocious' means prematurely developed.

preconscious: consists of information and ideas that could be retrieved easily from memory and brought into consciousness.

- Freud distinguished three levels of mind: *unconscious*, preconscious (or sub-conscious) and *conscious*. In this sense the preconscious is that area of the mind through which material must pass before it reaches the conscious mind.

predictive validity: a means of assessing the validity or trueness of a psychological test.

- It is the extent to which performance on the test predicts later performance on some other criterion.
- ***e.g.*** We would expect that people who do well on tests of engineering ability, later go on to be successful engineers.
- ***TIP*** See other forms of establishing validity: *content, construct, concurrent, criterion* and *face validity*.

prefrontal lobotomy: see *lobotomy* and *psychosurgery*.

pre-intellectual speech: *Vygotsky's* concept that language initially serves a social function.

- In Vygotsky's view, language and thought develop separately as there is also pre-linguistic thought.

prejudice: literally, a pre-judgement. It is a *biased* attitude held towards an individual or group prior to direct experience of that person/people.

- Such attitudes are often based on *stereotypes* and/or group characteristics. Individual attributes are ignored and prejudices are resistant to change and logical argument. A prejudiced attitude often leads to prejudiced behaviour (*discrimination*). This can be negative or positive (e.g. *ingroup favouritism*). Attitudes do not always result in behaviour; a trigger may be required, e.g. frustration. There are many explanations for the causes of prejudice, such as the *authoritarian personality, conformity, realistic conflict theory, scapegoat theory, social identity theory*.

Premack principle: with reference to education, Premack (1965) suggested that a behaviour that occurs frequently should be used to *reinforce* less frequent behaviour.

- ***e.g.*** We often reward ourselves in this way, for example watching TV after doing 2 hours of homework.

pre-menstrual syndrome (PMS): a phase in a woman's menstrual cycle, just prior to menstruation, when some individuals experience mood swings and increased aggression.

- At this time of the female cycle, levels of progesterone are high.

prenatal: before birth.

pre-operational stage: the second stage in *Piaget's theory of cognitive development* characterised by intuitive rather than internal logical thought.

preparedness: the concept proposed by Seligman that some conditioned responses are easier to acquire than others because an animal has an *innate* predisposition to acquire such responses.

- Animals tend to be able to acquire certain habits/associations faster than others, and this speed can be related to the *adaptiveness* of the behaviour.
- ***e.g.*** Rats exhibit 'bait shyness'. This is a tendency to sample unfamiliar foods cautiously. The rat learns quickly to avoid any food that causes illness. This predisposition is likely to be innate and adaptive because it enables them to avoid being poisoned.

presumptive consent: to obtain the views of other people about the acceptability of the experimental procedures as a substitute for the *informed consent* of a research participant.

- It is argued that if other people felt it would be acceptable to take part in a research study then we can presume that the actual participants would have felt this way if they had been asked.

primacy effect: refers to things that come first.

- (1) In relation to *memory*, a high level of free recall for the first items in a list. This is due to the extra rehearsal received by earlier items and is evidence of the effects of *long-term memory*. (2) In relation to *interpersonal perception*, the notion that first impressions have a stronger influence than those perceived later (*recency effect*). This would be important in an interview for a job.

primary caregiver: the child's main source of emotional comfort.

- Bowlby proposed that the child's primary attachment object is qualitatively different from all the other attachments. This has important consequences for the *internal working model* and later relationships.

primary emotion: an *emotion* that is universally experienced, such as fear, anger, sadness, joy and disgust.

- Psychological research has found that the expressions associated with these emotions can be distinguished by infants and also by people in different cultures. This suggests that such emotions are *innate* and universal, as opposed to *secondary emotions*. There is also evidence that primary emotions have a specific *physiological* 'signature', for example heart rate and blood pressure are low when a person is happy but high when they are angry. This suggests that primary emotions may be an innate 'read-out' of physiological states.

prior general consent: prospective participants in a research study are asked if they would take part in certain kinds of research, including ones involving deception. If they say 'yes' they have given their general consent to taking part in such research.

- This is an alternative strategy for obtaining consent when *informed consent* is not possible because *deception* is part of the design.

privacy: participants have a right not to be observed, for the purposes of psychological research, in situations where they would not expect to be seen/heard by strangers.

privation: the lack of any attachments, as distinct from the loss of attachments (*deprivation*).

- Rutter suggested that privation may lead to permanent emotional damage, whereas deprivation may have less serious consequences.

proactive interference (PI): a kind of *forgetting* due to *interference* where previous learning interferes with current learning/recall.

- ***e.g.*** A first list contains the following word pairs: AFR-table, STJ-shoe, VKD-lake. A second list has AFR-man, STJ-lake, VKD-chair. Proactive interference would affect your recall of the second list. (As distinct from *retroactive interference*.)

probability: the likelihood of an event occurring.

- A probability of 1% is very unlikely, whereas 99% is extremely likely.
- ***TIP*** The expression '$p < 0.01$' stands for a 'probability of less than 0.01 or 1%'.

problem-solving theory: Webb and Cartwright's (1978) *cognitive* theory of dreaming that suggests that dreams are a way of dealing with our problems, such as those relating to work and personal life.

problem–space theory: Newell and Simon's (1963) account of how people solve problems in terms of the strategies needed to find the shortest route between the current state and goal state.

- One possibility is means–end analysis: (1) identify the problem space, i.e. the distance between where you are now and the goal state; (2) create a subgoal to reduce this difference; (3) select a suitable method to solve the subgoal; (4) recalculate the problem space and set a new subgoal. This method has been supported by comparing human performance with computer performance (using the *general problem solver*) on certain tasks.

procedural knowledge: a subdivision of *long-term memory*, 'knowing how' as opposed to 'knowing that' (*declarative knowledge*).

- This is similar to *implicit memory*. Evidence for the existence of a separate declarative and procedural system comes from research into brain structures.

processing: changing the form or structure of something.

- ***TIP*** One way to understand this is to think of processed peas, which are peas that have been subject to a process that turns them into something slightly different. The same is true of *cognitive* processing and information processing.

process study: see *outcome study*.

programmed learning: a method of teaching based on *learning theory*.

- The system consists of breaking down a topic into individual 'frames' or very small steps. A correct response acts as a reward. The system may be linear (a list of questions) or branching (the programme can 'respond' to a student's needs by offering special help with a question the student got wrong).

projection: a form of *ego defence*, whereby one unknowingly displaces one's own unacceptable feelings onto someone else.

- This is a means of coping with feelings that cause anxiety and thus are threatening to the *ego*.
- ***e.g.*** An individual may project their own feelings of inferiority onto a minority group in the form of prejudiced behaviour. (*Displacement* can also be used to explain prejudiced behaviour.)

projective test: a measurement of *attitude* that involves asking respondents to give their interpretation of a picture.

- This means that the respondents 'project' their own attitudes onto the picture and reveal the attitudes in the descriptions provided.
- ***e.g.*** The *Rorschach* and *thematic apperception test*.

promiscuity: see *polygynandry*.

prosocial behaviour: behaviour which is beneficial to others and may not necessarily benefit the helper.

- Social behaviour is any behaviour involving one or more members of the same species and therefore prosocial behaviour promotes this in some way. The opposite is *antisocial behaviour*.
- ***e.g.*** Routine courtesies, friendship, cooperation, *helping behaviour*, *altruism*, *conformity*, *obedience* can all be prosocial in so far as they assist social interaction and are helpful to others.

prosocial reasoning: the way an individual thinks about prosocial and moral behaviour.

protest–despair–detachment (PDD) model: the child's response to prolonged separation from his/her primary caregiver.

- The three typical phases are: *separation protest*, despair (outward calm and/or apathy) and finally detachment (caregiver's return may be ignored).

prototype theory: an explanation for pattern recognition in which abstract forms (prototypes) are matched with the external stimuli.

- This is preferable to *template matching theory* but the details remain imprecise. The theory can account for how one deals with novel stimuli but not how expectations might affect pattern recognition.

proximal stimulus: that which is near, the sensory stimulation, as distinct from the *distal stimulus*.

psychiatry: the diagnosis and treatment of mental illness by a medically trained person, as distinct from a *clinical psychologist*.

psychic energy: a means of describing the force required to engage in psychological activity.

- ***e.g.*** Major *life events* absorb 'psychic energy', leaving less to cope with other matters such as physical defence against illness. Unpredictable noise has

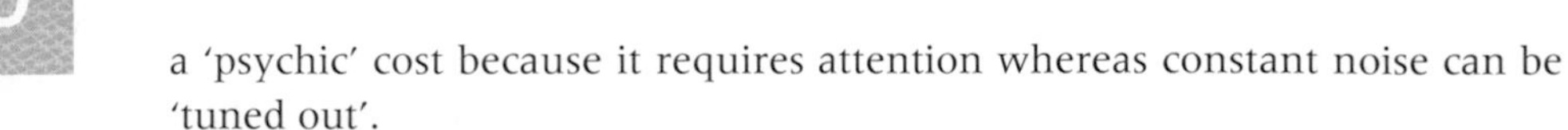

a 'psychic' cost because it requires attention whereas constant noise can be 'tuned out'.

psychoactive drug: a *drug* that alters one's thought or mental processes.

psychoanalysis: both the form of therapy derived from *psychoanalytic theory* and the theory itself.

psychoanalyst: a therapist who uses *psychoanalysis* to treat individuals.

psychoanalytic theory: Freud's explanation of how adult personality develops as a consequence of the interaction between biological (sexual) drives and early experience.

■ This is a *psychodynamic theory* because it describes behaviour in terms of the forces that motivate it (the dynamics of behaviour). According to Freud, personality develops through *psychosexual stages* (*oral, anal, phallic* and *genital*). At each of these stages the child seeks gratification through different body organs. Over- or under-gratification results in *fixations* and *repressions*. In addition the structures of the personality (the *id, ego* and *superego*) are inevitably in conflict. Conflicts cause the individual to experience anxiety, which the ego reduces using *ego defences*, such as repression and *denial*. These ego defences are unconscious and are a key dynamic of the personality. Thoughts that are repressed surface in other ways, such as through *dreams* and *regression* to earlier phases of life. In the long term, ego defences may cause abnormal personality development because they exert pressure through unconsciously motivated behaviour. Freud's psychoanalytic theory continues to have an enormous influence in psychology and beyond, despite being derived from Victorian culture. Some of the criticisms include a lack of empirical evidence and an overemphasis on deterministic, biological (psychosexual) factors. *Neo-Freudians* changed this emphasis to more social factors.

■ ***TIP*** The key strands of psychoanalytic theory are the dynamic process (motivation), early experience and fixations, ego defences, and the unconscious.

psychoanalytic theory of dreams: Freud's theory that dreams are the 'royal road to the unconscious'.

■ Dreams act as a psychic safety valve and allow a therapist to have insight into a patient's *unconscious* thoughts. Thus they are an important part of the therapy. Freud suggested that a dream has both manifest content (the actual content of the dream) and latent content (what the dream symbolises). However, the interpretation of a dream is highly subjective and makes the theory non-*falsifiable*.

psychodrama: a form of treatment for mental illness where patients act out their emotions and the emotions of others.

■ In a supportive environment, a patient is able to express deep feelings.

psychodynamic theory: any approach that emphasises the processes of change and development, i.e. the dynamics of behaviour.

■ 'Dynamics' are what *drive* us to behave in particular ways.

■ ***e.g.*** Freud's *psychoanalytic theory* is the best-known psychodynamic theory.

psychogenic illness: any illness which is primarily caused by psychological factors, such as stress at work or repressed thoughts. Contrast with *organic disorders*.

psychological altruism: see *altruism, psychological*.

psychology: the *science* of *behaviour* and experience.

- The term 'science' refers to objective study and a desire to describe and explain facts. The term 'behaviour' includes anything an organism does — blink their eye, think, pay attention, secrete hormones, get old, evolve and so on. Psychologists are also interested in 'experience' because a true understanding of behaviour requires us to consider what the experience is like for the individual doing the behaving.

psychometric test: a set of questions that tests some aspect of psychological functioning, such as intelligence or personality.

- 'Metric' refers to 'measurement' and 'psycho' is obviously 'psychological'.
- ***e.g.*** Aptitude, creativity, reaction time, *attitudes*.

psychoneuroimmunology (PNI): the study of the effects of psychological factors (such as *stress*) on the immune system.

psychopath: now called 'sociopath'. See *antisocial personality disorder*.

psychopathology: the scientific study of what causes mental disorders.

- The term 'pathology' refers to the study of diseases, including their symptoms and explanations. 'Psychopathology' is concerned with diseases that are psychological rather than physical.

psychopharmacology: the scientific study of the effects of *drugs* on behaviour.

psychosexual development: in *psychoanalytic theory*, the developmental stages that are related to the *id*'s changing focus on different parts of the body.

- 'Sexual' is roughly equivalent to 'physical pleasure'. Examples of the stages of psychosexual development: *anal, oral, phallic, genital stages*.

psychosis: a severe mental illness where the patient has lost touch with reality, the whole person is affected, behaviour is qualitatively different from before and the patient lacks insight into their condition.

- ***e.g.*** *Schizophrenia*.
- ***TIP*** Classification schemes traditionally distinguished between psychoses and *neuroses* but the current versions have dropped this. However, the terms remain in use, probably because they reflect some important characteristics of mental illness.

psychosurgery: a *somatic* method of treating psychological disorders where sections of the brain are removed or lesions (cuts) are made so that areas of the brain become separate to all extents and purposes (i.e. 'functionally').

- Psychosurgery was pioneered by Moniz (1937) who performed *lobotomies*. Now it is used in extremely rare conditions, such as for chronic pain where no other treatment seems appropriate. Lesions are still irreversible and may damage many aspects of behaviour aside from the target behaviour.

psychotherapy: any psychological form of treatment for a mental disorder, as distinct from medical forms of treatment.

■ ***e.g.*** *Client-centred therapy, cognitive restructuring, psychoanalysis.*

punishment: a procedure that decreases the likelihood that a behaviour will be repeated because the overall experience is unpleasant.

■ *Positive punishment* (punishment by application) occurs when you receive something unpleasant. For example, having to write 500 lines for being rude to a teacher. *Negative punishment* (punishment by removal) occurs when something desirable is removed. For example, losing your pocket money because you were rude to your father. Punishments do not always decrease the probability of a response because sometimes they act as a reward. For instance, a child may persist in being naughty because, when he/she is told off, this increased attention is enjoyable.

■ ***TIP*** Both *negative reinforcement* and negative punishment involve an aversive stimulus, which may make negative reinforcement sound like a punishment but it is not because the overall effect increases the likelihood of a response.

qualitative data: data representing how things are expressed, the feelings and thoughts that a person has, what something means to the individual, i.e. the quality of an experience or behaviour.

- The emphasis is on the stated experiences of participants and on the stated meanings they attach to the data. Such information is represented in words rather than numbers. The latter is typical of *quantitative data*.
- ***e.g.*** Qualitative data may be collected from unstructured *surveys, case studies, discourse analysis*. Methods of analysis include discourse analysis, *content analysis, thematic analysis* and *grounded theory*.
- ***TIP*** Sometimes the phrase 'qualitative research' is used though, strictly speaking, it is the data and not the research that are qualitative.

quantitative data: data representing how much there is of something, i.e. the quantity.

- Such data are represented in numerical form. The alternative is *qualitative data*.
- ***e.g.*** The use of descriptive statistics such as the *mean* or *bar charts*, recording the frequency of certain responses.
- ***TIP*** Sometimes the phrase 'quantitative research' is used though, strictly speaking, it is the data and not the research that are quantitative.

quasi-experiment: a research study that involves an *independent* and *dependent variable* but lacks some of the key characteristics of a true experiment.

- The key features are: lack of *random allocation* of participants to conditions, and/or lack of direct manipulation of the *independent variable* by the experimenter. The term 'quasi' means 'apparently but not really'.
- ***TIP*** A *natural experiment* is not truly a quasi-experiment because the experimenter cannot exert any control over the research environment, whereas in a quasi-experiment the researcher can exert some control.

quasi-interval scale: a term used to refer to a scale of measurement that is 'almost' an *interval* level of measurement but only because it has been *standardised*.

- ***e.g.*** Many psychological test scores, such as IQ test scores, are standardised so that the intervals can be claimed to count as equal. This is not necessarily true. For example, on an IQ test, the 'amount of intelligence' between a score of 85 and 90 may not represent the same thing as between 120 and 125, but we claim that it is the same.

quasi-random sampling: a *sampling method* that appears to be *random* but is not truly random.

■ ***e.g.*** *Systematic sampling.*

questionnaire: a method of written data collection that may form the basis of a research study.

■ See *survey* for a general discussion. Questionnaires may only be suitable for certain kinds of participants — those who are literate and willing to spend time filling in a questionnaire. This may lead to a *biased sample*. Designing questionnaires requires considerable skill but enables large amounts of data to be collected relatively easily.

quota sample: a *sampling technique* similar to a *stratified sample*, but where the sample is not randomly determined.

■ Having identified the key strata, the researcher finds a fixed quota of individuals satisfying each criteria.

■ ***e.g.*** In a study using the interview method, it is decided to collect data from ten people in each age group (10–19, 20–29, etc.). The interviewer just uses the first ten people found in each strata.

race: a subdivision of humankind which has distinct physical characteristics.

■ The concept of race is a *socially sensitive* issue. In terms of *genetics* there are only minor and nonsignificant differences between racial groups. However, in terms of superficial attributes, race is one of the main factors in our *social identity* and in *stereotypes, prejudice* and *discrimination*.

racism: *prejudice* and *discrimination* based on *race*.

radical behaviourism: the purist behaviourist view that there may be mental events but these are not relevant to any explanation of behaviour.

■ This was Skinner's position.

random: a term describing a process or sample where each item has an equal chance of being selected.

random allocation: a method of assigning participants in each *experimental condition/group* using *random* methods to ensure no differences between the groups.

■ Random allocation is important because only then can we be confident that participants in different conditions are comparable.

■ ***TIP*** In a *natural experiment* it is not possible to allocate participants randomly to conditions, which is one reason why this kind of experiment is not a 'true' experiment.

random error: *variables* in an experiment that occur with no pattern.

■ They occur equally in all conditions and are assumed to cancel each other out, unlike *constant errors* which need to be *controlled*.

random number: a number selected using some *random* process.

■ Tables of random numbers are generated by computers or can be found in books on statistics. These are used for *random allocation* procedures.

random sample: a *sampling technique* where every member of the population has an equal chance of being selected; therefore it is an *unbiased* sample.

■ This can be achieved with *random* number tables, or numbers can be drawn from a hat. One should be careful about the assumed lack of bias because the *population* from which the sample is drawn may be biased.

■ ***e.g.*** You could randomly select names from the phone book using random numbers to identify page numbers and then random numbers for the position on the page. However, the population is biased because it only includes those people with telephones.

range: a *measure of dispersion*. The distance between the lowest and highest value in the data sample.

- This has the advantage of being easy to calculate but it is affected by extreme values. This can be overcome using the *semi-interquartile range*.
- ***TIP*** It is desirable to add 1 to the difference, to account for possible measurement error. For example, the range between 4 and 16 is 12. However, the actual scores might have been 4.1 and 16.9, in which case the range was 12.8. Therefore 13 would have been a better estimate of the true range.

raphe nuclei (system): a small group of cells near the *pons* in the *hindbrain*, associated with the *reticular formation*. It is involved in the control of sleep.

- The raphe nuclei (RN) are inactive during *REM sleep*, similar to the *locus coeruleus*. The RN produces *serotonin* which helps to switch off REM sleep.

rapid eye movement sleep: see *REM sleep*.

rational–emotive therapy (RET): a *cognitive therapy* developed by Ellis.

- Irrational beliefs can be turned into rational ones using the ABC model: obstacles or activating events (A) lead to rational or irrational beliefs (B) about the event and finally this leads to emotional or behavioural consequences (C). The therapist aggressively challenges the beliefs so that more rational beliefs are developed.

ratio scale: a *level of measurement*. This is an *interval scale* with a true zero point, as in most measures of physical quantities.

- It is rare in psychological measurement.

raw data/scores: in *research*, the data that have been collected before being summarised in some way, such as placed in a frequency table.

- In other words, the data prior to *statistical* analysis.

reactance: in relation to *social influence*, a person's reaction against attempts to control or restrict his/her personal choices.

- This may be *independent behaviour* but is more likely to be *anti-conformity*.
- ***e.g.*** Everyone is wearing pink this summer so you react against this trend by wearing a different colour because you do not wish to feel pressured.

realistic conflict theory: an explanation for both *prejudice* and *discrimination*, that conflict stems from direct competition between social groups over scarce resources.

- The conflict does not create prejudice — this is pre-existing. Conflict leads to blame being *projected* onto scapegoats and then *intergroup* hostility towards the scapegoats. Scapegoats are likely to be *outgroups*.
- ***e.g.*** At times when unemployment is high, individuals compete for jobs, creating interpersonal conflict and hostility. Hostility is projected onto outgroups and expressed as *discrimination* towards the outgroup.

reality principle: in *psychoanalytic theory*, the drive to accommodate the demands of the environment in a realistic way.

- The *ego* is motivated by the reality principle.

recapitulation theory: a suggestion by Hall (1904) that adolescence is a time of 'storm and stress' during which the child must experience the turbulent history of the human race in order to reach maturity.

- This has little real foundation, but nevertheless the concept of 'storm and stress' has had a lasting influence. See *focal theory*.

recency effect: the influence of recent material.

- (1) In relation to *memory*, a high level of free recall for the last items in a list. Such items are the ones still in *short-term memory* that have not yet decayed. (2) In relation to *interpersonal perception*, the notion that more recent impressions have a stronger influence than those perceived first (*primacy effect*).

recessive gene: see *chromosomes*.

reciprocal altruism: a kind of *altruism* described by Trivers (1971), in which one individual helps another, at some cost to themselves, in the anticipation that the favour will be returned (i.e. reciprocated).

- This is *adaptive* behaviour because ultimately both individuals stand to benefit. It may be an *evolutionarily stable strategy*. However, it does depend on being able to recognise individuals in order to return the favour and it is also vulnerable to cheating.
- ***e.g.*** Grooming, acting as lookouts when feeding.

reconstructive memory: recall is achieved through reconstruction based on *stereotypes* and *schema*.

- Bartlett suggested that recall is not a matter of passively accessing a piece of information and 'reading it' (as suggested by the *multi-store model*). Instead, memory involves active reconstruction. Prior knowledge (schema) and expectations lead to distortions of memory during both storage and recall. This has good support from a variety of studies, such as those concerned with the effects of schema on recall. However, reconstructive theory cannot explain instances when memory is perfectly accurate, such as learning the lines of a poem.

recovered memory: one consequence of *psychotherapy* where an individual recalls a *repressed* and traumatic memory.

- ***e.g.*** The individual may have been sexually abused as a child but such experiences were repressed, leading to some form of mental illness or problem. During psychotherapy the individual is able to recall the earlier memory.
- ***TIP*** There is ongoing debate about the reliability of such recovered memories (thus called '*false memory syndrome*').

reductionist: an argument or theory which reduces complex factors to a set of simple principles.

- Such an approach is very appealing because it makes concepts more manageable and researchable, but at the same time it may result in oversimplification. Rose (1976) suggested that we should think in terms of 'levels of explanation' with reductionist explanations at the most fundamental level. Reductionist explanations are necessary but not sufficient to explain behaviour fully. The converse of reductionism is *holism*, a *gestalt* approach.

■ ***e.g.*** *Physiological* explanations reduce behaviour to a set of nervous impulses. The *theory of evolution* reduces behaviour to a set of functional principles.

reflex: an innate and automatic response to a stimulus.

■ ***e.g.*** Blinking your eye in response to a fast approaching object.

regression: returning to an earlier stage of development as a means of coping with anxiety.

■ *Psychoanalytic theory* proposes that when an adult is in a stressful situation, they may regress back to the psychosexual stage upon which they had previously fixated. The result would be that they behave as they would have done at that age.

reinforcement: an increase in the likelihood of a response because the response resulted in a pleasurable (not aversive) outcome.

■ Positive reinforcement occurs when there is a reward for doing something. For example, you work hard in school because your teacher starts to give everyone sweets for doing well. Negative reinforcement occurs when you avoid something that is unpleasant — but the consequence is pleasurable. For example, you learn to avoid doing the washing up by crying every time your parents ask you. If this ruse is successful it is likely that you will repeat it.

reinforcement–affect model: model of *interpersonal relationships*. We learn to associate positive feelings (affect) with people or situations that reward us (reinforcement).

■ The suggestion is that affection grows when it is associated with rewarding situations. Relationships may break down when the rewards stop.

■ ***e.g.*** You come to fall in love with someone because they are a member of your winning darts team. When the team starts losing, the love turns sour.

reinforcement schedule: the frequency with which a reinforcer is delivered.

■ ***e.g.*** A *continuous reinforcement schedule* is reinforcement every time the right response is made. *Partial reinforcement schedules* are most effective and most resistant to *extinction*, possibly because the animal does not expect the reinforcement on every trial and therefore does not 'notice' its absence so readily.

reinforcer: any response that creates *reinforcement*.

■ *Primary reinforcers* are things that are *innately* reinforcing, such as food or warmth. *Secondary* (or conditioned) *reinforcers* are things that are *learned*, such as money or a hot cooker. They work as reinforcers because at some time they have been paired with a primary reinforcer. Money might have been paired with obtaining food, and the hot cooker might have been paired with pain.

related *t*-test: see *t-test*.

relative deprivation theory: an *intergroup* explanation for *aggressive* behaviour based on the principle that a sense of having less than one feels entitled to leads to aggression.

■ One's feelings of deprivation are judged in terms of what other people might be perceived to have. This exacerbates pre-existing *prejudices* about an *outgroup*, especially at times of economic hardship, and is expressed as aggression towards that group. See also *scapegoat theory, frustration–aggression hypothesis*.

relearning savings: the concept that you may think you have forgotten something, but the next time you try to learn the same thing, it is easier.

- This suggests that some *memory trace* is there but it is either fragmentary or not accessible.

releaser: an *ethological* concept, a feature of the environment that triggers a *fixed action pattern*.

- All releasers are *sign stimuli*, but not all sign stimuli are releasers.
- ***e.g.*** If a young herring gull sees a red spot, this 'releases' a pecking response. The adult herring gull has a red spot on its beak and responds to being pecked with a regurgitation response, thus feeding the young. Young herring gulls will peck at any red spot. The red spot is both a sign stimulus and a releaser. The sight of a male peacock releases certain behaviours in the peahen but only when she is in a hormonally ready state. In this case, the sign stimulus (male peacock's fan) is not always a releaser.

reliability: the extent to which a method of measurement or study produces consistent findings across situations or over time.

- If something produces the same result each time it is used, then it is reliable, like a ruler. (1) Internal reliability is the extent to which a measure is consistent within itself. This can be checked using the *split-half method* or *item analysis*. (2) External reliability. The extent to which a measure varies from one use to another. This can be assessed using *test–retest, inter-rater reliability* and *replication*.

REM rebound: the need for greater amounts of *REM sleep* after a period of sleep deprivation.

- This suggests that REM sleep serves a vital function as distinct from the other *sleep stages*. Individuals who are sleep deprived also need more *slow wave sleep*.

REM sleep: the phase of sleep accompanied by rapid eye movement (REM).

- At the same time the body is in a state of paralysis, leading some to call this *paradoxical sleep*. REM sleep has been associated with dreaming, though people do dream during other *sleep stages*, and they are not always dreaming when awoken from REM sleep. REM sleep has also been associated with production of important proteins such as neurotransmitters, which would explain the *REM rebound* phenomenon. The onset, continuation and end of REM sleep is governed by the *neurotransmitters serotonin* (REM on), *acetylcholine* (REM on and continue) and *noradrenaline* (REM off). The *locus coeruleus* and *raphe nuclei* are also involved. See also *NREM sleep*.

repeated measures design: an *experimental design* where the same participants are used for each condition in the experiment.

- Each participant receives the *experimental treatment* (or *independent variable*) and also receives the *control condition*, or the participant may simply be tested before and after the experimental treatment. Performance on the *dependent variable* is compared. All participants are tested twice, and this may lead to *order effects* which act as a *confounding variable*. It is possible to *control* for these using *counterbalancing*, or leaving a time gap between testing. Alternatively, one can use an *independent measures design* or *matched pairs design*. Repeated measures design has the advantage of needing fewer participants and it offers good control for *participant variables*.

- ***e.g.*** A memory experiment to compare the effects of processing words at the shallow or deep level. Participants are given words in both conditions (shallow and deep) and tested on recall.

repertory grid: see *personal construct therapy*.

replication: the repetition of, for example, a research study to confirm the findings.

- If a finding from a research study is true (valid) it should be possible to obtain the same finding if the study is repeated. This confirms the *validity* of the finding. In order to replicate a study it is necessary to have a record of *standardised procedures*, otherwise any differences in findings may be due to different procedures rather than a lack of validity.

representativeness heuristic: a mental shortcut (*heuristic*) or rule that tells us to make judgements in terms of how likely something is, or how representative a thing is of the general population.

- We tend to make quick judgements about people based on a limited range of cues (*impression formation*) and, in doing so, draw on the most likely or representative explanations.
- ***e.g.*** In an experiment by Tversky and Kahneman (1973), participants were given a description of Steve: 'very shy and withdrawn, invariably helpful … a meek and tidy soul'. They were more likely to label him as a librarian rather than an artist, driver or surgeon because the characteristics are most representative of librarians.

repressed memory: an explanation for *forgetting* in terms of the influence of emotional factors.

- Freud argued that painful or disturbing memories are put beyond conscious recall as a means of *ego defence*. Such memories are those that are emotionally threatening. The memory is inaccessible but not unavailable. Freud aimed to access such memories through *psychoanalysis*.
- ***e.g.*** You might 'forget' an appointment with the dentist or, more seriously, might 'forget' an incident of sexual abuse from your childhood.

repression: in *psychoanalytic theory*, a form of *ego defence* whereby anxiety-provoking material is kept out of conscious awareness as a means of coping.

- Freud proposed that such repressed material surfaces elsewhere such as in dreams or *Freudian slips*.

research: the process of gaining knowledge and understanding via either *theory* examination or *empirical* data collection.

research aims: the purpose of a research study.

research hypothesis: the *hypothesis* written prior to conducting research.

- A general statement of what you aim to prove or disprove.
- ***e.g.*** 'Memory declines with age' (the *experimental hypothesis* would specify the variables more exactly).

research study: refers specifically to the acquisition of knowledge through empirical data collection.

resistant attachment (type C)**:** a type of *insecure attachment* of an infant to its caregiver.

- It is assessed in the *strange situation*. The type C infant is very distressed when the caregiver goes and is not easily consoled on his/her return and may resist contact. The infant seeks comfort and rejects it at the same time.

response bias: the tendency for interviewees to respond in the same way to certain questions.

- ***e.g.*** Certain questions will elicit a *social desirability bias* and this will lead most interviewees to respond in the same way, thus affecting the results. For example, asking parents 'Do you hit your children?' instead of 'What punishment do you use when your child is very naughty?'

response set: a tendency for interviewees to provide the same answers.

- ***e.g.*** Some people prefer to give the answer 'maybe' rather than 'yes'.

restoration theory of dreaming: Oswald's (1980) neurobiological theory of dreaming (*REM sleep*) that suggests that this stage of sleep is the time when the body replenishes its neurochemical supplies.

- This is supported by the fact that babies have more REM sleep than older people, which might be because babies are forming large numbers of neural connections.

restoration theory of sleep: this suggests that *sleep* provides an opportunity for *physiological* and psychological restoration.

- This can explain the effects of sleep deprivation, though it may be that only certain stages of sleep have a restorative function, e.g. *slow wave sleep* and *REM sleep*. See also the *evolutionary theory of sleep*.

restricted code: Bernstein's (1961) concept that some people use a form of language that makes it difficult to elaborate abstract concepts.

- 'Elaborated code' permits users to 'think' more easily and, Bernstein suggested, is more likely to be used by middle-class parents and their children, whereas lower-class families are more likely to use a restricted code.
- ***TIP*** Labov (1969) called this the 'verbal deprivation theory' and claimed that Bernstein had failed to recognise some of the subtleties of non-standard English, and also muddled social and linguistic deprivation.

reticular activating system (RAS): a system in the *midbrain* that links the *hindbrain* to the *forebrain* and monitors ascending (ARAS) and descending (DRAS) signals which are related to arousal.

- Damage to this area causes coma and stimulation causes wakefulness. The RAS contains important neurons related to sleep: those that produce *acetylcholine* (in the *pons*), *noradrenaline* (in the *locus coeruleus*) and *serotonin* (in the *raphe nuclei*).

reticular formation (system): an area in the brain containing the *reticular activating system*, adjacent to the *raphe nuclei* and the *locus coeruleus*.

retina: a layer of cells at the back of the eye that contains the *rods* and *cones*.

retinal ganglion cell: the third layer of cells in the *retina*, closest to the source of light.

retroactive interference (RI): a kind of *forgetting* due to *interference* where a second set of information 'pushes out' earlier material.

- ***e.g.*** In the example given for *proactive interference*, two lists were described: list 1 was AFR-table, STJ-shoe, VKD-lake; and list 2 was AFR-man, STJ-lake, VKD-chair. Retroactive interference would affect your recall of the first list.

retrograde amnesia: see *amnesia*.

retrospective: looking back into the past.

- A study that uses retrospective data is one where the data collected involves participants recalling past events. Such recall is likely to be inaccurate because it is affected by expectations and *schema*.

reverse learning theory: Crick and Mitchison's (1983) neurobiological theory of dreaming (*REM sleep*) whereby dreams are the result of erasing material from the brain which has been accumulated during the day and for which there is only limited space.

- The content of the dream is accidental and has no meaning. It is argued that animals with a very large cortex, such as the spiny anteater and the dolphin, do not need REM sleep because they do not have space problems in their brains.

revolving-door phenomenon: a term to describe the fact that mental patients may be repeatedly discharged and readmitted.

risky shift: a term coined by Stoner (1968) to describe the fact that groups tend to take more risky decisions than the members had previously indicated.

- Subsequent research showed that in fact group decisions tend to polarise the individuals' opinions, i.e. group decisions become more risky, or more cautious. Where the individuals were tending towards a cautious decision the group would make a more cautious decision. This can be explained, for example, in terms of *diffusion of responsibility*, social comparison (each individual finds that their decision was not so risky or cautious), persuasive arguments (the group members collectively develop more arguments for the direction they were tending towards) or *normative social influence*.

ritualisation (ritualised behaviour): behaving in a fixed pattern.

- In animal behaviour, the aim of a ritual is that a particular message is communicated to a receiver. In order to be successful, rituals need to be unambiguous so that the receiver does understand the message.
- ***e.g.*** (1) Ritualised fighting, such as the behaviour of opposing stags which start with a roaring contest, then a parallel walk to assess the size of the opponent, and finally a clash with antlers. The aim of this ritual is to prevent injury, because a weaker animal will back down before the actual fight. (2) Courtship rituals, such as the peacock strutting around with his fan up for a female. By doing this the male is advertising his genetic superiority as indicated by the fact that he can maintain such a plumage.

RNA (ribonucleic acid): a large molecule which is similar to *DNA*.

- RNA acts as a messenger by copying segments of genetic code contained on the strands of DNA (chromosomes) and passing this to other parts of the cell, so that the cell can manufacture appropriate proteins.

rod: a long and thin *photosensitive cell* found in the *retina*. Rods respond to shades of grey, movement and edges.

- The outer region of the retina consists mainly of rods. There are many more rods than *cones* in the retina.

role play: a technique used in research studies where participants are asked to imagine how they would behave in certain situations and act out the part.

- This method has the advantage of permitting one to study certain behaviours which might be unethical or difficult to find in the real world. A major limitation is the fact that individuals behave as they think they should, not how they would behave.
- ***e.g.*** Zimbardo's prison study involved role play from both prisoners and guards, and both took to their parts with alacrity. The result was some degree of concern about the ethics of the study despite using role play.

romantic love: see *passionate love*.

Rorschach test: a *projective* technique for measuring *attitudes* or feelings.

- Respondents are asked to describe a set of standardised ink blots. Their responses are interpreted in terms of, for example, whether they have used the whole blot in their response, whether they have included unusual detail, whether they describe something animate or inanimate and so on.

rote learning: material is reproduced in the exact form in which it was originally presented.

r-strategy: an *adaptive* reproductive behaviour where the individual protects its genetic line by having many offspring and devoting little energy to caring for them.

- The continuance of the individual's genetic line is guaranteed by strength of numbers rather than protecting the offspring.
- ***e.g.*** Fish.
- ***TIP*** The alternative strategy is the *K-strategy*.

runaway process: an explanation for elaborate sexual characteristics such as the peacock's tail.

- Fisher (1930) proposed that females mate with the most attractive males so that their own sons will inherit these characteristics and thus be attractive to other females — the sexy sons hypothesis. It is a 'runaway' process because the characteristics would initially have had some survival value but, because females actively select mates with this feature, it became exaggerated. As long as the advantages outweigh the disadvantages the bizarre characteristic will be perpetuated.
- ***e.g.*** The antlers of a stag.
- ***TIP*** *Handicapping theory* is an alternative suggestion.

sample: part of a population selected such that it is considered to be representative of the *population* as a whole.

- The population may be people (as in an experiment) or behaviours (as in an observational study). The key issue is using a *sampling technique* that draws a representative and unbiased sample.
- ***e.g.*** Selecting a sample of ten participants for your study from a group of 100 people (the population).

sampling bias: some participants (or things) have a greater or lesser chance of being selected than they should, given their frequency in the population.

- The data collected in this way cannot be claimed to be representative of the population and this challenges the *validity* of the research findings.

sampling technique: a method used to derive a representative and unbiased *sample*.

- ***e.g.*** In experimental or correlational studies: *random, systematic, opportunity, volunteer, stratified, quota* and *cluster sampling*. In observational studies: *point, event* and *time sampling*.

scaffolding: in relation to *Vygotsky's theory of cognitive development*, a metaphor for explaining how a tutor or 'expert' can advance a child's thinking by providing a framework on which the child can 'climb' or develop.

- There are five stages in the process: (1) gaining the child's interest; (2) breaking the task down into manageable steps; (3) encouraging and motivating the child until they have become self-motivating; (4) drawing attention to aspects of the problem which will help further progress; (5) demonstration — the tutor finishes the task off so that the learner can imitate this back in a better form. See *peer tutoring*.

scapegoat theory: a *psychoanalytic* explanation for prejudiced behaviour.

- A frustrated individual will become aggressive (*frustration–aggression* theory) and this aggression is *projected* onto other, less powerful people or objects (the scapegoat) rather than being turned onto oneself. Projection is a means of protecting one's *ego* from self-aggression.
- ***e.g.*** Frustration may arise as a result of economic pressures or overcrowding, leading to aggression, projection and discrimination.

scattergram (scattergraph): a *graph* that shows the *correlation* between two sets of data by plotting a dot to represent each pair of scores.

■ The scatter of the dots indicates the degree of correlation between the *covariables*. An inferential test is used to calculate the *correlation coefficient*, a measure of the extent of correlation that exists.

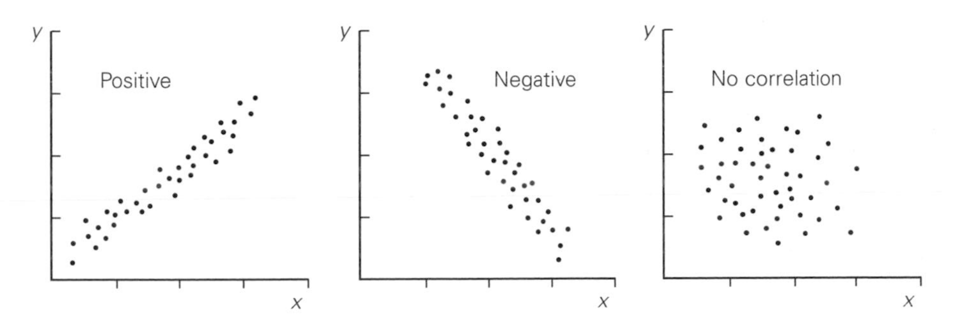

schedule of reinforcement: see *reinforcement schedule*.

schema: an organised packet of information stored in *long-term memory*.

■ A schema is more than a single fact. It is a cluster of related facts. It is a *cognitive* structure that contains knowledge about something, including its attributes and the relations among its attributes. Both schema and *stereotypes* provide a means of organising information and generating future expectations which simplify our social perceptions. At the same time they bias our perceptions because they are affected by culturally shared concepts. The 'schema' is a central concept in psychology. *Piaget* used it (schemata) to describe how knowledge develops. *Cognitive psychologists* use it to explain the organisation of *memory*.

■ ***e.g.*** Your concept of a waitress involves a cluster of facts about the kind of person who is a waitress and what a waitress does.

■ ***TIP*** See also *scripts*.

schema theory: the view that *memory* is affected by *schemas*.

■ This is related to the *reconstructive* theory of memory.

schizophrenia: a severe mental illness where contact with reality and insight are impaired; a kind of *psychosis*.

■ The main symptoms include: hallucinations, delusions, passivity phenomena (something or someone is controlling the individual's thoughts and actions), interference with thoughts (thoughts are being inserted or taken away), movement abnormalities (e.g. catatonia or giggling), emotional disturbances (e.g. blunted affect), language abnormalities (e.g. *echolalia* or word salad), lack of drive, intellectual impairment and mood symptoms. The features of schizophrenia can be divided into positive and negative types. There are four subtypes of the classification that are recognised: paranoid, hebephrenic, catatonic and simple.

■ ***TIP*** Explanations are either biological (e.g. the *diathesis–stress model* and the *dopamine hypothesis*) or psychological (e.g. the *double-bind theory, schizophrenogenic families* and the *EE model*).

schizophrenogenic families: a psychological explanation for schizophrenia, that families with poor communication systems and high conflict act as a causal factor in the development of schizophrenia.

■ It has been suggested that schizophrenogenic mothers are both cold and rejecting, and overprotective and domineering.

science: an organised body of knowledge conducted on objective principles.

scientific method: a series of steps used by scientists to construct and test theories.

■ (1) Make observations which are turned into potential facts. (2) Produce a *theory* based on the set of facts or observations. (3) The theory is then used to generate expectations (*hypotheses*). (4) An *experiment*, or other form of *research*, is designed to test the hypothesis. (5) Data are collected. (6) The theory is adjusted in response to the new set of data.

scientific research: the attempt to discover facts using objective techniques and to organise these facts into theories.

■ ***e.g.*** The *laboratory experiment* is the ideal method of conducting objective research but it is not the only method. Other research methods, such as *naturalistic observation* and *surveys*, aim to be objective and unbiased.

script: a *schema* about an event which serves as a plan for action.

■ A script contains details about the expectations of others and directions about how you should behave.

■ ***e.g.*** You have a script for what to do when going out for dinner to a restaurant.

search image: in relation to *foraging*, the mental image that an animal has of the food it is looking for.

■ Search images may be learned but some are also innate.

seasonal affective disorder (SAD): depression associated with seasonal changes, usually the onset of winter and increased darkness.

■ Some people experience a more manic phase in summer and others experience the reverse — depression in summer. The use of very bright lights may provide an effective treatment.

seasons of a man's life: an account of adulthood presented by Levinson (1966) which identifies potentially stressful periods of transition that are critical for healthy adjustment because they allow the individual to assess what has gone before.

secondary emotions: *emotions* that are learned responses to specific situations.

■ ***e.g.*** Contempt is a blend of the *primary emotions* of anger and disgust. Secondary emotions are specific to certain cultures. For example, 'hagaii' means helpless anguish, tinged with remorse for the Japanese, an emotion not experienced in the Western world.

■ ***TIP*** See *display rules*.

secondary reinforcer: a *reinforcer* that has no natural properties of reinforcement, but through association with a primary reinforcer has become a reinforcer.

- In other words it is *learned* or *conditioned*. It is sometimes called a conditioned reinforcer.
- **e.g.** *Behaviourists* suggest that *attachment* occurs because the mother is a secondary reinforcer. She comes to be associated with the supply of food (a primary reinforcer) and thus becomes reinforcing in her own right.

secure attachment (type B): a strong and contented *attachment* of an infant to its caregiver, related to healthy cognitive and emotional development.

- This is the optimal type of attachment. The securely attached infant is able to function independently because its caregiver acts as a secure base. In the *strange situation* the infant shows a moderate level of seeking closeness to the caregiver. The infant is upset by the caregiver's departure but greets him/her positively on reunion and is readily soothed. It has been suggested that secure attachment has implications for the quality of one's adult relationships (see *internal working model*).

sedative hypnotic drugs: see *anxiolytic drugs*.

selective pressure: in *evolutionary theory*, the force by which one individual is favoured over another.

- A behaviour which is *adaptive* leads to increased reproduction and therefore the *genes* for that behaviour remain in the population. Non-adaptive behaviours reduce reproductive success and therefore the associated genes decrease. Thus adaptiveness acts as a pressure on the selection of certain genes. This is the mechanism of *natural selection*.

selective serotonin reuptake inhibitors (SSRIs): *antidepressant drugs* which block the reuptake of *serotonin*, i.e. they prevent serotonin being taken back into the *terminal boutons* at the neuronal *synapse*.

- **e.g.** Fluoxetine (Prozac), tricyclics.

self: A sense of your unique existence, the inner agent.

- A person's attitudes and feelings about him/herself, and the group of psychological processes that govern behaviour and adjustment. There are a huge number of self-related concepts, some of which are considered below.

self-actualisation: a concept from Rogers' *self theory* and Maslow's *hierarchy of needs*, the notion that each of us has an innate drive for growth and fulfilment of one's potential.

- A lack of *self-esteem* and conditional love blocks the ability to self-actualise because the individual has to strive instead for acceptance. Once you feel accepted, then you can self-actualise. However, this may be an abstract ideal and only appropriate for *individualist* rather than *collectivist* societies.

self-concept: the self as it is currently experienced, all the attitudes we hold about ourselves.

- It incorporates many different things, such as *self-esteem* and *self-efficacy*, and is contrasted with the *ideal self*.

self-disclosure: see *disclosure*.

self-efficacy: the belief in one's abilities as distinct from the abilities themselves.

■ One's confidence in being able to do something. Such confidence generates expectations and these act as *self-fulfilling prophecies.*

■ ***e.g.*** This can be used to explain gender differences — boys and girls learn to have different beliefs about the abilities of boys and girls, and this leads to observed differences in their abilities.

self-esteem: the feelings that an individual has about himself or herself.

■ It is determined largely by the distance between your *self-image* and your *ideal self.* If this gap is large, your self-esteem will be low. Rogers suggested that low self-esteem also results from the conditional love of significant others. Low self-esteem leads to lowered expectations and poorer performance.

self-fulfilling prophecy: a prediction made about another comes true simply because of the expectation.

■ Our beliefs generate expectations which affect our own perception and other people's behaviour. This can be related to *experimenter bias* where the experimenter influences participants' behaviour as a consequence of the experimenter's expectations. See also *confirmatory bias.*

■ ***e.g.*** Guthrie (1938) told the story of a rather unattractive female whose male classmates decided to play a trick. They would all pretend that she was the most sought-after girl in the class and ask her out on a date. By the sixth date everyone felt that she had actually become more attractive. Presumably the attention she received increased her self-confidence and actually made her more attractive.

selfish gene: the idea put forward by Dawkins (1976) that individuals may appear to behave in an altruistic fashion but, at the level of their *genes,* they are in fact 'behaving' selfishly.

■ Note that a gene cannot be said to 'behave'; however, natural selection will favour individuals whose genes promote those behaviours that promote the survival (and reproduction) of the same genetic line (i.e. the individual and their genetic relatives = *kin selection*).

self-monitoring: the degree to which one is aware of one's own behaviour and uses this awareness to regulate one's behaviour.

■ This is an important part of *impression management.* Individuals who are high self-monitors shrewdly tailor their behaviour to fit the social situation.

self perception theory: Bem's (1967) theory of *attribution* that suggests we explain the causes of our own behaviour by observing the behaviour itself.

■ In other words, self-knowledge is not based on any internal insights. We use the same clues to find out about ourselves as we do in finding out about others.

■ ***e.g.*** You come to know yourself as a moody person because you observe that you often behave in a moody manner.

self theory: Rogers's (1951) theory of personality and personality development.

■ The theory is the basis of *client-centred therapy.* The core concept in this theory is the '*self*'. Rogers believed that the individual reacts as an organised whole, rather than a set of *stimulus–response* (S–R) links. The individual has one basic tendency and striving — to actualise. The best vantage point for understanding behaviour is from the internal frame of reference of the individual him/her self. Psychological maladjustment exists when the individual denies experiences which therefore cannot be admitted into the self-structure. Such experiences are 'threats' to self and this leads to psychological tension, blocking self-actualisation. Psychological adjustment occurs when all experiences can be assimilated into a consistent relationship within the concept of self.

semantic: the meaning of a thing.

semantic differential technique: a method of assessing *attitudes* by measuring the affective component using bipolar adjectives.

- This means that an attitude can be evaluated on a number of different dimensions whereas the *Likert scale* only represents one dimension of an attitude (agreement or disagreement).
- ***e.g.*** Respondents are asked to rate, on a scale from 1 to 7, an attitude object, such as a person or word, in terms of a set of bipolar adjectives, such as: generous–ungenerous; humane–ruthless; wise–shrewd.

semantic memory: a subdivision of *long-term memory* which contains organised knowledge about the world and about language, i.e. facts which have meaning.

- It is distinguished from *episodic memory*.

semantic processing: *processing* material according to its meaning.

- The *levels of processing theory* suggests that meaning creates a deeper and more lasting memory than *phonemic processing*. However, this may depend on how recall is tested.
- ***e.g.*** 'Does the word cat fit in this sentence: "Mary laid the table with a ... and fork"?' To do this task requires checking the meaning of the word 'cat'.

semi-interquartile range: a *measure of dispersion* which ignores the more extreme values in a set of data because it focuses on the 50% of scores closest to the median (the 25% above the median and the 25% below the median).

- In other words, it focuses on the central group of values. It is calculated by placing all scores in order and dividing them into equal quarters. This way you can identify the 25th percentile (the score that marks the first quarter of the data) and the 75th percentile (the score that marks three-quarters of the data). The semi-interquartile range is the distance between the 25th and 75th percentile score. The 50th percentile is the median. This measure of dispersion has the advantage of being fairly easy to calculate and it represents the central range. The semi-interquartile range can be represented graphically using a *box-plot* or an *ogive*.

sensitive: in *statistics*, 'sensitive' means more precise, i.e. able to reflect small differences or changes.

- See *powerful*.

sensitive period: a biologically determined period of time during which an animal is most likely to acquire certain behaviours.

■ This is in contrast to the concept of a *critical period*, which suggests a more finite period during which change can take place.

■ ***e.g.*** Sensitive periods have been proposed in the development of *imprinting*, *attachment* and language.

sensitive period hypothesis: see *skin-to-skin hypothesis*.

sensorimotor stage: the first stage in *Piaget's theory of cognitive development*. The infant practises and learns to coordinate sensory and motor responses, such as hand–eye.

sensory memory (SM): the store containing the *sensory* form of a stimulus.

■ This could be an auditory or visual trace. It remains unaltered in the mind for a brief time and then is rapidly lost through spontaneous *trace decay* unless it is further processed and passed to *short-term memory* (STM).

■ ***TIP*** The *multi-store model* proposes that there are three *memory* stores: SM, STM and *long-term memory* (LTM).

separation: the physical loss of a mother-figure, but not necessarily of maternal care, as other people may continue to provide mothering.

separation anxiety: the sense of distress felt by a child when separated from an attachment figure.

■ Separation anxiety first appears developmentally at about the same time that attachments are first formed, i.e. around the age of 7 months. It is taken as a sign of the onset of attachments and used as a means of assessing the strength of attachment (see *strange situation*).

separation protest: the infant's behaviour when separated from a caregiver.

■ A securely attached child first responds to its caregiver's departure with protest. The child cries and appears to be very distressed. They may be easily comforted, but are nevertheless inwardly angry and fearful. It is a natural response to loss and may last for a few hours or a few days. Some insecurely attached infants show no protest when left by their attachment figure. See *protest–despair–detachment (PDD) model*.

serial position effect: the fact that the earlier and later words (as distinct from those in the middle) are recalled best from a list of words.

■ This is illustrated visually with a U-shaped curve. See *primacy effect* and *recency effect*.

serial processing: an *information processing* concept that means someone dealing with one piece of information at one time, as distinguished from *parallel processing*.

■ ***e.g.*** Theories of focused *attention* suggest that information is processed in a serial fashion.

seriation: a child's ability to understand the relationships between objects or concepts, and place them in order.

■ *Piaget* claimed that this kind of thinking was typical of a child in the concrete operational stage of *cognitive development*.

■ ***e.g.*** Being able to use a time line to study history.

serotonin: a *neurotransmitter* of the monoamine (*catecholamine*) group that generally has an excitatory effect.

- High levels of serotonin are associated with sleep, whereas low levels are associated with depression and aggression. (1) Sleep. *Melatonin* is produced by the *pineal gland* as a response to low levels of light. The melatonin increases the production of serotonin which then accumulates in the *raphe nuclei*. The increased level of serotonin shuts down the *reticular system* and results in de-arousal. This triggers the onset of *NREM sleep* and may also act as a REM-off switch. (2) Depression. The *monoamine theory of depression* suggests that depression is the result of depletion of monoamine (*catecholamine*) neurotransmitters such as serotonin. *Antidepressant drugs* aim to increase these neurotransmitters, i.e. they act as *agonists*. (3) Aggression. Low levels of serotonin have been associated with aggression. Sugar substitutes, such as NutraSweet, interfere with serotonin production and have been associated with increased aggression. See also *selective serotonin reuptake inhibitors*.

set: the tendency to respond in a certain manner, in line with expectations built on past experience.

- **e.g.** *Perceptual set, mental set.*

sex chromosomes: see *chromosomes*.

sexual dimorphism: the physical distinction between males and females of the same *species*.

- Females tend to evolve good camouflage for protection against predators whereas males are *naturally selected* for exaggerated characteristics such as antlers or the peacock's feathers (see *sexual selection*). The result is a considerable difference between male and female members of the same species.

sexual imprinting: a young animal learns to recognise the characteristics of their own species (especially the opposite sex) during a *sensitive period* of early development as a consequence of their *innate* drive to *imprint*.

- This is an *adaptive* behaviour because otherwise the individual may not reproduce successfully.

sexual selection: the *natural selection* of traits that are solely concerned with increasing an individual's mating success.

- Any strategy that makes reproduction more likely is bound to be *adaptive* and naturally selected. Darwin claimed that the reason why males and females are so different is because there are different selective pressures on males and females. Males can potentially fertilise hundreds of eggs at little cost to future reproductive success (*r-strategy*) whereas females invest much more per offspring (*K-strategy*). Therefore it makes sense for females to be more choosy and for males to maximise the number of potential reproductions, which leads to competition between males. Therefore in males, selective pressure results in 'intrasexual' strategies, i.e. males compete against other males for the opportunity to mate. In females the pressures tend to be 'intersexual', i.e. females are more concerned with strategies that help them choose a member of the opposite sex.

▪ **e.g.** A male intrasexual strategy can be seen in the elaborate plumage of birds. A peacock's fan must confer distinct reproductive advantages because otherwise why would he invest so much energy in maintaining such a display? It enables a male to compete against other males by advertising his genetic fitness and perhaps securing his selection. A female intersexual strategy can be seen in the coy behaviour of females, which gives them the opportunity to assess a male's fitness.

sexy sons hypothesis: see *runaway process.*

shadowing: a method of testing *focused attention* by asking participants to attend to one particular stimulus and immediately repeating it.

▪ See *dichotic listening task.*

shallow processing: in *levels of processing theory,* shallow processing refers to a minimal amount of *processing,* such as in the physical analysis of information.

▪ *Deep processing* involves extracting meaning and leads to more enduring memories than shallow processing.

▪ **e.g.** Shallow processing might involve *phonemic processing* such as considering whether two words rhyme, or at an even more shallow level one might ask if a word is printed in capital letters.

sham rage: a kind of 'cool' aggression displayed by cats without a *cerebral cortex.*

▪ Such aggression occurs in response to almost anything and supports the idea that aggression is produced *subcortically,* but organised by the *cortex.*

shaping: learned behaviours are gradually built up through a process of successive reinforcements for behaviours that are progressively closer and closer to the desired behaviour.

▪ This explains how an animal acquires complex behaviours.

▪ **e.g.** The *behaviourist* account of language acquisition suggests that children start by producing sounds that sound vaguely similar to the real word. At first this vague approximation is reinforced, but gradually the parent only reinforces those sounds that are more and more similar to the real word.

short-term memory (STM): a temporary place for storing data where it receives minimal processing.

▪ The *multi-store model* proposes that there are three *memory* stores: *sensory memory* (SM), STM and *long-term* memory (LTM). STM has a very limited capacity and short duration, unless it is maintained through rehearsal. Six kinds of evidence are provided that distinguish STM from LTM: capacity (7±2 chunks in STM), duration (under 30 seconds in STM), coding differences (more acoustic coding in STM and less semantic), *serial position effect* (*recency effect* related to STM), evidence from studies of brain damage (*retrograde amnesia* affects STM), and differences in forgetting (*trace decay* in STM). The *working memory model* was an attempt to further subdivide STM. It portrays STM as a kind of work station for dealing with current material.

significance: the extent to which something is important. See *level of significance.*

sign stimulus: an *ethological* concept, an environmental cue that leads an animal to produce a *fixed action pattern.*

- *e.g.* The egg is a sign stimulus to the greylag goose and triggers off the egg retrieval behaviour (see *fixed action pattern*).

sign test: an *inferential* and *non-parametric test* of the difference between related samples.

- The reasons for selecting this test are: (1) a test of difference is required; (2) the samples used are related; (3) the data are at the nominal *level of measurement.*

single blind: a research procedure where the *participant* is prevented from knowing the key details of the experiment.

- In other words, they are rendered 'blind' to certain aspects of the experiment. This is done to reduce the effects of expectations on the *dependent variable.* In general, *deception* is used when explaining the experiment to the participants. See *double blind.*

single participant design: an *experiment* that uses one participant only.

- Sometimes it may only be feasible to use one participant, though this clearly affects the extent to which the results of the experiment can be *generalised.*
- *e.g.* Little Albert (conditioned emotional responses).
- *TIP* A single participant design is not the same as a case study because the former involves the manipulation of an *independent variable* and a case study involves collecting data about an individual.

situational explanation: this accounts for behaviour in terms of aspects of the environment.

- *e.g.* A situational explanation for the behaviour of prison guards in Zimbardo's (1971) study would be that the prison environment made them aggressive.
- *TIP* Contrast this with *dispositional explanation.*

situationalism: Mischel's view that *personality* is not an enduring trait. This is in contrast with other personality theories.

- Mischel argued that, in reality, people are only consistent in the same situations, but their behaviour varies from one situation to another. Any regularity of behaviour is due to the fact that we tend to find ourselves in similar situations. The notion of consistency is a useful tool in organising our perceptions about ourselves and others. But this is the way we think about personality, which according to Mischel does not really exist. We learn, through selective *reinforcement,* what behaviours are appropriate in what situations.
- *e.g.* Someone may be shy in class but quite *extrovert* amongst close friends.

situational variable: a feature of the research setting that varies and may act as a *confounding variable.*

- These may be *controlled* through the use of *standardised procedures.*
- *e.g.* Noise, lighting conditions, time of day.

skewed distribution: a frequency distribution where the data are not spread symmetrically around the mean.

- The bulk of the scores are concentrated at one end or the other. Data distributed in this way should not be considered for use with a *parametric test*.

Skill AO1: a cluster of skills used to assess examination answers, its focus is on knowledge and understanding.

- ***TIP*** The better you are able to organise the material and structure your answer, the more it appears that you are confident about what you know; it also shows that you understand it. An answer which is 'list-like' lacks detail and looks as if the student knows the material but doesn't actually understand it very well.

Skill AO2: the other main assessment criterion, which rewards *analysis* and *evaluation*.

- The intention is to encourage higher-level students to do more than just regurgitate knowledge. They should also recognise and express the 'value' of that knowledge. This can be achieved in many ways. (1) Positive: e.g. useful applications of the research, relevance to real life, *empirical* support, agreement with other theories. (2) Negative: e.g. failure to be demonstrated empirically, flaws in the argument, undesirable consequences, e.g. social sensitivity, contrast with other theories. Other features of Skill AO2: commentary, interpretation, effective use, appropriate selection.

skin-to-skin hypothesis: the view that skin-to-skin contact between mothers and their newborn infants promotes *attachment*.

- The period immediately after birth may be a *sensitive period* due to the presence of hormones. This would make both mother and infant more susceptible to irreversible *learning*.

sleep: a state when the body is relaxed, the nervous system is inactive and there is a loss of consciousness.

- There are two main theories to explain why animals sleep: the *restoration theory* and the *evolutionary theory of sleep*. See *REM sleep*, *NREM sleep*.

sleep stages: during sleep, brain activity changes and can be described in terms of stages, a regular *ultradian rhythm*.

- The first four stages are called *NREM sleep*. In stages I–III brain waves increase progressively in amplitude and have lower frequency. Stage I is associated with alpha waves (8–12 Hz), and stage II has theta waves (3–7 Hz) and sleep spindles (12–14 Hz in bursts that last at least half a second). Stage III is a continuation of this slowing down but external disturbance may prolong this stage or cause the individual to return to stage II or I, or even wake up. Stage IV is called *slow wave sleep* or deep sleep. There are large waves of very low frequency (delta waves — less than 2 Hz, i.e. less than 2 per second). After stage IV the individual goes back up the 'sleep staircase' to stage II and then there is a period of *REM sleep*, lasting for about 10–15 minutes. Sleep stages alternate through the night, starting with a rapid descent into slow wave sleep, followed by progressively increased episodes of lighter sleep and REM sleep. Each complete cycle takes about 90 minutes.

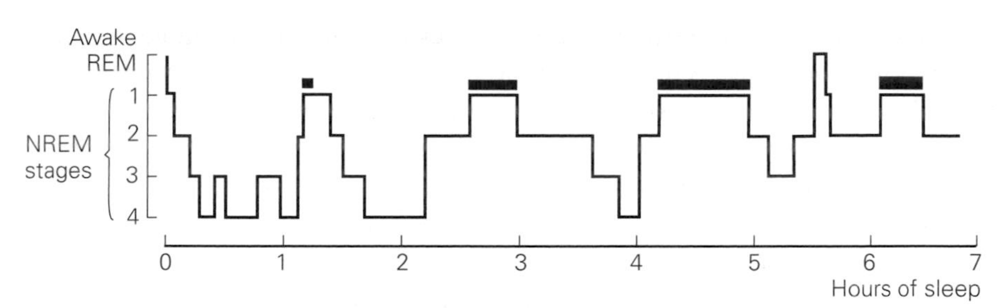

Sleep stages alternate through the night, starting with a rapid descent into deep sleep, followed by progressively increased episodes of lighter sleep and REM sleep (shaded areas).

sleep staircase: see *sleep stages*.

slow wave sleep (SWS): also called deep sleep, a *sleep stage* which probably serves an important core function.

- Growth hormone is secreted during SWS, as well as other restorative activities. This is what makes it *core sleep*. It is very difficult to wake someone up during this stage, which occurs more at the start of the night than towards morning. SWS is characterised by little brain activity and little sensory input to the *cerebral cortex*. The brain waves are highly synchronised, large amplitude delta waves.

sneak copulation: discrete copulation by secondary males when the first male is not looking.

- This is a useful *adaptive* strategy for secondary males. In order to counteract this, primary males must be very possessive of their females.
- ***e.g.*** Some male elephant seals pretend to be females and are then able to join a harem and engage in sneak copulation when the bull is occupied elsewhere.

sociability: the tendency to seek and enjoy the company of others.

- It has been suggested that this is an *innate* feature of our *temperament*. In other words, babies are born more or less sociable. A sociable baby will find it easier to form relations and become *attached* to his/her caregiver(s). Such babies may then be looked after better (in terms of food and protection). Therefore sociability is an *adaptive* behaviour because it is likely to promote survival.

social behaviour: interactions between two or more members of the same species.

- ***e.g.*** *Antisocial* and *prosocial behaviour, conformity, obedience, prejudice.*

social cognition: an attempt to use the models and methods of *cognitive psychology* to discover how cognition (i.e. thinking, beliefs, perception) influences social behaviour.

- The social world is less 'real' than the physical world and we interpret the information presented to our senses. In doing this 'interpreting', we bend reality according to our beliefs, expectations, *stereotypes* and so on.
- ***e.g.*** *Impression formation, attribution theory, social identity theory.*

social constructionism: a radical new approach in psychology, which takes the view that reality is socially constructed rather than being objective.

- Social constructionists disagree with the traditional view that psychologists should aim to make objective and unbiased observations about people. In fact social constructionists do not believe that it is possible to make such observations, because we can only see the world as it is represented in our culture and language. In order to understand behaviour, psychologists should seek explanations in terms of the social context in which behaviour occurs. This means that we should analyse research through, for example, *discourse analysis*.

social contagion: an explanation for *crowd behaviour*, the transmission of social behaviour from one person to another.

- Once antisocial behaviour has emerged, it is 'catching'. Individuals *imitate* the behaviour of others and it becomes the *norm* of the crowd.

social desirability bias: the tendency for a respondent to provide socially desirable answers on questionnaires or in interviews so that they appear in a 'better light'.

- This inevitably reduces the *validity* of the research findings. There are various methods used to try to detect this, such as a *lie scale*.

social disengagement theory: the view proposed by Cumming and Henry (1961) that psychological well-being in old age is promoted by a gradual withdrawing from personal contacts and world affairs.

- This may be true for some individuals but others thrive on being more active (see *activity theory*).

social exchange theory (SET): an explanation of behaviour in terms of costs and rewards, an 'economic' theory.

- (1) Social exchange theory is used to explain formation, maintenance and dissolution of *interpersonal relationships*. Homans (1961) suggested that, before embarking on a relationship, one calculates the potential profits in a relationship by working out the rewards minus the costs. Rewards include anything that makes you feel good and costs are anything that is unpleasant. Thibaut and Kelley (1959) suggested that it is not the actual costs and rewards that matter, but the comparative levels. Thus we assess costs and rewards by using (a) a comparison level (CL) which estimates the amount of rewards we think we deserve from the relationship, based on a comparison between what we have and what we expect out of relationships, and (b) a comparison level for alternatives (CLalt) which is the amount of costs and rewards available in other, alternative relationships. Criticisms of this model include the fact that it is very *mechanistic* and that costs and rewards are not so easy to quantify. (2) With regard to old age, social exchange theory has also been used by Dowd (1975) to explain the route to contentment in older people. Individuals enter into an informal contract when they get older, for example they exchange being an active member of society for increased leisure time and a pension.

social facilitation: the enhancement of an individual's performance when working in the presence of other people (an audience), a form of *social influence*.

- Social facilitation only occurs in some situations, when a task is relatively practised (or 'dominant'). When an individual has to perform a novel or difficult ('nondominant') task, then the presence of others reduces performance. This is called *social inhibition*. This can be explained in terms of *evaluation apprehension* and *arousal*. Both of these enhance performance when the task is easy, but reduce it when the task is difficult (see *Yerkes–Dodson law*). Social facilitation can occur when co-acting (working side-by-side) or in the presence of an audience (the *audience effect*). See also *social loafing*.

social identity theory (SIT): the view that *social perception* is influenced by social identity and social identity is a key part of personal identity.

- There are three causal processes in social identity. (1) Categorisation. We group people into social categories, which leads to the formation of ingroups and *outgroups*. This categorisation process simplifies interpersonal perception. (2) Comparison. Social comparisons are made between ingroups and outgroups in order to increase *self-esteem* (*ingroup favouritism* and *outgroup bias*). (3) Cognition. Social beliefs (cognitions) generate different social behaviours and perceptions.

social impact theory: a way of explaining *social influence* in terms of cumulative factors, proposed by Latané and Wolf (1981).

- Impact refers to the effect of one body on another and is jointly determined by strength (e.g. numbers of people present, consistency of message), status (high or low) and immediacy (the closer you are, physically or psychologically, to the influencer the more effect their message will have). This can explain both majority (*conformity*) and *minority influence*.

social influence: the effects one person or group has on the attitudes or behaviour of another.

- ***e.g.*** *Conformity, crowds, leadership, obedience.*

social inhibition: a form of *social influence*, where the presence of others results in a decrease in individual performance.

- The reverse of *social facilitation*. Inhibition occurs when tasks involve nondominant (novel or difficult) tasks or when quality rather than quantity is required. See also *social loafing*.

socialisation: the process by which individuals learn the social behaviours of their *culture*.

- The 'social behaviours' include *morals*, social skills, norms, *language* and so on.

social learning theory: the view that behaviour can be explained in terms of direct and indirect *reinforcement*.

- This is a modification of traditional *learning theory*. Learning theory proposes that we learn through association (*classical conditioning*) and direct reinforcement (*operant conditioning*). Social learning theory proposed that learning also occurs through indirect or *vicarious reinforcement*. In order for such learning to take place the individual must observe another person's behaviour (observational learning) and *imitate* this in the future. The fact that the behaviour is imitated means that a mental image (model) must have been stored. Thus social learning theory involves internal mental (*cognitive*) processes. The term 'modelling' is used to describe the process of imitation because the individual forms a mental model which is then used to generate subsequent behaviour. The concept of *identification* is also important. The individual is more likely to imitate someone that he/she identifies with, such as a parent or a film star.

social loafing: the reduction of individual effort when people work in groups as compared with when they work alone.

■ This involves the interaction of individuals rather than, in the case of *social inhibition*, the influence of others. Social inhibition can be explained in terms of arousal, whereas social loafing is probably due to *deindividuation* and a lack of coordination between the individual performances.

■ ***e.g.*** In a tug of war team the actual pull exerted does not equal the sum of all the individuals' maximum potential pulls. This was demonstrated by Ringlemann (1913 — the Ringlemann effect) when he attached a pressure gauge to a rope and measured the pull exerted by teams and individuals.

socially sensitive research: research that has direct *social* consequences.

■ Such research creates particular problems because it often concerns issues over which there is little agreement in society generally and therefore people look to psychologists for 'facts'. However, the data produced in psychological research are never certain and may be unreliable. Furthermore, the data are often based on *correlational* analyses and cannot inform us about cause and effect relationships. Nevertheless, such research may have wide-reaching consequences.

social perception: any aspect of *perception* that has a social element.

■ The process is similar to that of visual perception. Both are influenced by expectations and past experience. However, in the case of physical perception there is a physical reality against which to test one's perceptions.

social psychology: the study of *social behaviour*, i.e. how two or more members of the same *species* interact and influence each other.

■ This branch of psychology includes the study of *social cognition, social influence, interpersonal relationships, prosocial* and *antisocial behaviour*.

social readjustment rating scale (SRRS): a *psychometric test* devised by Holmes and Rahe (1967) to assess the *stress* experienced by an individual in the recent past.

■ The scale was compiled by analysing 5000 patient records and identifying 43 *life events* which appeared to precede illness. Then 400 people were asked to rate the events using marriage as a reference point with an arbitrary value of 500. The 43 events were listed in order and each given a value in terms of 'life change units' (LCUs). The LCU is an estimate of the amount of stress you have experienced. To use the scale one must circle those events that have happened to you in the last 12 months, and this can then be correlated with some measure of illness to assess the relationship between stress and illness.

■ ***e.g.*** On the final scale, death of a spouse is 100 LCUs, marriage is 50 and Christmas is 12.

■ ***TIP*** Both negative and positive events require readjustment.

social releaser: a social behaviour or characteristic which elicits a caregiving reaction.

- Bowlby suggested that these were *innate* and *adaptive*, and critical in the process of forming *attachments*.
- ***e.g.*** Smiling, crying, the 'baby face' (large eyes, small nose, big forehead).

social representation: a shared belief within a social group that is used to explain social events.

- These explanations evolve through conversation and media reports (i.e. non-specialist and specialist individuals moulding our knowledge). Eventually the explanations are regarded as 'fact', though they still may continue to evolve.
- ***e.g.*** Individuals' knowledge about AIDS is in part based on 'fact' but more largely derived from various social representations of the facts. A 'conservative' representation would suggest that AIDS is related to membership of social fringe groups and promiscuity. A 'liberal' view would suggest that AIDS is a more mainstream phenomenon. Such representations affect the way subsequent data are processed and remembered so that the representations are self-perpetuating.

social skills training: a *behavioural* approach to treatment that involves teaching appropriate social skills by using rewards, *modelling* and *conditioning*.

- ***e.g.*** Programmes designed to help disruptive pupils which teach skills such as listening, apologising, and dealing with teasing and bullying.

sociobiological theory of interpersonal relationships: this suggests that the main reason why individuals form relationships is for reproduction.

- Relationships are a kind of *adaptive* behaviour which differs in males and females. Men produce many sperm and usually do not need to rear their young, whereas the opposite is true for females, who invest much more in each reproduction. Sociobiological theory therefore predicts that men look for attractive females who can bear good offspring, thus enhancing the males' genetic line. Females, on the other hand, seek males with resources to help provide for the female during pregnancy and child-rearing. This can only explain reproductive relationships and not those between same-sex partners or close friends.

sociobiology: an approach to explaining social behaviour in terms of *evolutionary* processes.

- The key difference between sociobiology and the *theory of evolution* is that the former uses the *gene* rather than the individual as the basic unit of evolution.
- ***e.g.*** Sociobiologists suggest that animals are *altruistic* because such behaviour benefits their gene pool rather than the individual. This is *kin selection* in addition to *natural selection*. The animal behaves the way it does in order to promote the survival of genetic relatives. Kin selection promotes *inclusive fitness* — it promotes the survival of all genetic relatives, not just one individual. The theory of evolution was centred on the concept of individual fitness.

socio-emotional leader: see *contingency theory*.

sociopath: see *antisocial personality disorder*.

soft determinism: see *determinism*.

somatic: related to the body ('soma' = body).

■ Somatic treatments for mental illness involve physical intervention, such as *electroconvulsive shock therapy*, the use of *drugs* and *psychosurgery*.

Spearman's rho: an *inferential* and *non-parametric test* of the *correlation* between covariables.

■ The reasons for selecting this test are: (1) a test of correlation is required; (2) the data do not fit *parametric* assumptions (e.g. the distribution is not *normal* and the *level of measurement* is ordinal).

species: a group of *organisms* that share the same *genetic* characteristics and are able to breed successfully among themselves.

speciesism: the view that prejudices against 'lower' species are based on arbitrary and unreasonable assumptions.

■ It is increasingly recognised that many primates are genetically very close to human beings and that they share key characteristics, such as consciousness. This may extend to other animals. Such prejudices against other species allow us to deny certain rights to other groups of animals, in the same way as humans once denied rights to people of different racial groups (*racism*).

split-brain procedure: a surgical procedure to separate the two *cerebral hemispheres* by severing the *corpus callosum*.

■ This is done, for example, to alleviate the symptoms of severe *epilepsy*. An epileptic fit is caused when there is a storm of electrical activity in the brain. In severe cases, severing the connections between the right and left hemisphere to limit the electrical storm reduces the fits which in themselves cause brain damage. The resulting 'two brains in one head' permits some interesting research to be conducted on the brain. When the fibres are cut, the patient cannot tell you what they see in their left visual field (speech is produced in the left hemisphere and the left visual field is connected to the right *visual cortex*). Such research can be criticised because it relies on data from abnormal brains; however, it has been confirmed in other studies of normal people who had one hemisphere of their brain anaesthetised using a harmless drug (the Wada test).

split-half method: a method of assessing the internal *reliability* of a psychological test, i.e. the extent to which the test measure is consistent within itself.

■ The items on the test are *randomly* assigned to two halves so that each half is equivalent. The same person does both sub-tests simultaneously and their scores are compared to see if they are similar, which would suggest that the test items are reliable.

spontaneous recovery: in *conditioning*, when a new *stimulus–response link* reappears after having been extinguished.

■ If a *conditioned* response is not reinforced, it is extinguished. But after a rest period the response may reappear.

spontaneous remission: recovering from an illness (or experiencing reduced symptoms) as a consequence of the passage of time rather than any treatment.

sport psychology: the branch of *applied psychology* that seeks to understand psychological influences on sporting behaviour.

- The concerns of sport psychology include the effects of personality, aggression, motivation and self-confidence, arousal and anxiety, on sporting performance. It also involves the study of group behaviour, leadership and imagery.

S–R link: see *stimulus–response link*.

standard deviation (σ): a *measure of dispersion* which reports the spread of the data around the *mean*.

- The standard deviation is calculated by working out the difference between each value and the mean. These differences are squared and then the mean of these squared differences is worked out. This produces the *variance* for the data. The standard deviation is calculated by obtaining the square root of the variance. (This last step is done so that the standard deviation is of the same magnitude as the actual deviations.) The advantage of using the standard deviation is that it is the most accurate measure of dispersion, because it takes the distance between all values into account. The disadvantage is that it requires calculation and does not reflect the range. It is useful to give both the standard deviation and the range for any set of data. Note: the *mean deviation* is a different measure of dispersion.

standardised instructions: the predetermined instructions given to each participant before and during a research study.

- These are kept identical to help to prevent *experimenter bias*. If the instructions varied, this might act as a *confounding variable*.
- ***e.g.*** One group of participants might be told that they should try as hard as possible to recall the words given in the stimulus list, whereas another group was told to do the test quickly. This might lead to better performance from the first group.

standardised procedure: a fixed series of actions conducted in a certain order and manner.

- In a psychometric test, it is important that every individual is tested in the same way and under the same conditions. The smallest variations may have important effects. In a research study, the same procedures are used with every participant to ensure that no *confounding variables* affect the *dependent variable*. Such confounding variables might include the researcher's manner towards participants, *experimenter bias*, and the setting of the study. Standardised procedures also include the use of *standardised instructions*.
- ***TIP*** Standardised procedures are important for *replication*.

standardised tests: the result of using psychological tests with large groups of individuals in order to establish a set of 'standards' or *norms*.

- This means that, later, any individual taking the test can be compared with the norms and their score given in terms of how far above or below average they are. The drawback is that the population used to establish the standard may be *biased* and therefore the individual may be unfairly compared with this standard. For example, the individual might belong to a different *culture* or *sub-culture* and differences in performance would not be due to individual characteristics but instead to differences between the populations.

standard score: a score that has been standardised.

■ This enables a score on one test to be compared with a score on another test because both are expressed in terms of the number of standard deviations that the score is from the mean for their own population. Also called a z-score.

state-dependent recall: see *mood-dependent recall*.

statistical significance: see *level of significance*.

statistics: a method of collecting, summarising and analysing data for the purpose of drawing some conclusions about the data.

■ ***e.g.*** *Descriptive* and *inferential statistics*.

stem and leaf diagram: a way of representing data in a histogram-like form but retaining the actual data.

■ The advantage of this method is that it often reveals patterns in the data. The 'stem' is the element that certain data items share. For example, the scores 1.3, 1.5, 1.9 all share the unit 1. The scores 23, 25, 29 all share the base of 20. So that is their stem. The 'leaf' is the individual element to each score. In both examples the leaves would be 3, 5 and 9.

stereotype: a social perception of an individual in terms of some readily available feature, such as their group membership or physical attractiveness, rather than their personal attributes.

■ Stereotyping is a feature of our *cognitive processing*. Stereotypes summarise large amounts of information and provide an instant picture from meagre data. We are 'cognitive misers' and stereotypes allow us to conserve cognitive energy. Stereotypes can be positive and can be at least partly accurate. The fact that they contain a 'grain of truth' leads to their perpetuation (see *confirmatory bias*). On the other hand, stereotypes are at least partly inaccurate because they do not allow for exceptions and are based on superficial characteristics. They tend to be irrational, resistant to change and to lead to prejudice and discrimination.

■ ***e.g.*** If a character is described as 'an Italian mother' we all have an immediate impression of this individual, even if one has never met an Italian woman.

stimulation effect: the view that watching television is beneficial because it is an ideal medium for educational information.

■ Contrast this with the *displacement effect*.

stimulus: a feature of the environment that elicits a response (*stimulus–response link*).

■ Stimuli may also arise from within the organism.

stimulus discrimination: *learning* to differentiate between two stimuli that are similar, because one is associated with a conditioned stimulus or reward and the other is not.

■ ***e.g.*** A pigeon will learn to peck at a circle rather than an elliptical shape if only the circle is rewarded.

stimulus generalisation: see *generalisation.*

- ***e.g.*** A pigeon is rewarded for pecking at a circle and will generalise this to all circular-shaped objects such as an ellipse, until it finds that no reward is received from such objects — then the pigeon will discriminate.

stimulus–response link: *learning.*

- It is the outcome of *conditioning;* a stimulus has become associated with a new response.

stooge: see *confederate.*

'storm and stress': a phrase coined to describe *adolescence.* See *recapitulation theory.*

stranger anxiety: the distress experienced by a child when approached by a stranger.

- Stranger anxiety first appears developmentally at about the same time that attachments are first formed, i.e. around the age of 7 months. It is taken as a sign of the onset of attachments, like *separation anxiety.*

Strange Situation: a method of *controlled observation* used to test the security of an infant's attachment to a caregiver. It has been adapted to be used with older children.

- The procedure consists of seven episodes each lasting about 3 minutes. (1) The mother (or caregiver) carries the infant into a *laboratory* room. She puts the infant on the floor and sits quietly in a chair. (2) A stranger enters the room and talks with the mother. The stranger gradually approaches the infant with a toy. (3) The mother leaves. The stranger interacts with the child if the infant is passive or distressed. (4) The mother returns and the stranger leaves. (5) After the infant has again begun to play, the mother also departs. (6) The stranger re-enters the room and behaves as described in 3. (7) The mother returns and the stranger leaves. The key features are: what the child does when it is left by the caregiver (*separation anxiety*); the child's behaviour at reunion; responses to the stranger (*stranger anxiety*); and willingness to explore.
- ***TIP*** There are objections related to the validity of this measure, both in terms of whether it actually measures something inherent in the child (or whether it is just measuring one relationship) and to what extent it is culturally biased. In some cultures an infant is never left with a stranger.

stratified sample: a *sampling technique* where groups of participants are selected in proportion to their frequency in the population.

- The aim is to identify sections of the population, or strata, that need to be represented in the study. If employment status was regarded as an important *participant variable,* then the same proportions of employed and unemployed people should be represented in the sample as in the actual population. This ensures representativeness. The actual sample of employed people would then be *randomly* selected from the 'employed' population, and the same for the 'unemployed' population. If the sample is not randomly selected from the strata it is then a *quota sample.*

■ ***e.g.*** If unemployment levels were 10%, then your sample should contain 10% unemployed and 90% employed people, both randomly selected.

stress: a state of physiological arousal produced by the demands of the environment (*stressors*).

■ The term 'stress' is used in engineering terms to describe a force which causes some significant modification of form to a system, such as stress causing a bridge to become deformed. Selye (1936) first suggested the psychological use of the term 'stress' to describe how an animal responds to 'acute nocuous agents' such as cold, surgical injury, excessive exercise, or sublethal doses of various drugs. Selye described the *general adaptation syndrome* which suggested that stress is, initially, an *adaptive* response which is vital to the survival of an animal. The *autonomic nervous system* is activated and this makes the animal ready for *fight or flight*. Individuals who have no *innate* stress response would die. Stress can also be understood in terms of an interaction between the individual and his/her environment. Cox (1978) produced a *transactional model* of stress which proposed that stress is only experienced when the perceived demands of the environment are greater than the individual's perceived ability to cope.

■ ***e.g.*** If you have never been in an aeroplane before you may find the experience stressful. This is because the perceived demands are greater than your ability to cope, whereas a frequent flyer does not experience stress.

stress inoculation therapy: a *cognitive therapy* devised by Meichenbaum.

■ A technique to reduce stress through the use of stress management techniques and self-statements which aim to restructure the way the client thinks.

stress management: techniques to take charge of stress responses and regulate them so they are less harmful.

■ ***e.g.*** *Anxiolytic drugs, biofeedback, hardiness training, stress inoculation therapy.*

stressors: events which throw the body out of balance and force it to respond.

■ ***e.g.*** Environmental factors such as noise, cold, pain, overcrowding, pollution, or viruses; *life events* such as marriage, death of a loved one, redundancy.

striate cortex: the outer surface of the *cortex* where the cells are organised in columns.

Stroop effect: the conflict experienced when trying to perform two conflicting tasks.

■ Stroop (1935) found that participants were slower when naming the colours of a list of colour words when the colour and the word were in conflict ('red' written in orange ink) than when they were not in conflict ('red' written in red ink). This is because reading is an automatic activity (see *automatic processing*).

structuralism: any theory that aims to study the relationship among phenomena rather than the phenomena themselves and the systems formed by these relations.

■ ***e.g.*** The structure of the eye, rather than how vision works (*functionalism*).

subconscious: an alternative word for the *preconscious*.

subcortical: a description of parts of the frontal region of the *brain* that are not part of the *cerebral cortex*. They lie under the cortex.

■ ***e.g.*** The *thalamus, hypothalamus, pituitary gland, hippocampus* and *limbic system*, and the *basal ganglia*.

sub-culture: a term used to refer to subgroups within one *culture*.

■ A sub-culture is a group of people who share a distinct set of rules, morals and so on. It is not always possible to distinguish between cultures and sub-cultures. For example, are the Scottish a separate cultural group from the British or are they (and the English) actually sub-cultures? In practice the same principles apply to cultures and sub-cultures.

subject: a non-human animal *participant* in a research study.

■ The distinction between 'subject' and 'participant' is one of passive involvement. A subject is ruled by its superior. It does not seem appropriate or desirable to think of human subjects in psychological research.

subjective: from a personal view, likely to be *biased*. See *objective*.

superego: a personality structure identified in *psychoanalytic theory*. It is the part of the mind that embodies one's conscience and sense of right and wrong.

■ Freud proposed that the superego forms during the *phallic stage*, around the age of 3. At this time the *id* derives satisfaction from the genital region, and is also becoming aware of a three-way conflict between the child and its parents. This conflict is resolved differently in boys and girls (see *Oedipus complex, penis envy, Electra complex*). For both sexes, resolution leads to *identification* with the same-gender parent. Identification results in taking on the attitudes and ideas of that other person, including their notions of right and wrong.

■ ***TIP*** Freud referred to the ego as 'I' and the superego as 'above I'.

superordinate goal: an aim which is shared by all group members.

■ This serves to unite a group and encourage cooperation, rather than emphasising individual goals and competition. This is useful in reducing *prejudice* and *discrimination*, as employed in the *jigsaw method*.

suprachiasmatic nucleus (SCN): a small group of neurones in the *hypothalamus* that act as a *biological clock* and help regulate the *circadian rhythm*.

■ The SCN rhythms are set by: (1) Light. *Axons* from the optic nerve extend into the SCN so that light can reset the biological clock. Light is a *zeitgeber*. The SCN is called 'supra-chiasmatic' because it is located just above the *optic chiasma*. (2) Protein synthesis allows the SCN to generate rhythms itself, so that there is a free-running clock which can be reset by light. (3) *Melatonin* which is produced in the afternoon causes a phase advance, i.e. makes you feel sleepy earlier. Melatonin in the morning causes a phase delay.

surface structure: see *transformational grammar*.

survey: a method of data collection that may form the basis of a research study.

- 'Survey' is an umbrella term for *interviews* and *questionnaires*. They are all essentially questionnaires because they involve questions. Such methods make it possible to collect data that are not accessible through direct observation. However, people do not always know what they think and therefore their answers may be influenced by *interviewer bias* and *social desirability bias*. Ethical considerations include issues of privacy and confidentiality. The differences between surveys, interviews and questions lie in: (1) The amount of structure. Questionnaires tend to be more structured because of their written form. In a structured interview all or most of the questions are decided beforehand. An unstructured interview starts out with some general aims, and lets the interviewee's answers guide subsequent questions. It has the advantage of collecting a rich amount of data but requires well-trained interviewers and may lack *reliability* because different interviewers ask different questions (low *inter-interviewer reliability*). (2) The mode of data collection. Interviews are conducted face-to-face whereas surveys may be conducted at a distance, such as by post or telephone, and may be affected by *interviewer bias*. Written questionnaires enable large amounts of data to be collected relatively easily, though there may be problems with *sampling bias*. (3) Kind of data. Unstructured interviews are more likely to produce *qualitative* data whereas structured questionnaires with closed questions produce *quantitative* data.
- ***TIP*** In postal surveys there is often quite a low rate of return. This means that the data tend to be collected from a *volunteer sample* — individuals with special characteristics.

SWS: see *slow wave sleep*.

sympathetic nervous system (sympathetic branch): a division of the *autonomic nervous system* which activates internal organs for vigorous activities and emergencies, such as the 'fight or flight' response.

- It consists of nerves that control, for example, increased heart rate and breathing, and decreased digestive activity. The sympathetic branch works in opposition to the *parasympathetic* branch of the ANS.
- ***e.g.*** Other examples include the dilation of the pupils, release of glucose for activity, and contraction of the bladder — all the things that happen when you feel 'excited'.
- ***TIP*** *Adrenaline* is a hormone that has the same effect on target organs as the sympathetic nervous system.

synapse: the junction between two neurones.

- The synapse includes the *terminal bouton*, the *synaptic cleft* and the *postsynaptic membrane*. *Neurotransmitters* are released from the synaptic vesicles in the presynaptic neurone when the vesicle is activated by a raised *action potential* in the neurone. The neurotransmitter enters the synaptic cleft and acts on the postsynaptic membrane or another organ.
- ***TIP*** A picture is worth a thousand words! Sometimes it is more helpful to produce a drawing as an additional means of explanation.

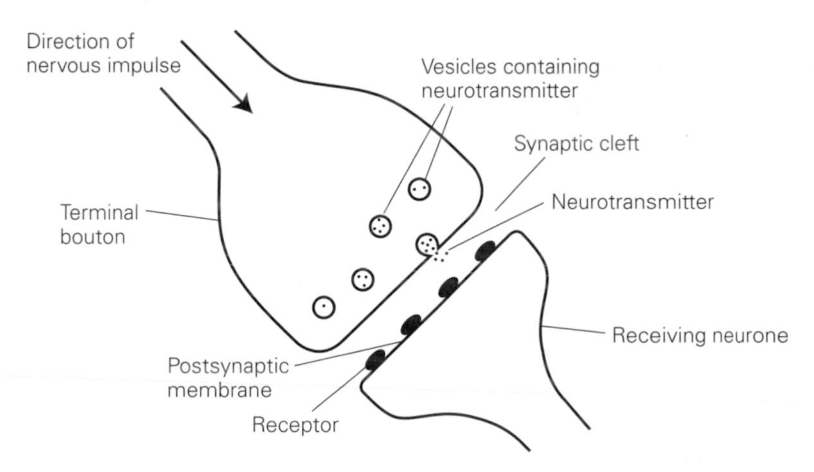

synaptic cleft: the gap between the presynaptic membrane (at the *terminal bouton*) and the *postsynaptic membrane* (the dendrite) across which *neurotransmitters* travel.

- This gap is microscopic, measured in angstrom.

synaptic transmission: the process of conducting information from one *neurone* to another, across the *synaptic cleft*.

synoptic: a summary view. An understanding and critical appreciation of the breadth of theoretical and methodological approaches, issues and debates in psychology.

- The synoptic element of the A-level examination, tested in the A2 part of the examination, assesses the candidates' understanding of the connections between the different elements of the subject, ensuring that they have an overall grasp of the subject. All A-levels are required to include a minimum of 20% synoptic assessment.

systematic desensitisation (SD): a form of *behavioural therapy* for treating phobias.

- The patient learns to pair the feared object or situation with relaxation rather than anxiety, following the principles of *classical conditioning*. (1) The patient learns deep muscle relaxation. (2) The patient constructs a hierarchy of increasingly threatening situations. (3) The patient is asked to imagine each scene while deeply relaxed. At any time, if the patient feels anxious, the image is stopped and relaxation regained. The concept of 'reciprocal inhibition' describes the fact that it is impossible to maintain two incompatible emotional responses simultaneously (anxiety and relaxation).

systematic sample: a *sampling technique* where some system is used to select the *sample*.

- There is no bias in selection; however, every person does not stand an equal chance of being selected. Therefore this is called a 'quasi-random' technique as distinct from a *random sample*.
- ***e.g.*** Selecting every tenth name in the school register.

table of random numbers: see *random numbers*.

tabula rasa: the Latin for a 'blank slate', a phrase used to describe the *neonate*'s mind as being empty of ideas. Experience is then 'etched in'.

■ This is the view held by *behaviourists*.

tachistoscope: an instrument which presents visual stimuli for controlled, very short periods of time. Used in memory research in the days before computer technology took over.

target population: see *population*.

task-oriented leader: see *contingency theory*.

teaching style: an identifiable and related set of teaching strategies.

■ There are two main dimensions: (1) teacher-centred: formal, direct, authoritarian, traditional; (2) pupil-centred: *discovery learning*, informal, democratic, progressive. Formal methods have been associated with greater academic achievement, whereas informal methods foster greater creativity and higher self-esteem.

■ ***TIP*** One should also consider *learning styles*.

temperament: an individual's characteristic modes of emotional response which are inherited.

■ Five major dimensions of temperament have been identified: activity level, emotionality (how easily the infant can be upset), soothability (how easily the infant can be calmed down), fearfulness and sociability. These dimensions create three main clusters or temperamental types: (1) the easy child: even-tempered, positive, adaptable, predictable; (2) the difficult child: active, irritable, irregular, finds newness distressing and responds by withdrawing; (3) the slow-to-warm-up child: inactive, moody, slow to adapt but responds with passive resistance rather than crying like the difficult child.

temperament hypothesis: the view that a child's temperament is responsible for the quality of attachment between the child and his/her caregiver.

■ The alternative view is that strength of attachment can be explained in terms of the sensitivity of the caregiver (see *caregiver sensitivity hypothesis*).

template matching theory: a *bottom–up* explanation for pattern recognition in which external stimuli are matched with an internal template of the pattern.

■ The drawback is that one would have to have an enormous number of templates if this were the only method of pattern recognition. In addition it is a very inflexible system, as something that was slightly different to the template would not be recognised. An alternative is offered by the concept of *geons*.

■ **TIP** Contrast with *feature detection theory* and *prototypes*.

temporal lobe: a region in each *hemisphere* of the forebrain (see the *brain*).

■ The temporal lobe is separated from the frontal and parietal lobes by the lateral fissure. It contains part of the *association cortex*, which is involved with sensory processing. It is also concerned with memory, emotional behaviour, face perception, auditory perception and speech comprehension (*Wernicke's area*).

terminal bouton: a swelling at the end of the *axon*.

■ The terminal bouton contains synaptic vesicles which produce neurotransmitters.

territory: a portion of land belonging to an individual or a group, that can be defended.

■ The concept of a 'primary territory' refers to an area over which one has a sense of ownership, such as your bedroom. 'Secondary territories' are spaces you use a lot, such as where you sit in class. 'Public territories' are available to everyone. In non-human animals, territories are important to ensure adequate food resources. Territorial behaviour involves control of access, marking the boundaries and defending against intruders.

■ **TIP** Territory differs from *personal space* in that the former involves land — they both are exclusive and defensible areas.

testicular feminising syndrome: a condition that results from an insensitivity to the male hormone *testosterone*.

■ The consequence is that the testes do not develop even though the individual is genetically male (XY rather than XX).

■ **TIP** Such cases can shed light on the determination of *gender identity*. If it is biology that matters, such individuals should still feel as if they are a male; if it is *socialisation* that matters, then they should feel as if they are a female.

testosterone: a male sex hormone produced mainly in the testes.

■ In males, testosterone governs the appearance of secondary sexual characteristics (such as beard growth and muscular development). It is also responsible for producing sperm and is associated with increased levels of aggression. Testosterone is present in small quantities in females.

test–retest: a method of assessing the external *reliability* of a psychological test, i.e. the extent that a test gives consistent results.

■ This is done by testing the same person twice over a period of time on the same test. Similar scores demonstrate high external reliability. To reduce the *practice effect*, it may be desirable to use *split-half* forms of the test.

texture gradient: the texture of an object appears to get smoother with distance, which acts as a depth cue.

thalamus: a structure in the centre of the subcortical area of the *forebrain*; one in each *hemisphere*.

■ Each thalamus is quite large and shaped like an avocado. The right and left structures are joined. It has been described as the great relay station of the brain because most sensory information first goes to the thalamus, where it is processed and sent on to the *cerebral cortex*.

thanatos: a term used in *psychoanalytic theory* to represent the death wish.

■ Thanatos was the Greek god of death. Freud suggested that living things have a drive to return to their inorganic state. This results in a death *instinct*. The consequences of this drive include *denial*, *aggression* and turning away from anything pleasurable. The life instinct prevents the death instinct from destroying the individual.

thematic analysis: a form of *qualitative analysis* where textual material is organised in relation to certain research questions or themes that had been identified before the research started.

■ The 'text' may come from, for example, an interview or a recorded conversation. This approach is different from *grounded theory* in that, in thematic analysis, the themes arise prior to the research.

thematic apperception test (TAT): a *projective* technique for measuring *attitudes*.

■ A series of pictures is presented and respondents are asked to make them into a story. The individual's story reflects their attitudes because pictures are vague and open to all sorts of subjective interpretation.

theory: a systematic collection of interrelated facts put forward as a description and/or explanation of a set of observed phenomena.

■ Distinct from a *model*.

theory of evolution: a *theory* that accounts for the diversity of living species and the fact that the characteristics of individuals change (i.e. evolve).

■ Darwin proposed a theory to account for the forces behind the change: as the environment changes (or an individual moves to a new environment), new traits are needed to ensure survival. New *genetic* combinations produce *adaptation* and the individual who best 'fits' the environmental niche will survive ('survival of the fittest') through the process of *natural selection*.

■ ***e.g.*** One reason proposed for why the dinosaurs became extinct was that, as the environment changed, they were unable to adapt quickly enough because there was not enough genetic variation to produce new, better adapted forms. It could be argued, however, that birds, which evolved from dinosaurs, were the 'new variation'.

■ ***TIP*** Always be careful about describing this process as any kind of conscious activity: the process of natural selection happens through *selective pressure*.

theory of mind (ToM): an individual's understanding that other people have separate mental states and that they see the world from their point of view, which differs from one's own.

■ Young children do not have this theory of mind and cannot imagine that someone else is experiencing different feelings or thoughts. By the age of 4, children have begun to develop a theory of mind. The key importance of this development is that, in order to conduct relationships, you need to be able to predict how others will behave and have an understanding of someone else's emotional state. Some psychologists believe that *autistic* children lack a ToM, and this would explain why they find social contact so difficult. ToM is also a criterion used in considering the intelligence of non-human animals. There is evidence that they do have mental representations of themselves and others from studies of self-recognition, imitation, role-taking and social relationships.

therapeutic community: a group of people living together in a social environment that is designed to have a beneficial and therapeutic impact on the residents.

therapy: a treatment for psychological or physical disorders.

thinking: the processes that are going on in the mind which are unobservable, symbolic and involve the manipulation of some content.

- ***e.g.*** Decision making, problem solving, reasoning, *convergent* and *divergent* thought, *means–end analysis*.
- ***TIP*** Intelligence is a measure of the quality of your thinking.

time-out technique: a method of *behaviour therapy* used to remove undesirable behaviours.

- When a child behaves uncontrollably he/she receives attention which, despite being negative, is positively *reinforcing*. In order to break this cycle, unacceptable behaviour is treated with time in temporary isolation until they calm down. To be effective this should be accompanied by attention for good behaviour.

time sampling: a method of collecting data in an *observational study* where observations are made at regular intervals, such as once a minute.

- See also *event sampling* and *point sampling*.

token economy (TE): a form of *behaviour modification*, where desirable behaviours are encouraged by the use of selective reinforcements.

- The system works well in institutions where patients are given rewards (tokens) as *secondary reinforcers* when they engage in correct/socially desirable behaviours. The tokens can then be exchanged for primary reinforcers — food or privileges. This mirrors the system of rewards often used by parents. The drawback to this therapy is that it may fail to transfer to life outside the institution when the behaviours are no longer reinforced.
- ***e.g.*** Giving a patient a reward for making their bed every day and gradually building this up so that they are capable of self-care.

tolerance: in relation to *drugs*, the fact that the body increasingly adapts to the substance and needs larger doses to achieve the same effect.

top–down processing: *processing* that is concept-driven and affected by expectations, as distinct from *bottom–up processing* which is data-driven.

- ***e.g.*** The *constructivist* theory of perception is a top–down theory.

trace decay: the idea that *forgetting* is due to the spontaneous physical disappearance of the *memory trace*.

■ It is difficult to know whether the disappearance of a *memory trace* is due to spontaneous decay rather than interference. If nothing else entered *short-term memory*, would the trace disappear? Trace decay is unlikely to apply to *long-term memory* because some kinds of memory clearly do not decay. For example, (it is said) you never forget to ride a bicycle (*procedural* memory). It is hard to know if a memory has actually disappeared or is simply not accessible.

trait theory: a theory of *personality* based on the different traits possessed by individuals.

■ Traits are essentially adjectives such as 'serious' and 'trusting'; they describe tendencies to act in a particular way. Such theories have the advantage of reflecting our natural tendency to categorise people using traits, such as talkative or shy, and are useful for developing personality tests based on a list of adjectives. However, they are not very sophisticated, little more than a list of adjectives which describe but do not explain how behaviour develops.

■ ***e.g.*** Cattell's (1965) theory based on the factor analysis of 4500 traits identified 16 source traits (such as self-assured) and eight surface traits (such as depression).

transactional analysis (TA): a form of *psychodynamic* and *humanistic* therapy which aims to analyse the 'crossed' transactions between people; 'uncrossing' them enables the individual to return to normality.

■ Berne (1964) suggested that adults operate at any time in one of three ego states: parent (doing what society says), child (pleasure-seeking) and adult (rational). Individuals move between these and in a sense play 'games' with others.

■ ***e.g.*** You take on a 'child' state in order to elicit a parent role from another person. This is especially relevant to *interpersonal relationships* because such relationships develop elaborate 'games'. Games become 'crossed transactions'. The aim of TA is to focus on the present and teach the individual to regain social control by becoming more adult and rational, and to become more aware of the games he/she plays.

transactional model: an explanation for behaviour that emphasises an interaction between various factors.

■ ***e.g.*** Cox's transactional model of *stress* describes stress in terms of an interaction between the individual's ability to cope and the demands of the environment.

transference: displacing the feelings about one person onto another.

■ It is a problem that occurs during *psychoanalysis* when a patient may transfer their feelings about others onto the therapist. The therapist then has to deal with this as an additional 'problem'.

transfer of learning: when learning on one task affects the learning of another task.

■ Positive transfer occurs when learning on task A has a positive effect on learning task B. Negative transfer occurs when learning on task A has a negative effect on learning task B. Both imply some *cognitive* activity is mediating performance (in contrast with *learning theory*).

- ***e.g.*** An example of positive transfer would be learning to swim backstroke after learning to swim breaststroke. There may also be some negative transfer because of the different arm movements.

transformational grammar: a concept from the *nativist theory* of language acquisition, it is an *innate* set of rules for combining words to produce meaning.

- Transformational grammar transforms surface structure (the actual words used) into deep structure (the actual meaning) and vice versa. This is how we produce sentences with meaning (deep to surface structure) and understand what others say (surface to deep structure).
- ***e.g.*** 'The peasants are revolting' has two deep structures. 'The cat chased the dog' and 'The dog was chased by the cat' have two surface structures but the same deep structure.
- ***TIP*** It is this transformational grammar which is not present in non-human animals and could explain why non-human animals can never get beyond a certain level of acquiring human language.

trial and error learning: a method of learning by which the organism tries a behaviour and learns whether it has positive consequences (and is then likely to repeat the behaviour) or negative consequences (and is then not likely to repeat the behaviour).

- Gradually this results in learning an appropriate response and underlies the process of *instrumental learning*.

trichromatic theory of colour vision: this proposes that there are three kinds of *cone* cell; we are able to see the full range of colour by mixing signals from each cone cell.

- ***TIP*** It is probable that this explains initial colour perception and *opponent–process theory* explains subsequent processing. The trichromatic theory cannot explain colour blindness or negative afterimages.

trigram: see *nonsense syllable*.

true experiment: an experiment where the *independent variable* is manipulated and participants are randomly allocated to conditions/groups. This is distinct from a *quasi-experiment*.

***t*-test:** an *inferential* and *parametric test* of the difference. The related *t*-test assesses the difference between related samples and the unrelated *t*-test is for unrelated samples.

- The reasons for selecting the related or unrelated *t*-test are: (1) a test of difference is required; (2) the samples are related or unrelated (respectively); (3) the data do fit parametric assumptions (e.g. the distribution is *normal* and the *level of measurement* is at the interval or ratio level).

twin study: research conducted using twins.

- *Monozygotic* (MZ) *twins* have the same *genes* (100% *concordance*) whereas *dizygotic* (DZ) *twins* are genetically 50% similar. It is presumed that all twins share a similar environment, so by comparing MZ and DZ twins, this means that one can conduct a natural experiment, where the *independent variable* is genetic similarity (MZ twins are the same, DZ twins are different), to see how this influences behaviours such as IQ or personality characteristics. Furthermore, where MZ twins have been reared apart, one can study the effects of the environment. In this case the independent variable is environmental differences, because genetic similarity has been kept constant. Such research suffers from the problems of all natural experiments, namely that the independent variable has not been directly manipulated and participants have not been randomly allocated to conditions. Therefore we cannot claim to have identified a cause-and-effect relationship. The assumption that MZ and DZ twins reared together both share the same environment may not be justified. MZ twins look more similar and this may create a more similar environment because people treat them the same, whereas DZ twins are treated differently and therefore experience a different microenvironment.

two-tailed hypothesis: see *non-directional hypothesis*.

two-tailed test: used when carrying out a test of significance on a *non-directional hypothesis*.

type A, B, C, D: a typology used to characterise an infant's attachment to his/her caregiver, based on their response in the *strange situation*.

■ Type A is insecure–*avoidant attachment*, B is *secure attachment*, C is insecure–*resistant attachment*, and D is *disorganised attachment*.

type A, B, C personality: someone who demonstrates characteristic responses to emotional pressure.

■ Type A personalities are typically impatient, competitive, time pressured, hostile and more prone to suffering from coronary heart disease (CHD). Type B personalities lack these characteristics. Type C personalities are industrious, conventional, sociable and tend to have repressed emotional reactions and react to stress with helplessness. This type has been associated with cancer risk.

type I error: an error that may occur when using a *level of significance* (for example 10%) that is too high (lenient).

■ A *null hypothesis* (H_0) that is true is rejected.

type II error: an error that may occur when using a *level of significance* (for example 1%) that is too low (stringent).

■ A *null hypothesis* (H_0) that is false is accepted.

■ ***TIP*** To help you remember:

	H_0 is accepted	H_0 is rejected
H_0 is true	OK	Type I error
H_0 is false	Type II error	OK

type theory: a theory of *personality* based on the notion that each person can be categorised as one or another qualitatively different type.

■ A 'type' is a cluster of traits. Like *trait theory*, this is useful for developing personality tests. In addition, types may be linked to a biological basis.

- ***e.g.*** Eysenck's type theory identified three continuums or dimensions on which individuals could be measured: *extravert/introvert,* neurotic/stable and intelligent/psychotic. Your 'type' can be measured using *Eysenck's personality inventory* (EPI). This is both a *behaviourist* theory (because behaviours are learned through *reinforcement*) and a biological theory (because introversion/extroversion are proposed to have an *innate* biological basis).

ultradian rhythm: a *biological rhythm* that occurs or recurs in a cycle of less than 24 hours ('ultra' and 'dies' = above or higher frequency than a day).

■ ***e.g.*** Sleep stages, basic rest activity cycle (BRAC), tidal rhythms in marine animals. See also *circannual, circadian* and *infradian rhythms.*

unbiased: without distortion or prejudice. See *bias.*

unconditional positive regard: providing affection and respect without any conditions attached.

■ Rogers proposed, in his *self theory,* that healthy personality development depends on unconditional positive regard from significant others. If love is conditional, then the individual must strive for social approval and this striving blocks the individual's ability to self-actualise, leading to maladjustment. The therapy derived from this theory, *counselling,* proposes that maladjustment can be reversed by supplying positive unconditional regard. The counsellor aims to listen to the client with total acceptance, regardless of what the client says, and in this way it is unconditional. This enables the individual to become self-accepting of all those areas of self previously excluded and which therefore were threatening. Finally, this enables self-actualisation.

unconditioned response/stimulus: *innate* reflex responses to a stimulus. See *classical conditioning.*

■ ***e.g.*** A loud bang (unconditioned stimulus, UCS) creates a reflex response to be startled (unconditioned response, UCR).

unconscious: lacking *consciousness* or awareness.

■ In *psychoanalytic theory,* the unconscious part of your mind contains information that is either very hard or almost impossible to bring into conscious awareness. It holds your *repressed* thoughts which are too anxiety-provoking to allow into one's conscious. However, such material exerts a powerful influence over behaviour. In a *physiological* sense, the term is used to refer to a loss of consciousness such as in a coma or deep sleep. The mind may maintain some awareness of the environment but cannot be aroused. See also *preconscious.*

understudied relationships: those which have tended to be overlooked in the psychological research on *interpersonal relationships.*

■ Psychologists have tended to 'overstudy' traditional relationships such as marriage and same-sex friendship, and ignored homosexual relationships, long-term partners who are not married (cohabitation), arranged marriages or other involuntary relationships, 'electronic' friendships and so on. This means that theories of interpersonal relationships focus on a rather narrow band of experiences.

undisclosed observation: a kind of *observational study* where participants are not aware of being observed.

- The observations may be through a one-way mirror or in a public place. There are ethical concerns about such methods, although it is considered to be acceptable to make observations without the consent of participants as long as they are observed in a situation where they would normally expect to be seen by others (i.e. a public place).
- ***e.g.*** In Bandura et al.'s (1961) study of aggression the children were observed playing with toys through a one-way mirror.

unfalsifiable: refers to a hypothesis or theory which is impossible to *falsify*, i.e. prove false.

- ***e.g.*** Freud argued that if a client accepted his interpretation of the client's dream, then the interpretation was probably correct. However, if the client rejected the interpretation, this demonstrates resistance to an unacceptable but entirely accurate interpretation. The result is that Freud's theory of the meaning of dreams cannot be falsified.

unipolar depression: see *depression (unipolar)*.

unrelated *t*-test: see *t-test*.

validity: the extent to which something is true.

■ It is used to describe: (1) The soundness of the measurement tool, such as a psychological test, i.e. the extent to which it is measuring something which is real or true (see *internal validity*). For example, *content, construct, concurrent, criterion, face, predictive validity*. (2) The soundness of an experimental procedure in terms of both what goes on within the experiment (*internal validity*) and its relevance to other people and situations (*external validity*).

Valins effect: experiencing an *emotion* in the absence of physiological arousal.

■ It is sufficient to **think** that one is physiologically aroused in order to seek a label for the emotion. Valins (1966) showed male participants slides of semi-nude women and gave them false feedback about their heart rate. Ratings of attractiveness were positively related to supposed increases in heart rate.

variables: things which vary or change.

■ ***e.g.*** In an experiment we are primarily concerned with manipulating the *independent variable* and observing changes in the *dependent variable*. We control *extraneous variables* as far as possible (if this is not successful they are called *confounding variables*).

variance (abbreviated as ***s***)**:** a *measure of dispersion* of a set of scores. It is the square of the *standard deviation*.

variation ratio: a *measure of dispersion*. It is the ratio of non-modal scores to the total number of scores.

■ ***e.g.*** In the set of data '2, 3, 5, 5, 7, 8', four out of six scores are non-modal.

ventromedial hypothalamus (VMH): possibly a satiety centre in the brain.

■ Animals that have *lesions* to the VMH overeat. The VMH acts in a *homeostatic* fashion in conjunction with the *lateral hypothalamus*.

vicarious reinforcement: *reinforcement* that is received indirectly, by observing another person being reinforced.

■ See *social learning theory* and *observational learning*.

visual cortex: the region of the *occipital lobe* in the *cerebral cortex* that processes visual data.

■ The primary visual cortex, also called V1 or the *striate cortex*, receives the visual input from the *thalamus*. Data is processed and sent on to the secondary visual cortex (V2) where it is further processed and returned to V1 or sent on to other areas of the brain for further processing. V1 contains simple cells, which respond to the orientation of lines. V2 contains complex cells which receive input from simple cells, and hypercomplex cells, which receive input from complex cells.

visual illusion: an unconscious 'mistake' of perception.

- In fact visual illusions are not really mistakes, but are normal, relatively consistent phenomena which are subject to regular rules of perception. Illusions are distinct from hallucinations or delusions and usually associated with an element of surprise. However, many commonplace visual techniques, such as using shadow to infer 3D in pictures, are also illusions.
- ***e.g.*** Ponzo, Müller–Lyer and Titchener illusions. The two horizontal lines in the first two and the two central circles in the third are in fact the same size as each other.

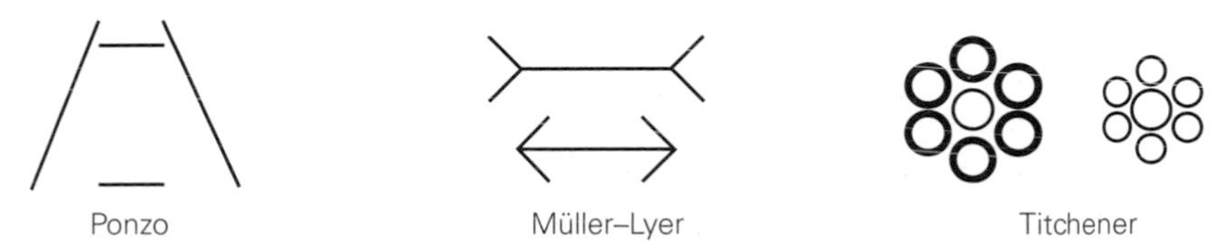

Ponzo Müller–Lyer Titchener

visuo-spatial sketchpad: a system within *working memory* designed for spatial and/or visual coding.

volunteer sample (self-selected): a *sampling technique* where participants become part of a study because they volunteer when asked or in response to an advertisement.

- Such participants have special characteristics. They are usually more highly motivated and perform better than an *opportunity* or *random sample*. This is likely to *bias* the findings of the study.
- ***e.g.*** The participants in Milgram's classic obedience study (1963) were a volunteer sample.

Vygotsky's theory of cognitive development: Vygotsky proposed that *cognitive development* occurs as a consequence of the influence of culture, as opposed to Piaget's view that biological maturation was the mainspring of cognitive development.

- Vygotsky suggested that we are born with elementary mental functions (e.g. attention), which are present in all animals. There is some natural development but the agent of change is mainly *culture*, which transforms the elementary functions into higher mental functions. 'Culture' includes concepts and tools which are embodied in language and passed on by 'experts' (anyone who knows more). Experts lead the child through his/her *zone of proximal development* (ZPD). See *pre-intellectual speech*.
- ***TIP*** The current popularity of Vygotsky's work is in part due to its emphasis on social influences and relevance to education. He argued that it is educationally more valuable to know what children can do with some assistance than what they can do unaided.

weaning conflict: an example of *parent–offspring conflict* which occurs in mammals where offspring wish to prolong their easy and rich food source, whereas the mother needs to wean in order to prepare for the next pregnancy and conserve resources (lactation is a greater drain than pregnancy, and suppresses ovulation).

Wernicke's area: an area in the *temporal lobe* of the forebrain, usually in the left *hemisphere*, related to speech comprehension. See also *Broca's area* and *aphasia*.

Whorfian hypothesis: see *linguistic relativity hypothesis*.

Wilcoxon signed ranks test: an *inferential* and *non-parametric test* of the difference between related samples.

■ The reasons for selecting this test are: (1) a test of difference is required; (2) the samples are related; (3) the data do not fit *parametric* assumptions (e.g. the distribution is not *normal* and the *level of measurement* is ordinal).

working memory model: Baddeley and Hitch's idea that *short-term memory* is more accurately represented in terms of a set of separate stores which handle different modalities (sound and visual data) rather than a single store, as in the *multi-store model*.

■ The use of the term 'working memory' reflects the idea that this is the area of memory that is active when you are working on information. Working memory consists of: a *central executive* (the modality-free organiser), a phonological loop (verbal material) and a *visuo-spatial sketchpad* (visual memories). The phonological loop is further subdivided into a phonological store (speech perception) and an articulatory process (speech production).

■ ***TIP*** This model has many strengths: it can explain how we can do two tasks at one time if they involve different stores and why we have trouble with some tasks which involve the same store. It also concerns active processing and therefore is relevant to a wider set of activities than the STM model, such as verbal reasoning and comprehension. However, the most important component, the central executive, is rather vaguely defined and may require further subdivision.

X-chromosome: see *chromosomes*.

X-ray tomography: see *CAT scan*.

XXY syndrome: Klinefelter's syndrome, an abnormality of the sex chromosomes where the individual is a male but also has some female characteristics, such as breast development.

XYY syndrome: another abnormality of the sex chromosomes which results in males who are abnormally tall and have reduced sperm production.

- ***TIP*** At one time this abnormality was associated with aggression and criminality, but the research has not been replicated.

Yale model of persuasion: Hovland et al. (1953) explained persuasion in terms of four basic variables in all persuasion situations: the source, the message, the receiver and the context ('who says what to whom and with what effect').

Y-chromosome: see *chromosomes*.

Yerkes–Dodson law: describes the *curvilinear* relationship between arousal and performance.

- When arousal is very low or very high, performance is poor. Performance is highest at a medium level of arousal.

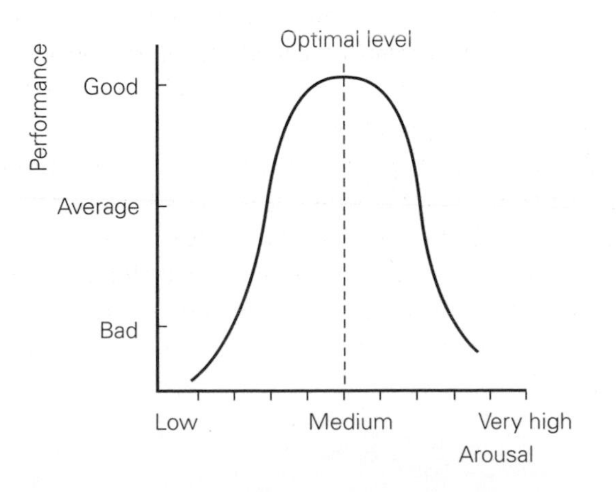

Zeitgeber: the German word for 'time giver'. An external cue that sets the *biological clock*.

■ ***e.g.*** Light is the main Zeitgeber, but there are many others such as seasons, weather, temperature, phases of the moon, tides (in aquatic animals), availability of food, pheromones and social stimuli.

zero correlation: no consistent relationship between *covariables*.

■ When there is a complete lack of relationship the *correlation coefficient* would be zero. In reality this never occurs. A low value, such as ±0.20, would usually indicate a non-*significant* correlation — though this varies depending on the amount of data collected! If you have 20 pairs of data, then a correlation of 0.4 would be significant. If you have 10 pairs of data, then 0.5 would be significant. See *positive* and *negative correlation*.

zone of proximal development (ZPD): in *Vygotsky's theory of cognitive development*, the distance or space between what the child currently can do and is currently capable of, given instruction by experts (sources of greater knowledge).

■ At any time a child is performing at a certain level but, at the same time, has a capacity to be able to do more. Without experts the child would not move through the ZPD. This is a key concept in Vygotsky's theory because it describes how experts intervene in the development process. In time, one learns to move oneself through the ZPD.

zoom-lens model: a model for focused visual *attention*, proposed by Eriksen (1983), suggesting that visual attention acts like a spotlight where the 'beam' can be adjusted to cover a greater or smaller area.

z-score: see *standard score*.

zygote: the cell produced by the union of an egg and sperm.

■ The term is used in 'monozygotic' meaning 'one fertilised cell', where twins develop from one cell and thus share identical genes. 'Dizygotic' means that twins are created from two fertilised cells, each with different genetic characteristics.